OTIS FELLOWS

From Voltaire to *La Nouvelle Critique*:

# PROBLEMS AND PERSONALITIES

WITH AN INTRODUCTION BY
NORMAN L. TORREY

LIBRAIRIE DROZ, GENÈVE
1970

HISTOIRE DES IDÉES
ET CRITIQUE LITTÉRAIRE

N° 105

OTIS FELLOWS

From Voltaire to *La Nouvelle Critique*:

# PROBLEMS AND PERSONALITIES

WITH AN INTRODUCTION BY
NORMAN L. TORREY

LIBRAIRIE DROZ, GENÈVE
1970

© 1970, Librairie Droz S.A., 11, rue Massot, Genève

Printed in Switzerland

# CONTENTS

|  | Page |
|---|---|
| Introduction by Norman L. Torrey | 9 |

## I

### THE EIGHTEENTH CENTURY

| | |
|---|---|
| Voltaire in Liberated France | 13 |
| Voltaire and Buffon: Clash and Conciliation | 22 |
| Buffon and Rousseau: Aspects of a Relationship | 33 |
| Buffon's Place in the Enlightenment | 54 |
| The Theme of Genius in Diderot's *Neveu de Rameau* | 72 |
| *Jacques le fataliste* Revisited | 94 |
| Metaphysics and the *Bijoux indiscrets*: Diderot's Debt to Prior | 103 |
| Molière à la fin du siècle des lumières | 125 |

## II

### THE NINETEENTH CENTURY

| | |
|---|---|
| Rachel and America: A Re-appraisal | 143 |
| *Madame Bovary*, cent ans après | 154 |
| Maupassant's *Apparition*: A Source and a Creative Process | 159 |

## III

### THE TWENTIETH CENTURY

| | |
|---|---|
| Master of Real Fiction | 175 |
| Un Critique littéraire de la nouvelle vague: Jean-Paul Weber | 179 |
| La Nouvelle Critique: ou la mésentente cordiale | 195 |

# INTRODUCTION

By Norman L. Torrey

The essays here presented are concerned with the last three centuries of French literature. All but one have been published in European or American reviews, collections, and professional journals; however, some have been revised for this volume. With their variety of approaches and moods, these articles in both French and English represent the wide range of Professor Fellows' interests and contributions to scholarship. Specialists in the eighteenth century and students of French literature in general can profit from the original insights contained within these pages.

The author's broadly based humanistic interests are focused on the history of ideas, as it is revealed in literary and critical theories and especially in the fluctuations of literary fortunes. This approach was first manifested in his dissertation, *French Opinion of Molière (1800-1850)*, handsomely published by Brown University in 1937 and now out of print. This careful investigation showed conclusively that Molière's position as France's leading dramatist was firmly established during the period considered. Illustrations in the present volume include essays on " Molière à la fin du siècle des lumières," " Rachel and America: a Re-appraisal " (which inspired the book on that subject by M<sup>me</sup> Chevalier, Directrice de la Bibliothèque de la Comédie Française), " *Madame Bovary*, cent ans après," and " Voltaire in Liberated France," an on-the-spot account of the celebration of Voltaire's two hundred and fiftieth anniversary. The changing reputations of Molière and Voltaire in particular were clearly not based entirely on literary merit, but were in part determined by sociological, political, and religious situations.

Another group of essays is definitely in the Lansonian tradition of historical scholarship. Outstanding among these are the articles on Buffon in his relations with Voltaire, Rousseau, and the Encyclopedists. As noted by the editors of *The Year's Work* (1963, XXV, 81) " O. Fellows' sure and suggestive study of ' Buffon's Place in the Enlightenment ' is an important step towards the rehabilitation of this rather devious figure in the history of scientific ideas in the 18th century."

Mr. Fellows' thorough command of Diderot scholarship, past and present, is exemplified in " Metaphysics and the *Bijoux indiscrets*: Diderot's Debt to Prior." From the latter's light and hudibrastic poem on the soul, Diderot developed the chief metaphysical ideas of his most important and original philosophical works, the *Interprétation de la Nature* and *Le Rêve de d'Alembert*. With meticulous scholarly procedures, Fellows sums up the already known before adding the discoveries of his own research. A briefer essay with a similar approach is devoted to " Maupassant's *Apparition*: a Source and a Creative Process." Here, the elusive source of one of his most tantalizing tales has—for the first time—been revealed. This insight into the famous *conteur's* creative processes has not been sufficiently taken into account by Maupassant specialists, but it could, I think, serve as an example for future studies.

More akin to the new criticism, which results from the close reading of texts, are essays on two of Diderot's contributions to eighteenth-century fiction: " The Theme of Genius in Diderot's *Neveu de Rameau*," and " *Jacques le fataliste* Revisited." These essays present new interpretations of Diderot's satirical masterpiece and his most intriguing novel. An essay on Simenon, " Master of Real Fiction," brings the reader well into modern times and modern methods.

Finally, two essays are concerned with the most recent critical theories: " Un Critique littéraire de la nouvelle vague: Jean-Paul Weber " (published in *Saggi e Ricerche di Letteratura Francese*, 1965) and, in a more playful mood, a short history of critical theories from the past to the present, " La Nouvelle Critique: ou la mésentente cordiale." Delivered orally and unpublished, this discourse might well represent the " scholar's holiday."

Readers who might wish there were more are reminded that this volume contains merely a representative selection, and although other articles on diverse topics have appeared through the years, Otis Fellows' time and ideas have been offered primarily to his students. During the last ten years he has sponsored thirty doctoral dissertations (five with co-sponsors) of well above average quality. Ten have already been published, four more are " sous presse," and two have won Columbia University's coveted Ansley Awards. A compulsive worker, he spends his " spare " time as general editor of the well-established *Diderot Studies*, for which he has been able to elicit the cooperation of the leading scholars in the field in Europe and America.

Jaffrey Center
New Hampshire
October, 1968.

# I

# THE EIGHTEENTH CENTURY

# VOLTAIRE IN LIBERATED FRANCE*

That a year and a half after the liberation of Paris Voltaire's pedestal on the Quai Malaquais should still remain empty is, paradoxically enough, a tribute to the man's greatness. His statue, like those of so many other illustrious Frenchmen, had fallen prey to the Nazi quest for non-ferrous metal. Under the Vichy regime it was decided that the missing monuments, which included those of Rousseau, Corneille, Lamartine, Béranger and Voltaire, should be replaced by statues in stone. When the list was submitted to the approval of Abel Bonnard, so the story runs, the Vichy minister of Education drew his pencil through the name of the philosopher of Ferney, declaring dryly: " Voltaire ? N'existe pas." [1]

Delivered of the enemy and the men of Vichy, French writers in the winter of 1944 were quick to stress that, of the masters of French thought, Voltaire had been one of the most feared opponents of Maurras, Fay, Bonnard, their " valets de plume," and the Nazi masters. Hitler's advocates, asserted the leftist weekly, *L'Avant-Garde*, avoided like the plague all mention of him whose name symbolizes freedom of thought, and hatred of prejudice, superstition and injustice. [2] The militant daily, *Franc-Tireur*, was still more categorical when on its masthead for November 22, 1944, it bluntly stated:

*Si Pétain est par terre,*
*C'est la faute à Voltaire....*

As a matter of fact, the author of *Candide* was the most widely discussed figure of the country's past in French periodicals during the winter of 1944-1945. Because Hitler detested Richelieu, Vichy had passed over in silence the tercentenary of the Cardinal's death. Likewise, the centenary of Anatole France's birth, falling in April 1944, was ignored except for a number of derogatory articles appearing in the enemy controlled Vichy

---

* Reprinted from *The Romanic Review* (April 1946), 168-176.

[1] Cf. Marcel Perier, " Voltaire n'a jamais existé," *Ici Paris*, June 13, 1945.

[2] J. D., " N'oublions pas Voltaire," December 1, 1944. Cf. Cécile Angrand, " Pour le 250e anniversaire de Voltaire," *La Pensée, Revue du Rationalisme moderne*, October-December, 1944; Auguste Gallois, " Voltaire, 250e anniversaire," *Le Peuple*, December 2, 1944; Pierre Paraf, " Voltaire résistant," *Radiodiffusion Française*, November 22, 1944.

press.[1] But as the dramatic critic, Robert Kemp, pointed out to a singularly appreciative audience at the Comédie-Française on December 2, 1944, Voltaire had had the excellent taste to be born on a date of which the 250th anniversary could be celebrated in a liberated France. Emile Moussat noted in typical comment: " Ce n'est pas un des moindres avantages ni une des moindres joies de la liberté retrouvée, que l'on puisse enfin évoquer le passé, fêter les gloires nationales et célébrer les jubilés." [2]

In the case of Voltaire, the occasion was seized upon with avidity by a press whose voice had been stifled during four years of oppression. Voltaire was fêted, but not with serenity, and the fact that he became the subject of heated controversy in the winter of 1944, is, doubtless, added proof of Voltaire's perennial youth.[3] It also suggests, however, that his acceptance or rejection was, in part, motivated by partisan passions which were flaring up anew in France after the long months of united resistance against the invader and his collaborating henchmen.

In early September, the French were already being told of the preparations under way in the Soviet Union for a fitting commemoration of Voltaire's birthday. When in Russia the last week of November was devoted to a nationwide recognition of this " symbole de la liberté, " as *Nouvelles Soviétiques* put it, the French leftist press gave columns to the event.[4] Moreover, the temptation was too strong not to publicize the heirs of Peter the Great as paying enthusiastic homage to a Frenchman unjustly neglected by his compatriots.[5]

---

[1] Cf. Claude Aveline, " Anatole France sous l'occupation," *Les Lettres Françaises*, December 9, 1944.

[2] " Voltaire," *L'Enseignement*, December 15, 1944.

[3] Cf. Auguste Gallois, *loc. cit.*, " On en est encore, il faut bien le dire, à se servir de ce nom comme d'un instrument de guerre, les uns s'en faisant un signe de ralliement et les autres une pierre de scandale."

[4] Chief articles giving detailed description of the Voltaire celebrations in the Soviet Union are: " Le 250ᵉ Anniversaire de la naissance de Voltaire," *Nouvelles Soviétiques*, November 25, 1944; Victor Vrassilnikov, " A la mémoire de Voltaire," *La Marseillaise*, December 28, 1944; Jean-Richard Bloch, " Voltaire a été fêté avec éclat en U.R.S.S.," *Ce Soir*, December 2, 1944; Fernand Caussy, " La France et la Russie célèbrent Voltaire en U.R.S.S.," *Gavroche*, December 7, 1944.

[5] Cécile Angrand protested (*loc. cit.*): " Novembre 1944 ! Aucune cérémonie vraiment nationale n'a consacré en ces jours le 250ᵉ anniversaire de l'immortel Voltaire ! A l'occasion du 150ᵉ anniversaire de sa mort, Edouard Herriot dénonçait déjà cette volonté de silence sur le patriarche de Ferney: ' Voltaire n'est plus guère à la mode; on le redoute; on cherche à le faire oublier ! ' Serait-ce encore plus vrai aujourd'hui, après ces quatre années d'obscurantisme et de barbarie ? " According to Fernand Caussy (*loc. cit.*), " Le gouvernement français a décidé de commémorer ce grand anniversaire par des cérémonies de deuxième classe," while the Soviet Union " le fête comme un héros national." Pol Gaillard complained in *L'Humanité* (November 22, 1944): " Malgré l'exemple de l'U.R.S.S., qui aurait dû pourtant, semble-t-il, stimuler l'amour-propre de nos ministres, aucune manifestation vraiment nationale n'a été prévue chez nous pour célébrer cet anniversaire comme il méritait de l'être." " Hélas," said J. D., *loc. cit.*, " notre pays, qui a donné le jour à ce grand écrivain, n'a pas marqué comme il convenait cet important anniversaire."

Such was not entirely the case, however. The Comédie-Française, the Odéon and the Bibliothèque Nationale in turn commemorated the famous anniversary,[1] while the Lycée Louis-le-Grand paid fitting tribute to its illustrious former student who was also the subject of numerous broadcasts by the government-controlled radio.[2] At the Maison de l'Université Française a Voltaire-Lamarck exposition was organized by the Front National Universitaire. This and similar acclaim culminated in a "séance solennelle" held in the Grand Amphithéâtre of the University of Paris on December 10.[3]

What do the thousands of spoken and written words poured out in liberated France on this 250th anniversary indicate regarding the current attitude or attitudes towards Voltaire? When Paul Valéry told the closely packed auditorium at the Sorbonne[4] that Voltaire is "indéfiniment actuel," Pierre Leuwen explained the assertion as meaning that today, as well as 200 years ago, one is obliged to take sides for or against him.[5]

In its broader aspects, the debate which centered around Voltaire's name in 1944 and 1945 passed judgment upon whether the great eighteenth-century figure was still abreast of the times or whether he was obsolete. " Voltaire a 250 ans, et il n'a jamais été aussi jeune," remarked one writer.[6] " Ci-gît Voltaire," retorted another.[7]

---

[1] In the presence of René Capitant, Georges Duhamel, Fernand Gregh, Emile Henriot, Robert Kemp and others, the Comédie-Française offered on December 2, 1944 a " matinée poétique " entitled " Voltaire, ou la passion de la liberté." Particularly acclaimed by the audience were readings from the " Traité sur la Tolérance," the " Saint-Barthélemy " fragment from *La Henriade* and scenes from *Brutus*. (Cf. Réné Lalou, " Hommages à Voltaire à la Comédie-Française," *Gavroche*, December 7, 1944 and " Le 250ᵉ Anniversaire de Voltaire," *Le Parisien Libéré*, December 3, 1944.) Speaking of *Zaïre* which opened at the *Odéon* on November 22, 1944, P.-A. Touchard told readers of *Gavroche* (December 7, 1944): " Telle qu'elle est, il faut bien le dire, la pièce qui est habilement construite et excite jusqu'au bout l'intérêt de curiosité a rencontré un grand succès près d'un curieux public." The Voltaire exposition which opened at the Bibliothèque Nationale on November 22, 1944 was held in the grand vestibule and overflowed into the " secrétariat." Here were exhibited rare editions, manuscripts, letters, medallions and engravings related to the writer. (See: *L'Aurore*, November 22, 1944; *Front National*, November 22, 1944; *Gavroche*, December 7, 1944.)

[2] Besides such broadcasts as Pierre Paraf's " Voltaire résistant " (November 22, 1944), Pierre Desgraupes' " Connaissance de Voltaire " (December 5, 1944) and Jacques Dapoigny's " Voltaire en Angleterre " (December 6, 1944), *Radiodiffusion Française* presented with outstanding success adaptations of " Candide " (December 2, 1944) and " Micromégas " (December 9, 1944).

[3] The speakers on this occasion were Emile Henriot, Henri Wallon, Paul Valéry and René Capitant. Valéry's talk was to constitute his last published book, *Voltaire*, Editions Domat-Montchrestien, Paris, 1945. Also members of the Comédie-Française read the following texts from Voltaire: " Portrait de Mazarin," " Memnon," " Lettre à l'Abbé Trublet," " Epître du Vous et du Tu," and " Prière à Dieu." A symphony orchestra under Roger Desormières presented selections from the music of Rameau and Grétry, while the band of the Garde Républicaine played " La Marseillaise " and " Le Chant du Départ."

[4] See footnote 3.

[5] " Voltaire notre Voltaire," *Action*, December 15, 1944.

[6] *La France au Combat*, November 30, 1944.

[7] Armand Hoog, *Carrefour*, December 2, 1944.

15

France, once again free, was justly proud of its Resistance movement, and it was altogether natural that its representatives should place on their roll of honor the one who had prided himself upon being in the vanguard of the eternal combat for justice and liberty. "Voltaire," said René Capitant, " est le prototype des écrivains de la résistance." [1] Contending that Voltaire's sojourn in London had marked his " entrée dans la dissidence," Emile Henriot observed: " Aimer Voltaire, c'est se refuser à l'automatisme, à l'intolérance et au mensonge, c'est vénérer l'intelligence, c'est savoir dire non quand il faut, c'est par-dessus tout, aimer la France." [2] For the critic and essayist Pierre Paraf, the word " résistance," so brilliantly illustrated by the French under four years of occupation, is the very essence of Voltaire's genius.[3] Stressing Voltaire's irony and his critical spirit, Jean Cassou, the famous " Jean Noir " of French clandestine poetry, commented: " N'avons-nous pas toujours la présence de Voltaire dans nos combats? " [4] Nevertheless Valéry had told his Sorbonne audience that were Voltaire confronted by the millions of Calas and Chevaliers de la Barre created by the Nazi conquest of France, he might have lost courage and said in the words of Christ: " They know not what they do." This was not the general opinion, however, and *Action* replied: " Peut-être, mais s'il s'en tenait là, ce ne serait plus le Voltaire que nous connaissons." [5] Even the anti-Voltairian, André Rousseaux, refusing to believe that Voltaire would have made any sort of compromise with Hitler's Germany, conceded: " Il n'est pas permis de douter de notre Voltaire." [6] Replying to those compatriots who dared suggest the defender of the Calas family out of date, *Les Lettres Françaises* exclaimed: "Voltaire pas actuel? Allons donc! Et d'abord, si la France avait été un peu plus voltairienne, la Révolution Nationale ne s'y serait pas étalée." [7]

A frequent inference in December 1944 was that if Voltaire had been a guide to patriotic Frenchmen during the occupation, his sagacity and vigilance were equally essential at the time of France's recovery. Whether one likes it or not, it was reiterated, Voltaire represents in the world the liberal concept of French civilization; moreover, he remains one of the great artisans of national unity. Also reminded that Voltaire had repeatedly urged his friends in Paris to unify their strength and their intelligence

---

[1] " Séance solennelle à la Sorbonne." Cf. J. D., *loc. cit.*: N'oublions pas que Voltaire fut, en quelque sorte, l'inventeur de la littérature clandestine, par ses pamphlets qui circulaient sous le manteau, pour dénoncer la tyrannie et l'arbitraire! Les dignes héritiers de Voltaire, les Politzer, les Decour, les Solomon, tous les martyrs de la pensée française, continuèrent cette tradition pour la même cause."

[2] " Séance solennelle à la Sorbonne."

[3] *Loc. cit.*

[4] " Présence de Voltaire," *Confluences*, January, February, 1945.

[5] Pierre Leuwen, *loc. cit.* Recalling the Sirven and Calas affairs, Emile Moussat (*loc. cit.*) said: " La fusillade des otages, le massacre des innocents paraît à un Allemand un acte normal; c'est un scandale pour toute âme française qu'un innocent puisse payer pour un coupable. Et là encore Voltaire est bien de chez nous."

[6] " Un Philosophe impertinent," *Les Lettres Françaises*, December 2, 1944.

[7] Pierre Lœwel, " Le Premier Historien moderne," December 2, 1944.

in the struggle for justice and human dignity, Frenchmen were admonished to listen to Voltaire's appeal today and remain united.[1] Furthermore, since Voltaire was on the side of true Frenchmen against duplicity, his inspiration was still desperately needed as an antidote for the spiritual contamination resulting from the years of enemy occupation. Regarding this latter exigency, Emile Henriot was expressing the concern of many of his compatriots when he openly declared: " Pour la desintoxication des esprits, il nous faudra un nouveau Voltaire." [2]

Critics discussing Voltaire's works late in 1944 agreed that the Voltaire most generally appreciated in present-day France is he whom the reader finds in " Candide " and other tales, his volumes on history, *Charles XII* in particular, his " *poésies légères* " and his correspondence.[3] Writers of the extreme left coupled Voltaire's name with that of Diderot, although the latter, who is currently serving as an inspiring example for the French marxist project, *L'Encyclopédie de la renaissance française*, was acknowledged much more profound.[4]

That the anti-clericalism of Voltaire should have become an issue on this 250th anniversary was, perhaps, inevitable. Had the socialist organ, *Le Populaire*, however, proceeded with more circumspection, the reaction of certain French Catholic critics might have been less violent. In a front page article, Fernand Caussy had told readers that French socialists were anxious to honor the liberator of human thought and the destroyer of primitive superstitions as they are perpetuated " dans nos climats par la religion chrétienne." Describing the Church in France as still " destructrice de la morale," Caussy ended his diatribe with Voltaire's rallying-cry, " Ecrasons l'infâme." [5] The response of defenders of Catholicism was immediate. On the following day, François Mauriac wrote in *Le Figaro* that the position of *Le Populaire* had undermined his faith in socialism, while the Dominican-inspired *Temps Présent* asserted that such an attitude was enough to make one loathe socialism forever.[6] Denouncing what it called socialism's frontal attack against Christianity, the influential *Courrier Français du Témoignage Chrétien* warned Catholics against allowing the name and the glory of Voltaire to be appropriated by " ces nouveaux fanatiques " only too anxious to launch sectarian campaigns such as that

---

[1] Among those holding such views were: Pierre Lœwel, *loc. cit.*, René Capitant, *loc. cit.*, Henri Wallon, " Séance solennelle à la Sorbonne," Bernard Grœthuysen, " Voltaire le fervent," *Les Lettres Françaises*, December 16, 1944.

[2] *Loc. cit.*

[3] Cf., René Groos, " Le Romancier de ' Candide '," *Les Lettres Françaises*, December 2, 1944; J. D., *loc. cit.*; Pol Gaillard, " Voltaire l'éducateur," *L'Humanité*, November 22, 1944; Pierre Lœwel, *loc. cit.*; Dominique Aury, " Voltaire," *Femmes Françaises*, December 7, 1944; Auguste Gallois, *loc. cit.*

[4] See especially: *L'Avant-Garde*, December 1, 1944; *L'Humanité*, November 22, 1944; Paul Langevin, " L'Encyclopédie, ou la solidarité de l'action et de la pensée," *Les Lettres Françaises*, June 16, 1945.

[5] *Loc. cit.*

[6] Hubert Beuve-Mery, " *Le Populaire* rajeuni...," November 24, 1944.

of secular versus Church education, for instance. Let us rather, stated *Témoignage Chrétien*, ourselves adopt Voltaire as the adversary of violence, the defender of the oppressed, the apostle of peace and the missionary of brotherhood.[1] *Le Populaire* itself attempted to make amends by publishing an article by Jean Guéhenno who, following in Victor Hugo's footsteps, compared Voltaire with Christ. In conclusion, Guéhenno admitted that stupid interpretations of Voltaire may have produced a few Homais, but that no master was ever responsible for all his disciples, no pastor for all his flock.[2]

The damage had been done, however, and the battle was on. In a particularly scathing article, Armand Hoog asked: " Comment ce capitaliste haineux et étroit a-t-il pu devenir une des idoles de la Révolution, c'est-à-dire de l'amélioration humaine, et cela jusqu'à nos jours? " According to Hoog, the permanent trilogy of Voltaire's greatest enemies consisted of Pascal, Rousseau and Shakespeare. Then calling the reader's attention to Henri Guillemin's book *Cette affaire infernale, les philosophes contre Jean-Jacques*, which had appeared in 1942, Hoog portrayed Rousseau, rather than Voltaire, as the true humanitarian, the real revolutionary. *Carrefour*'s literary critic concluded truculently: " Jean-Jacques dans l'éternité rejoint Shakespeare et Pascal, ceux qui ont cru que l'homme était beaucoup plus que l'homme, et Voltaire qui a écrit: ' Le paradis terrestre est où je suis ' ricane dans l'enfer bourgeois." [3] The Catholic weeklies were outspoken in their defense of Pascal against what some considered the sophistry and incompetence of Voltaire who, according to André Frossard, had called himself a deist in order to be more effectively anti-Christian.[4]

Those who with reluctance acknowledged the 250th anniversary of Voltaire's birth emphasized that the author of " Candide " represented the most typical form of the bourgeois mind. Consequently, reasoned *Volontés*, since the present century seems to be the age of decline for bourgeois thinking and ideals, may we not conclude that Voltaire is out of date?[5] For André Rousseaux, one of those to support the thesis that Voltaire has but little current interest, the twentieth century is one of faith, whether it be that of Christian dogma, communism or the monstrous doctrine of fascism. In a France which conceives of the Resistance movement under the occupation as the fanaticism of patriotic faith, he adds, in this age of

---

[1] Louis Herland, " A propos de Voltaire," December 15, 1944.

[2] " Voltaire et Jésus," December 2, 1944.

[3] " Ci-gît Voltaire," *Carrefour*, December 2, 1944. Already in 1876 Flaubert had noted this tendency to supplant Voltaire by Rousseau. In an attack on Thiers, Flaubert wrote to Jules Duplan (*Correspondance*, III, 138, Librairie de France, Paris, 1924): " Si on avait continué par la grande route de M. de Voltaire, au lieu de prendre par Jean-Jacques le néo-catholicisme, le gothique et la fraternité, nous n'en serions pas là." Cf. Flaubert's letter to Amélie Bosquet (*idem*, 141): " Je crois même que si nous sommes tellement bas moralement et politiquement, c'est qu'au lieu de suivre la grande route de Voltaire, c'est-à-dire celle de la Justice et du Droit, on a pris les sentiers de Rousseau, qui, par le sentiment, nous ont ramenés au catholicisme."

[4] " Voltaire, ou l'esprit est utile à tout," *Le Temps Présent*, December 11, 1944.

[5] *Loc. cit.*

conformist creeds, Voltaire would have felt piteously out of place.[1] Nor does Frossard see why this friend of a Prussian prince, this voluble partisan of enlightened despotism, this " âme vulgaire " should be a source of inspiration for a new-born France.[2] This rich, bigoted bourgeois, who disdained the proletariat as foul-smelling rabble, declared Hoog, survives only through a sparkling prose and a certain view of " la condition humaine." [3] *Le Canard Enchaîné* impatiently dismissed *Carrefour's* critic as an undertaker's assistant suitable for third class burials.[4] More temperate, Jean Cassou explained to the anti-Voltairians why their *bête noire* was and is respected by the common man. This lofty ironist, this *roué*, this friend of the worst princes, this insolent aristocrat of the intelligence, observed Cassou, has been able to become so popular with the masses because he is the first French writer to have engaged in the fight for the oppressed, victims of intolerance and injustice.[5]

Present-day adversaries of Voltaire found a dubious ally in Julien Benda who readily agreed with them that the eighteenth-century philosopher was no longer acceptable to many Frenchmen. Yet Benda's line of reasoning could have proved only disconcerting to such critics as Hoog and Frossard. Posing the question, " Voltaire est-il des nôtres," Benda asserted that Voltaire's literary position, that of uniting good taste and ideas, had made him the spiritual father of nineteenth-century French writers and at the same time extremely remote from such twentieth-century figures as Gide, Valéry and Suarez, who have not produced " un seul livre d'idées." Stressing Voltaire's " posthumous productivity," Benda developed the point that those whom the eighteenth-century writer attacked are chiefly men who have come after him and who are " en grande partie nos contemporains." In conclusion, Benda declared that Voltaire would have turned against the bourgeoisie of the Third Republic, who, terrified by the prospect of losing its prerogatives, had with sided the military in the Dreyfus case, had hoped to see the new Russian Republic crushed, had assassinated the Spanish Republic while applauding the totalitarian regimes, and had attempted to establish fascism in France.[6]

Viewing with dismay the partisan inspired difference of opinion on Voltaire in liberated France, Emile Moussat asked: " Quand donc feronsnous l'unanimité sur nos grands hommes? " [7] There were those, not-

---

[1] *Loc. cit.*

[2] *Loc. cit.*

[3] *Loc. cit.*

[4] Henri Jeanson, " Lettres ou pas lettres," December 13, 1945. Cf. *idem*, December 20, 1944: " Voltaire est un mort qu'il faut tuer tous les vingt-cinq ans, car tous les vingt-cinq ans, Voltaire renaît de ses ennemis depuis longtemps oubliés "

[5] *Loc. cit.*

[6] " Voltaire est-il des nôtres," *Confluences*, January, February, 1945.

[7] *Loc. cit.* Cf. Luc Estang, " A travers la presse littéraire: Pour et contre Voltaire," *Poésie 45*, February 1945: " Tout le monde y est allé de son article à l'occasion du 250e anniversaire de M. de Voltaire. M. Paul Valéry, dans le *Figaro*, le compare à Janus. De fait, selon l'humeur et les affinités spirituelles, deux visages de Voltaire s'opposent à travers les études qui lui sont consacrées. Du coup la justice et la liberté révèlent chacune une double face ! "

withstanding, who made a sincere effort to find a common ground upon which Voltaire might be accepted as an integral part of the national patrimony. Many agreed with Henriot that Voltaire's religious polemics no longer correspond to the needs of our times.[1] With the tyranny of clericalism a thing of the past, commented René Lalou, anticlericalism has lost its utility and modern Frenchmen have a common basis for their ideals founded on their faith in human progress. " Sur cet accord, " Lalou suggested, " s'instituera une tolérance sans abdication et Voltaire ne sera plus parmi nous un sujet de discorde." Then developing the argument that France's great men have often moved forward in couples, the critic stated that France should now invoke Voltaire and Rousseau in the same breath as had done Hugo's street urchin Gavroche.[2] Paul Valéry also indicated the point of reconciliation between believers and non-believers when he analyzed Voltaire's metamorphosis into a friend and champion of the human race.

It was in this same Sorbonne speech that Valéry put forth the most generally used plea for current acceptance of Voltaire when he asserted that the eighteenth-century philosopher was peculiarly representative of the French.[3] Observing that a great writer becomes immortal when his thought sinks into anonymous consciousness, Jean Guéhenno declared that Frenchmen had become " voltairiens " without even being aware of the fact.[4] Calling Voltaire the most representative of French writers, and agreeing in theory with Guéhenno's hypothesis, Emile Henriot reasoned, however, that the French were, in general, " voltairistes," since the term " voltairien " had become too specialized an attribute.[5] Today more than ever, Frenchmen were warned, the country needs the gay, shrewd, active, practical, industrious, typically French genius of Voltaire as well as its counterpart which, from Pascal to Péguy, has exalted the soul. Not only France, insisted Paul Angoulvent, but all of Europe, whose abandonment of the critical spirit exemplified by Descartes and Voltaire had led to one of the most terrible catastrophes of history, should set its intellectual house in order before it is too late.[6]

We see, then, that a liberated France was extremely articulate upon the occasion of the 250th anniversary of Voltaire's birth. Though here and there certain echoes of the controversy between M. Homais and the Abbé Bournisien continued to be apparent, the general impression obtained

---

[1] *Loc. cit.* Cf. Bernard Grœthuysen, *loc. cit.*, " L'Infâme qu'il a combattu n'est pas le nôtre. Le grand malentendu qui si longtemps a pesé sur la France s'est dissipé. Tout cela est devenu du passé. Mais la lutte pour la liberté continue."

[2] " Voltaire et nous," *Gavroche*, December 7, 1944.

[3] " Voltaire avait, je le crains, presque tous les défauts qu'on se plaît à nous donner... et certaines de nos qualités à une haute puissance " (*loc. cit.*). Cf. M. Thouret, " Voltaire en Sorbonne," *L'Enseignement*, December 15, 1944.

[4] *Loc. cit.*

[5] *Loc. cit.*

[6] " Trois Siècles après Descartes, deux Siècles après Voltaire," *Les Nouvelles Littéraires*, August 2, 1945.

that a sincere effort had been made to evaluate the philosopher of Ferney in terms of contemporary interest. Moreover, overwhelming evidence was brought to bear that Voltaire was still topical, and that the spirit of Voltaire was vital to a rejuvenation of France. For, as Pierre Lœwel asserted, one does not reign as Voltaire has reigned over France and the world without representing something steadfast, universal and permanent.[1]

---

[1] *Loc. cit.*

# VOLTAIRE AND BUFFON:
# CLASH AND CONCILIATION*

A few years past, Albert Einstein, in a provocative little essay entitled 'Principles of Research,' had this to say on the nature of man: " Man tries to make for himself in the fashion that suits him best a simplified and intelligible picture of the world; he then tries to some extent to substitute this cosmos of his for the world of experience, and thus to overcome it. This is what the painter, the poet, the speculative philosopher and the natural scientist do, each in his own fashion. He makes this cosmos and its construction the pivot of his emotional life, in order to find in this way the peace and security which he cannot find in the narrow whirlpool of personal experience."

The present inquiry attempts to examine two superior minds within the framework of the French Enlightenment, egotists both, who, in one phase of their intellectual and emotional activity, strikingly illustrate Einstein's assertion. Now each, by striving to fashion an intelligible picture of the world about him that would be consonant with his own personality and aspirations, was inevitably to come into conflict with the other. In its general lines, this is, to be sure, an often repeated story in the history of mankind.

In 1785 the twenty-four-year-old Hérault de Séchelles made his famous pilgrimage to the Burgundy estates of the aged Buffon. Buffon had three more years to live; Voltaire had died some seven years before. It was a time when both Voltaire, the Patriarch of Ferney, and Buffon, the Sage of Montbard, were hailed throughout Europe as men of genius and, in some quarters, as geniuses of the first magnitude. If we are to believe Séchelles, the great naturalist counselled the younger man to read assiduously only the greatest geniuses. Buffon is presumed to have added: " Il n'y en a guères que cinq: Newton, Bacon, Leibniz, Montesquieu et MOI."

So far as I know, there is no record of Voltaire's own limited listing of the greatest European minds. Had he had occasion to pass on Buffon's list, we may assume that Newton's name would have remained—and perhaps that of Bacon. Doubtless Montesquieu's presence would have

---

\* Presented as the second of the ' 1955 Series of University Lectures' at Vanderbilt University, February 14, 1955. Reprinted here from *Symposium*, IX (Fall, 1955), 222-235.

been greeted with raised eyebrows, though Voltaire recognized his enduring qualities as a man of the Enlightenment. Leibniz, however, so markedly the butt of Voltaire's satire, would have been given short shrift. Still, to see Buffon proposing his own name would assuredly have caused Voltaire to reach for his most vitriolic inkpot. The explosion, though, would probably have taken place in a letter to some discreet friend.

So unimpeded was Buffon's rise to fame, so great the weight of his authority, so imposing his very presence, that few were those during his lifetime to attack him frankly, openly, fiercely. If we except early attacks of the Jansenists and the Sorbonne, much of the criticism levelled against Buffon in the 18th century occurred behind the closed doors of drawing rooms, in the exchange of unpublished correspondence, or through general indirection. Of the latter, one example might suffice. Linnaeus, a bitter rival of Buffon's in natural history, had discovered an new variety of skunk cabbage—repugnant in appearance and odor—in the swamps of his native Sweden. This he named BUFFONIA.

Today, it is Voltaire who is generally known, not Buffon. Yet, in their day, each in his own way represented in considerable measure the aims and aspirations of the Age of Enlightenment. But among much else, Buffon was a man of hypotheses; Voltaire was not. Certain of Buffon's hypotheses, like those of his contemporaries, Diderot and Rousseau, were brilliantly prescient, while others were absurd. And Buffon, again like Diderot and Rousseau, sensed a truth to which Voltaire was blind. Today, as with Buffon, in the world of science as in that of the humanities—and even life itself—a fruitful hypothesis is judged on its merits, and a poor hypothesis is considered better than none at all.

Before examining the steadfast yet fluctuating relations that existed between these two men for more than forty years, I should like to touch upon the parallel, superficial but curious, which may be traced in lives marked by opposing temperaments. To begin at the beginning, François Arouet was born in 1694; it was the assumed name of " Voltaire " that was to become so famous. Georges Leclerc was born in 1707, but it was the name of " Buffon " that he was to make illustrious. While both were educated in Jesuit colleges, each was to make organized religion uneasy through his writings. The youthful Voltaire attempted to fight a duel—it was over his name—and found exile in England. Young Buffon fought a duel—but over a woman—and fled Angers. Soon thereafter, he too was to spend time in England. It was there that both seem to have discovered the great Issac Newton. Voltaire was to make him popularly known in France with his *Eléments de la philosophie de Newton*, published in 1738. The following year, Buffon added to French knowledge of Sir Issac by bringing out a translation of Newton's *Treatise on Fluxions*. Both were elected to the Académie Française—Buffon without having solicited the honor. Both were raised to the nobility with the title of " count "—though only Buffon accepted the distinction in all seriousness. Among their contemporaries, friend and enemy alike acknowledged them to be, though at times grudgingly, two of the greatest stylists of the age. Both were gifted in public relations, showed remarkable business acumen and amassed large fortunes. Each, during his lifetime, saw a statue raised in his honor—an unusual distinction then as now. In their declining years as Lord of Ferney and Lord of Montbard, respectively, pilgrimages were made to their estates from all over the world. It may be added, for what it is worth, that the venerable Buffon had his feet washed daily in a silver basin by a *valet de chambre* who had left the employ of Voltaire. Voltaire died in his 84th year and Buffon at 81, and all Europe was stirred at the death of each.

In 1910, Professor Daniel Mornet carried out a curious piece of research on the 18th century and, at the time, the results were greeted with a certain astonishment. Examining 500 published catalogues of private libraries sold in Paris between 1750 and 1780, he counted the number of times various titles appeared, to establish what works had been most commonly owned. M. Mornet discovered that the *Dictionnaire* of the 17th-century savant Pierre Bayle led the list. Second were the works of the Renaissance poet, Clément Marot. But in third place, ahead of all other 18th century writings, was Buffon's *Histoire naturelle*. And in fourth place was the Abbé Pluche's *Spectacle de la nature*. These findings do not prove that Buffon and Pluche were more generally read than those we now consider the giants of the French Enlightenment: Montesquieu, Voltaire, Diderot and Rousseau; that would be going too far. But the findings of Mornet go a long way toward suggesting that two works on natural science may have been more widely read by French contemporaries than any other *single* work of the 18th century.

There are a number of reasons why this should perhaps be so. Through the greatly increased use of telescope and microscope alike, man's awareness of a universe expanding in all directions and from the infinitely great to the infinitely small, became increasingly acute. Present day historians are cognizant of the fact—but so were Buffon, Diderot and other 18th-century thinkers—that the scientific interests of the age were moving away from mathematical abstractions toward the realm of living things, past, present and future. This was particularly true in the fields of geology and biology with all their suggested implications. The mathematical stability and order of the Newtonian system of the universe was giving way to a world of organic phenomena suggesting at every turn the dynamic creativeness of nature. Indeed, it was a trend manifest on many fronts, for this was a critical and transitional period devoted in no small measure to the revaluation and devaluation of established intellectual, artistic and spiritual traditions. It was an age in which the French, among others, participated in a change which not only enlarged their mental horizon, but awakened new capacities, new ideas, and new modes of activity.

In his *Histoire d'un bon brahmin*, Voltaire confessed: " I am sometimes on the point of falling into despair when I think that after all my diligent inquiries, I do not know whence I came, what I am, nor whither I go, nor what will become of me." There were those of his contemporaries, though— less dismayed—who were constantly seeking through inquiry, speculation and experimentation in the field of the natural sciences, not only answers to man in the universe, but to the origin and continuity of life in *all* its manifestations. And chief among those in the 18th century to hold that natural science is life itself was Buffon.

A problem confronting us is how to sum up Buffon's significance in a few words. A brief résumé of the *Histoire naturelle* itself would be quite impossible. The complete work has appeared, depending on format, in anywhere from 14 to 127 volumes. It stands as a great monument in the 18th century and, in its way, stands alone, though the century was full of compendia. What is unique is that it not only presented a most ambitious compilation on natural science, but that at the same time it offered theories on and insights into cosmology, geology, physiology, and biology that challenged the thinking of the day and, upon occasion, provided the spark for other boldly speculative minds.

It can be demonstrated that scientific inquiry had previously been pretty generally under the tutelage of theology. But with the rise of scientific naturalism, science became autonomous, and one of the great currents of the Enlightenment. Buffon is here a collaborator of such as Diderot, D'Holbach, La Mettrie and Boulanger. Scientific theories advanced by Buffon were, more often than not, quickly taken up by the " philosophes." Buffon seemed to be well aware of what use was being made of them. Thus, his ideas, when placed in the framework of the 18th century and in the cumulative interest in science, achieve an importance which has sometimes been denied them. Moreover, Buffon himself was often the first to obscure their importance. In so doing, he was able, in some measure, to escape the numbing censure of tradition and dogmatic authority. It is he who confessed to a close friend, and thus to us: " Sur la scène du monde, je m'avance masqué."

From our vantage-point in the 20th century, however, the careful reader may get a more knowing glimpse of the man behind the mask. Those who have looked with care, agree with Saint Hilaire that his glory lies in what he prepared for his successors: bold and seminal views on the common character of life's origin, laws of geographical distribution, a geological record of the earth's evolution, extinction of old species, the successive appearance of new species, the unity of the human race—in sum, the creation of a whole philosophy of science with emphasis on process rather than function. In the light of historical perspective, one example in detail of Buffon's impact on others has its diverting side. In his *History of New York*, Washington Irving, in 1809, ironically commented on " the startling conjecture of Buffon... and Darwin, so highly honorable to mankind, that the whole human species is accidentally descended from a remarkable family of monkeys." After a moment's pause the casual reader is aware that Irving could hardly have foreseen Charles Darwin's eruption upon the world. The reference is, of course, to the great evolutionist's grandfather Erasmus, whose own scientific theories often followed close in the footsteps of Buffon.

In concluding this summary of Buffon's significance, we might call on two recent historians of science, one in the field of geology and the other in biology—for it was here that Buffon and Voltaire were to come into sharpest conflict. Sir Archibald Geikie has stressed the significant rôle

Buffon played in laying some of the foundation-stones of modern geology, while Henry Fairchild Osborn asserts that Buffon asked almost all the questions that science has since been striving to answer.

Buffon was a remarkable theorist with a bold and quick imagination highly stimulating to the thought of his contemporaries. But this fertile imagination represented at once his strongest virtue and his most conspicuous shortcoming, touching, in turn, as it did, on his soundest and his most faulty speculations. It was a time when science had made remarkable strides, even though there as elsewhere wisdom and absurdity went hand in hand. The distinguished naturalist Réaumur, in studying hybridization, claimed to have seen with his own eyes a rabbit mating with a hen. He fully expected chickens with fur or rabbits with feathers to emerge. In this he was disappointed.

But, for the greater part of the century, Voltaire was at hand with intelligence and wit ready to lash out against the foibles and aberrations of the human mind whether manifest in man's relation to God, to his fellowmen or to nature. God, man and nature were all to figure in Voltaire's views on science.

Why was Voltaire drawn to science? What were his titles in this field of inquiry? A remarkably acute mind and a strong, stubborn curiosity, combined with an ambition to be outstanding wherever honors were to be won, inevitably led him to devote some of his amazing intellectual vitality to one of the most passionate pursuits of the age—the search for scientific truth.

In England and in Holland, during the first part of the 18th century, the disciples of Newton were many, and thus there was a strong insistence upon the use of mathematics and experimentation in all sciences with special emphasis on physics. Voltaire had probably had but little training in mathematics and he never did seem to be particularly fond of figures. But in 1721—he was twenty-six—at a time when he was studying law, he ended a letter to his friend Thieriot with, " here you see me as a poet and physicist "—" poète et physicien." If his letters from Holland the following year revealed no interest in science, the exile in England proved to be another story. There he met Newton's eminent disciple, Dr. Samuel Clarke whom, later in life, he was to refer to as *maître*. Moreover, he was already working on the *Lettres philosophiques* where, among other things, he was to extol Newton to the detriment of Descartes. And by 1732, with the *Lettres philosophiques* soon to appear in print, he had been completely won over to the Newtonian system by his present mentor and future enemy, Maupertuis. Still Voltaire had not yet committed himself wholeheartedly to science, and in 1735 he confessed to Cideville that though everyone was beginning to play the geometer and the physicist he, personally, preferred to pass from an experiment in physics to an opera to avoid becoming dull and wanting in taste. But he was already living with Mme. du Châtelet with whom he had set up a physics laboratory and was seeking out, as he expressed it, " truths founded on experiments." He also continued to meditate on Newton and, in 1738, published his widely read treatise on the Newtonian system which was such a revelation to many of his countrymen.

This successful attempt to set himself up as the champion of Newton's theories in France fanned smoldering ambitions. No longer satisfied with popularizing, he determined to make an all out attempt to achieve acclaim as an original investigator, and so be accepted as a member of the learned Académie des Sciences. Doubtless he felt he had already set its doors ajar for, in the same year, he had published a lyric outburst with the succinct title of 'Ode à Messieurs de l'Académie des Sciences, 1738, qui ont été sous l'équateur et au cercle polaire mesurer des degrés de latitude.'

Voltaire felt the opportunity at hand to secure distinction in science, when, also in 1738, the Académie des Sciences held a competition on the subject of the "Nature and propagation of fire." Immediately Voltaire engaged in a far-ranging correspondence with leading physicists for information concerning fire, read widely on the subject and conducted experiments on his own in the laboratory at Cirey. Meanwhile Mme. du Châtelet, herself preparing an essay for the same competition, kept the fact from her friend, co-scientist and potential rival, by carrying out no experiments whatsoever. As matters turned out, the prize was evenly divided among three others. Voltaire's experiments on fire had offered him the opportunity for original comment, perhaps even new discoveries, but, with a prudence he did not always observe in other fields of endeavor, he refused to commit himself and was content with repeating the scientific thought of his time.

He made one more serious bid as an original scientist when, in 1741, he presented a second memoir to the Academy, this time a paper on 'Motive forces.' Certain members acknowledged that he had a fair understanding of the subject, but Voltaire found this hardly sufficient recognition for his efforts. The doors of the Academy remained closed to him, while an upstart like Buffon, who was only twenty-six when he had been received as an *adjoint* in 1733, became a full member in 1738.

So, by the early 1740's Voltaire had abandoned all specialization in science. To the end of his days, however, he remained intensely interested in what the scientists had to say. He constantly weighed their judgments and voiced his own approval or disapproval in no uncertain terms. In doing so, he was to be both conservative and consistent in inveighing against all conclusions not reached by mathematics and experimentalism. At the same time he advocated almost total scepticism whenever scientific hypotheses or systems were presented. But he was often guided by wit and pure prejudice as well. It was then that his native cleverness and his scintillating style led him to epigrammatic phrases more for their own sake than any deep-seated conviction. And his prejudices induced him to attack and seek arguments against those scientific theories which ran counter to his own bias whether natural or supernatural.

Voltaire first took public notice of Buffon, then thirty-two years old, in a way that seemed auspicious for their future relations. In 1739, Voltaire published his *Défense* of Newtonian principles, in which he briefly paused to single out young Buffon for praise as one who, courageously embracing the new physics and the experimental method, had succeeded in introducing these truths into the Cartesian-dominated Académie des Sciences.

But it was a time when Voltaire saw with increasing alarm the rise of a far greater danger to scientific truth than mere Cartesianism. It lay in those cosmogonies, of naturalistic and theological scientists alike, which put particular stress on prehistoric seas or the biblical deluge. The abundance of fossils on every hand and, in particular, the repeated discovery of fossilized marine life far inland, struck both naturalistic scientists and defenders of Genesis as convincing proof that the earth had once been covered, or nearly so, with water. Furthermore, that something of the earth's history could be read in fossils of any form seemed to many a definite step forward in natural science. It was no longer commonly believed that fossils were stones which had sprung from the seeds of minerals, that they were endowed with virtues, that they were God's handiwork at the moment of Creation, or that they were simply "jeux de la nature." As late as 1696, the fossil skeleton of the elephant found at Tonna had been solemnly dubbed by the medical college of Gotha as a " sport of nature ". And Professor Beringer of Würzburg acquired a dubious sort of immortality when he published a book in 1726 describing such sports or tricks of nature as fossilized crosses, petrified flowers, images of saints and of stars which he and his students had found buried in the ground. The book received wide acclaim. That the students had played an elaborate hoax on him and a considerable reading public did not immediately occur to the learned professor. It was only when these same students later led him to a spot where he dug up his own petrified name that he realized the awful truth. He is supposed to have died of chagrin.

Fossils wilfully fabricated were no concern of Voltaire's, but the significance of petrified marine life, especially shells, was quite another matter. On the one hand, he wished to give small comfort to the quasi science of the theologians who maintained that fossilized shells found in mountain passes, crevasses and in quarries, were tokens of Noah's flood. On the other hand, he wanted to demolish those systems that interpreted the shells as being one indication that the earth had already passed through several stages of development.

By 1746, Voltaire's thoughts and prejudices on the whole question were organized in a fundamentally definitive form. It was then that he presented, but anonymously, a dissertation in Italian to the Academy of Bologna, and well pleased with his display of erudition in natural science, translated it into English for the Royal Academy of London under the resounding title of ' On the changes which have taken place in our globe and on the petrifications which are supposed to be witnesses of this.' He also set about preparing a Latin version of the memoir for the St. Petersburg Academy in Russia. Finally, it was to appear even in French. Here, in a tone of utmost confidence, Voltaire lashed out against those systems which suggested that the world was not once what it is today. With remarkable self-assurance, he found preposterous any theory inferring that great stretches of land now inhabited by man might once have been covered by seas, or that rocks and mountains had not always been in their present places, or that the earth, in any way, bore scars of past upheavals. He found particularly absurd the idea that all life might once have had its origin in the sea. He tells us, such theories merely showed that "philosophes" insisted on stupendous changes on the world's stage in the same way that Parisian playgoers demanded spectacular changes of scenery in the theatre. No, said Voltaire, from the very beginning, the universe was arranged in an orderly and permanent way. The mountain ranges had always been an essential part of the world's machinery. And the laws of gravity also prove that the oceans have remained unchanged. If fossil shells have been found in mountain passes, they are only the remains of lunches discarded by pilgrims returning from Jerusalem. Nor is man descended from porpoises or whales—or codfish. Indeed, upon various occasions, Voltaire was often to declare wittily and firmly that he recognized no cod or any other sort of fish among his own ancestry. We can well imagine, then, the horror and dismay with which he would have greeted the title and contents of Homer Smith's recent book *From Fish to Philosopher*. In fact, we are told: " Rien de ce qui végète, et de ce qui est animé n'a changé; toutes les espèces sont demeurées invariablement les mêmes.... "

Unwittingly Voltaire had set the stage for a first clash with a formidable opponent. He was unaware that the still youthful Buffon had long been busily engaged upon a work which, in boldly speculative terms, was to push still further the ideas so strongly decried by Voltaire and to add new ones of his own on the earth's origins and its subsequent history. Buffon's *Théorie de la terre* appeared in 1749, and in it, among other things, the many readers, including Voltaire, saw the clearest expression yet of the meaning of fossil shells found among rocks of the earth's surface. As explained by Buffon, they appeared as irrefutable evidence that the earth's crust contained a record of its ever-changing history. Here, Buffon paused to comment on an anonymous dissertation to the Academy of Bologna. So the presumed Italian scientist maintained that marine fossils discovered in the Alps were merely oyster shells that had fallen from the cloaks of wayfarers! In a tone that easily matched Voltaire's for flippancy, Buffon suggested that the author would have done well to add that monkeys had carried shells to parts of the mountains most inaccessible to man. Such an explanation would not have done any harm and would have seemed still more plausible. In a later volume, whether sincerely or not, Buffon protested for all to read, that he had been entirely ignorant of the authorship of the Italian dissertation, and that he would never have thought of attacking such a genius as Voltaire had he known. Nevertheless, Voltaire had been deeply humiliated, and he whose wit had sought out so many victims, never pardoned Buffon's little jest at his expense. True, Voltaire declared in 1767, in the *Défense de mon oncle*, that he had not wanted to quarrel with Buffon over a handful of shells, but down through the years to the end, and with ingenious variety, he jeered at what he liked to call " le galimatias physique du comte de Buffon." Pages would be required to record all his jibes at the expense of the author of the *Histoire naturelle*, which the Patriarch of Ferney enjoyed referring to as " pas si naturel."

To be sure, the clash over petrified shells was merely symptomatic, or, if you like, symbolic of a far deeper conflict between the two men. Newtonian science had considered the world a vast machine already assembled, and did not attempt to explain how. This was good enough for Voltaire. Not so Buffon! For him, emphasis was to remain on process, not function. And each successive volume of the *Histoire naturelle* came nearer to explaining the workings of nature, and was a serious threat to Voltaire's own neatly Newtonian universe.

It will be recalled that following the terrible earthquake and tidal wave at Lisbon in 1755, Voltaire wrote his eloquent and deeply moving poem *Le Désastre de Lisbonne*. In his despondency over the needless loss of so many lives, he turned against philosophers and theologians alike, and even questioned the benevolence of God:

> Ou l'homme est né coupable, et Dieu punit sa race,
> Ou ce maître absolu de l'être et de l'espace,
> Sans courroux, sans pitié, tranquille, indifférent,
> De ses premiers décrets suit l'éternel torrent.

Jean-Jacques Rousseau, on the other hand, in his *Lettre sur la Providence*, laid the blame squarely on social man who had compounded the tragedy by living in congested cities. But metaphysicians, theologians, social man or God himself, were no concern of Buffon's in such matters as earthquakes and tidal waves. Phenomena of this sort were simply natural processes in the history of the earth's ever-changing crust, and should be so explained. Furthermore, man's possible attainment of happiness and his drive toward perfectibility depended precisely on his better understanding of the natural processes at work in the universe. In other words, Buffon would have fully agreed with George Gaylord Simpson writing in the 20th century that: "The meaning of human life and the destiny of man cannot be separated from the meaning and destiny of life in general."

Voltaire's philosophy simply could not conceive, as Buffon's did, of the terrestrial globe coming into being, evolving through successive stages, and destined, ultimately, to sink into icy oblivion. Still less was he able to keep abreast of Buffon's even more complicated concepts of a world of living organisms undergoing, with astonishing results, much the same change. All that Voltaire could do with reasonable consistency was to attack Buffon's biology in its most vulnerable spot. It had to do with one aspect of procreation. By the 18th century, scientists were split into two great camps on the problem of generation. Voltaire belonged to the group that believed in preformation: that is, the theory that Mother Eve, for instance, had within her all the members of the human race already fully formed, much as a Chinese box encloses a myriad of other, progressively smaller Chinese boxes. Buffon's camp held to epigenesis, a theory that maintained that in each individual animal the organs are always formed anew.

Today we know that here it was Buffon who stood on firm ground. Considerably less firm, though, was the ground on which he stood in support of spontaneous generation. Ever since Aristotle, there were those who had held that dead and decayed matter could bring forth life. Upon occasion, this view had been pushed to such extremes that a late 17th-century German *savant* declared that a wad of cotton and a piece of cheese together in an old stocking could engender a mouse. But experiments of Francesco Redi and others had been so successful in disproving spontaneous generation that by 1745 the theory had fallen into almost complete disrepute.

Precisely in 1745, however, the English scientist and devout Catholic priest, John Needham, again set the world of science agog with new revelations on spontaneous generation. He found that mutton juice or barley water in sealed vessels previously subjected to heat, if set aside for a few days, would produce swarms of microscopic creatures. Buffon, peering through Needham's microscopes, was greatly impressed, for the supposed evidence of spontaneous generation lent added weight to his own theory of organic molecules. This theory maintained that the coalescence of matter caused all species of life to come into being. When Needham's experiments and Buffon's related speculations were published in the second volume of the *Histoire naturelle*, many were deeply impressed, but Voltaire was appalled. Openly and in print he denounced Needham again and again, not as an English scientist but as an Irish Jesuit and a charlatan who had seduced a great naturalist into believing his wild stories about microscopic eels. Privately and in his correspondence he condemned Buffon as a quack and a madman forever discredited by this tale of organic molecules based on alleged experiments of a wretched Jesuit. If Voltaire was wrong in claiming that there were no " eels " in the flasks, he was right in saying they were not spontaneously produced.

It was not Voltaire the scientist, though, but Voltaire the enlightened deist who so vehemently rejected spontaneous generation. As with fossil shells, so with Needham's infusoria, Voltaire's violence struck out in two directions. It fell on those literal-minded theologians who found support for their views in the Bible. Genesis told of the plague of locusts, clearly spontaneously generated. In the Judges, Samson saw a swarm of bees rising from the carcass of a lion, clearly spontaneously generated. But Voltaire was particularly perturbed by those who pointed to the verses in *St. John*: " Verily, verily I say unto you, Except a corn of wheat fall into the ground and die, it abideth alone: but if it die, it bringeth forth much fruit." Needham was one of these, an ardent Catholic who turned to the Bible for justification of his findings. Still, the Church was now with Voltaire whose violence also fell on those materialistic atheists who seized upon spontaneous generation to prove that life could spring from dead matter without the intervention of God, Creator of all life. La Mettrie, among others, had hinted as much, and here was Buffon, who had long since incurred Voltaire's jealousy, now boldly assuming that life could rise from direct creation with Nature, not God, the motivating force.

And with diabolical cleverness Voltaire for years held up before his reading public the two great advocates of spontaneous generation: Needham, now become the atheistic Jesuit, and Buffon—since he was an opponent more to be feared—the misguided genius.

By now, Buffon's eyesight had grown so weak that he was reading little else besides the tables of contents in books of science and poems penned in his honor—of which there were many. But he knew of Voltaire's published innuendoes or scathing sarcasms all pointed in his direction. He brushed them aside with lofty contempt. In a letter to de Brosses he says: " Comme je ne lis aucune des sottises de Voltaire, je n'ai su que par mes amis le mal qu'il a voulu dire de moi; je le lui pardonne...."

It was perhaps inevitable that some sort of conciliation should be effected between two such urbane men of the world as these. It was Buffon who made the first gesture. He sent his *Histoire naturelle* to Ferney as well as a letter addressed to " Voltaire Premier ";—" but of course," added Buffon, " there would never be a Voltaire the second." Voltaire's lost reply was apparently couched in equally flattering terms. When Buffon could not accept Voltaire's invitation to Ferney, he sent his eleven-year-old son in his stead. According to accounts, Voltaire solemnly placed the boy in his own armchair, and with head bared stood in silent reverence before the youthful representative of absent genius. Obviously, despite the passing years, Voltaire had not lost his touch for the theatre.

So reconciliation was reached—or nearly so. Despite these gestures on the part of one and the other, their relations remained politely distant. As Voltaire's life drew to a close, only in letters to a sympathetic Condorcet did he refer to the charlatan that was Buffon. And in 1777, Buffon wrote his friend Mme. Necker: "...Voltaire et Jean-Jacques ne feraient pas un sillon d'une ligne de profondeur sur la tête massive des pensées des Bacon, des Newton, des Montesquieu."

One final point. Early in 1778, Buffon was correcting new verses in his own praise composed by his personal poet laureate, Lebrun, when he heard that Voltaire was soon to make what proved to be his final and triumphant entry into Paris. Buffon charged Lebrun to rush into print the poem entitled ' Ode à M. de Buffon.' In it is this line with specific reference to Voltaire:

Partage avec Buffon le temple de Mémoire.

In a way, the verse is prophetic, for in the recent past there has come a new awareness among historians of science and scientists alike of Buffon's real significance—while, as we know, Voltaire belongs to the ages—but not in science.

# BUFFON AND ROUSSEAU: ASPECTS OF A RELATIONSHIP *

It seems safe to say that no writer of the French Enlightenment, with the possible exception of Voltaire, has received so much attention as that strangely paradoxical genius Jean-Jacques Rousseau. We know he was born in Switzerland of French blood, was largely self-taught, and made his vagabond way across eighteenth-century France, leaving in his wake a considerable number of works, the best known of which were all highly incandescent: the two Discourses, *Lettre sur les spectacles*, *La Nouvelle Héloïse*, *Le Contrat social*, *Emile*, and the *Confessions*.

Born in 1707 and so five years his senior, Georges-Louis Leclerc, comte de Buffon, offers in many ways a striking contrast to the turbulent, anguished Jean-Jacques so familiar to his contemporaries and to posterity. During the last 50 years of his life—50 years of perseverance that marked his climb to fame, Buffon experienced no appalling vicissitudes, no quick turns of fate; rather, France and Europe witnessed the majestic and ordered unfolding of half a century of ambition and intelligence. Raised with every advantage available to the *haute bourgeoisie* of Burgundy—wealth, education, travel, prestige—he was the exemplification of self-confidence, tact, and the social graces as he frequented the salons of Paris and the provinces, sat in the Academies to which he had been duly elected, or lorded it over the Jardin du Roi. Striking in bearing and handsome in appearance, he resembled, as David Hume observed, a marshal of France rather than a writer; while Lelarge de Lignac, one of the most severe critics among his contemporaries, admitted: " Quand on a de si heureuses dispositions, il est naturel de les faire valoir." [1] And this Buffon did, for not the least of his aims was to present to his age and to posterity an artfully designed likeness of himself, no matter how overdrawn it might be, but one of his own making—a picture, moreover, reflected in scores of portraits, busts and statues, as well as miniatures on countless medallions and snuffboxes which he distributed with a lavish hand. This image was that of one of God's most sublime creations, a peerless gentleman under the

---

* Reprinted from *PMLA*, LXXV (June 1960), 184-196.

[1] Joseph-Adrien Lelarge de Lignac, *Lettres à un Amériquain sur l'"Histoire naturelle générale et particulière" de M. de Buffon* (Hambourg, 1751), II, 414.

ancien régime, a great mind in eighteenth-century Europe. The evolution of man, if such evolution exists, could hardly be expected to advance further.

"Vanity," saith the preacher, "vanity." As for Rousseau, he knew excess of pride and, at least in some measure, it helps explain the " moi, Jean-Jacques " he wished the world to remember. Self-avowedly different from his fellow men, he felt compelled to live independently and in poverty, a creature apart, on the outer edge of eighteenth-century society—early, " notre cher ours " of Mme. d'Epinay's entourage, late, the "Je suis autre " of the *Confessions*. In contrast, Buffon held himself to be first and foremost of the species Man, and then a Frenchman of his age. If he looked upon himself as different at all, it was in degree rather than in kind—similar to most of his contemporaries, and yet also superior to them.

Nevertheless, it is not surprising that the names of Buffon and Rousseau have, upon occasion, been linked together. They were, in the eighteenth century as today, held to be two of the great stylists of their age. Both had achieved, each in his way, more than passing fame from writings on man and nature in a changing universe; one from the objective and methodical point of view of the scientist, the other as an impassioned social critic and *homme révolté*. But the linking of the two names has heretofore, with a few exceptions, been established merely to touch upon fleeting comparisons.[1] Any attempts made to examine or even speculate upon the personal and intellectual relations of the two men have encountered serious obstacles. It can be said that, for the most part, these were not of Rousseau's making. Marguerite Richebourg, in her *Essai sur les lectures de Rousseau*, has found in Jean-Jacques's voluminous correspondence, his *Confessions*, and other writings, some fifty references to the author of the *Histoire naturelle*. Conversely, mention of Rousseau by Buffon is extremely rare, and even then it is more often than not an oral judgment or confidence subsequently reported by some contemporary.

A partial explanation for this reticence on the part of Buffon lies in his relation to the age. With few exceptions, the aims and achievements of the century's most daring leaders came into unremitting conflict, during the age of Louis XV, with disintegrating yet oppressive authority in civil and ecclesiastical matters alike. An unavoidable result was that Voltaire, Diderot, Helvétius, D'Holbach, Rousseau, and others were, despite the public admiration for their works, insurgents against the imposed traditions. The place of Buffon in this picture has remained somewhat ambiguous. If, on the one hand, his independence of thought and his ill-concealed cooperation with the *philosophes* belong to the current of the Enlightenment, on the other hand, his personal conduct, social position, and official functions may be identified with the interests of the privileged aristocracy and an intolerant authoritarianism. Only by handling with uncommon judgment and tact all controversy and all controversial figures—and who was more controversial than Rousseau?—could Buffon maintain that delicate equilibrium which enabled him to pursue his aims among the

---

[1] An early and little known exception is H. Piguet, " De Buffon et de Jean-Jacques Rousseau," in *Mélanges de littérature* (Lausanne, 1816), 259-280.

opposing forces of the day. And his aims were manifest: to increase his already considerable fortune, to hold on to the many honors and titles acquired through the years, and, above all, to carry on peacefully his monumental work in natural history.

Moreover, not only his habitual reticence in personal relationships, but his deliberate suppression of pertinent papers and documents as well, were part of his character and procedure. In particular, scholars have deplored his practice of destroying letters once he had read them through. Thus there is evidence that he received correspondence from Diderot, Voltaire, and, most probably, Rousseau himself, though not a line of it has come down to us. Small wonder, then, that he has been called one of the most neglected and least understood of the great men of the century.[1] Where facts were wanting, legend was quick to take over; so much so that, among biographers, there is little agreement concerning the truth or falsity of the many anecdotes revolving around Buffon's name.

One of these legends concerns us for the three following reasons: it expresses a viewpoint of our own time; it involves both Buffon and Rousseau; and it indicates quite clearly that there is need of re-examining the relationships of these two eminent personalities.

Throughout France plans for a suitable observance of the bicentennial of Rousseau's birth had been afoot for some time, and in 1912 a "Comité Central" was set up in Paris, The province of Burgundy felt especially involved since it was the "Académie de Dijon" that had drawn Jean-Jacques out of obscurity and skyrocketed him to fame by selecting his *Discours sur les sciences et les arts* in its prize contest of 1750. For some, however, this reflected glory in which Burgundians were to bask during the bicentennial was not sufficient, and they were intent on making new revelations. It was known, for instance, that Buffon was born at Montbard, some thirty miles from Dijon, that the "Académie de Dijon" counted him among its most illustrious members, and that, in 1770, Rousseau had paid a brief visit to Buffon at the "Château de Montbard." But why this visit by the antisocial Jean-Jacques, now fifty-eight years old who, moreover, although famous, was broken in body and spirit? Was it because he wished to pay homage to one whom he considered as one of his masters? Quite possibly; after all there long remained inscribed on Buffon's *cabinet de travail* for all to see the following couplet by an unknown hand:

Passant, prosterne-toi; c'est devant cet asile
Qu'aux pieds du grand Buffon tomba l'auteur d'Emile!

Then too, Rousseau's visit might have been motivated by gratitude. But gratitude for what? The stage was now set for a plausible hypothesis. Could Buffon have had a hand, for instance, in the crowning of Rousseau's First Discourse? It remained now for someone with enough insight and imagination to come forth with credible and perhaps convincing arguments

---

[1] Cf. Ch. Barthélemy, "La Religion de Buffon," in *Erreurs et mensonges historiques* (Paris, 1877), 94.

to prove Buffon's intervention in 1750. The person to do so was M. Marcel Mayer, a journalist of Dijon who, upon presenting the almost inevitable hypothesis, became, overnight as it were, an *érudit*. It was M. Mayer's belief that the best of the competitive essays submitted to the Académie de Dijon were passed on to Buffon for his opinion. Struck by the stylistic qualities and original ideas that set one manuscript apart from the others, the author of *L'Histoire naturelle* presumably told his fellow academicians: " N'hésitez pas ! Voilà le manuscrit qu'il faut couronner." It was a striking enough phrase and one easily remembered. But a new development occurred before it could be generally accepted as Buffon's own. Montbard, not wishing to be left out of the bicentennial celebrations, organized a ceremony to fête Rousseau's anniversary. The Comité Central sent down from Paris one of the eminent Rousseauists of the day, M. Hippolyte Buffenoir, to be the principal speaker. M. Buffenoir's commission was a delicate one—to speak on Rousseau in the town of Buffon's birth, and to link decisively the two names without doing too much violence to the truth. But M. Buffenoir was a man of urbanity and a speaker of eloquence— quite capable of rising to the occasion. Before the gathered Montbardois he related Rousseau's visit in 1770, and here he was on solid ground, as Jean-Jacques himself tells of the incident in his *Correspondance*.[1] Furthermore, he read with feeling and effectively commented on the only known letter from Buffon to Rousseau, the famous letter so full of sympathy and understanding for a persecuted fellow man (*C.G.*, XIV, 195-196). He also stated, however, that " plusieurs érudits " were of the opinion that Buffon had interceded in behalf of Rousseau as early as 1750. Again the words which M. Mayer had put into the mouth of the long dead Sage of Montbard rang out: " N'hésitez pas ! Voilà le manuscrit qu'il faut couronner." But, among other things, Hippolyte Buffenoir was a prudent man and a scholar, and he immediately added: " Le fait n'est point nettement prouvé." Still, he admitted, Buffon's influence in Dijon was impressive at the time Rousseau submitted his prize-winning essay.

Among those who listened enthusiastically to M. Buffenoir's speech was a journalist from the *Progrès de la Côte d'Or*. The newspaperman, in an unsigned article, though the author was unquestionably the by-now-famous M. Mayer, told readers that M. Buffenoir had established a " fait historique," to wit: " L'influence de Buffon (qui, bien que non prouvée, semble néanmoins indéniable) sur l'esprit de ses confrères de l'Académie de Dijon, qui couronnèrent l'ouvrage de Rousseau." Other journals, both in Paris and the provinces, picked up the story and at least two stressed in headlines that Buffon had been the " lanceur " of Rousseau. And so another legend was born.[2]

---

[1] *Correspondance générale de J.-J. Rousseau*, ed. Théophile Dufour and Pierre-Paul Plan (Paris, 1924-34), 20 vols. Hereafter the letters " *C.G.* " in the text will be used in referring to this work. References to other writings of Rousseau have been drawn from the Hachette edition of the *Œuvres complètes*, which will be designated by the letter " H."

[2] The above account has been pieced together almost entirely from *Le Progrès de la Côte d'Or*, " Le Bi-Centenaire de J.-J. Rousseau à Montbard " (12 juillet 1912); *Le Temps*, " Les Manuscrits de J.-J. Rousseau et l'Académie de Dijon " (13 juillet 1912);

It was a legend because Buffon had no relations with the Académie or its members in 1750. It was, moreover, a time when his two close friends of Dijon, and the only ones with whom he was then in regular contact, De Brosses and Ruffey, were hostile to and even contemptuous of that august body. We may also read in Ruffey's *Histoire secrète de l'Académie de Dijon* his opinion of Rousseau and the First Discourse: " Il employa de mauvaise foi, à soutenir le mensonge, une plume qu'il aurait dû consacrer à la vérité " (p. 95). Of the Académie and its award, Ruffey was somewhat more charitable: " Il y avait de la gaucherie, de l'imprudence, de l'inconséquence, mais sûrement aucune prétention, aucune mauvaise foi, aucune malice " (p. 44).

But none of these facts was to be brought up during the bicentennial year, either by those prone to enticing suppositions, or by anyone else. Indeed, as late as 1923, in the *Mémoires de l'Académie de Dijon*, M. Buffenoir was able to return to the subject without challenge. But this time he even went so far as to improve upon the by now famous " Mayer-Buffon " phrase by shortening it to, " N'hésitez pas, couronnez ce discours ! "

Only in 1950 was a serious attempt made to refute these declarations linking Buffon with the Academy award two hundred years before. It was undertaken successfully by M. Marcel Bouchard, Recteur de l'Université de Dijon, in his excellent, though little publicized monograph, *L'Académie de Dijon et le Premier Discours de Rousseau*. Still, a rapport, though tenuous, could have been established between Buffon and Jean-Jacques's famous Discourse which the enthusiasts of the 1912 bicentennial might have used to some advantage had they but known. In September 1741, Buffon wrote a letter to the Doyen du Parlement de Bourgogne which reveals the important rôle he played in bringing into being the medal with which, down through the years, the Dijon Academy was to reward winners of its prize competitions. But it was a time when neither Buffon nor his contemporaries could foresee that the twenty-eight year old bohemian, reaching Paris in the autumn of 1741, with fifteen *louis d'or* in his pocket, the comedy *Narcisse*, and a musical scheme, as sole resource, would nine years later be launched to fame as recipient of the gold medal then being planned.

From the available material, leaving many gaps as it does, what are we able to say about the mutual relationships of these two personalities? Rousseau quarreled and broke ties, often definitively, with almost every outstanding thinker of the age with whom he came into contact. The list is long, and Voltaire, Diderot, d'Alembert, and Hume are but a few of the names that could be cited in this respect. On the other hand,

---

*Le Radical*, " Rousseau et Buffon, les deux manuscrits de l'Académie de Dijon " (15 juillet 1912); *Les Droits de l'homme*, " Le ' Lanceur ' de J.-J. Rousseau " (21 juillet 1912); *La Dépêche*, Toulouse, " Le ' Lanceur ' de J.-J. Rousseau " (21 juillet 1912); *Revue de Bourgogne*, " Buffon et le prix J.-J. Rousseau à l'Académie de Dijon," 1912, t. II, 304-306; Hippolyte Buffenoir, " Les Manuscrits de J.-J. Rousseau et l'Académie de Dijon," *Journal des Débats* (31 juillet 1912); Hippolyte Buffenoir, "Jean-Jacques Rousseau à Dijon et à Montbard du 10 au 17 juin 1770," *Mémoires de l'Académie des sciences, arts et belles-lettres de Dijon*, janvier 1923, 15-20.

admirers of Buffon have frequently stated, though only incidentally and with scant evidence, that Rousseau had respect, even veneration, for the author of the *Histoire naturelle*, an admiration he maintained to the end of his days. What is curious is that these assertions of Rousseau's deep regard for Buffon may be supported by an accumulated weight of evidence covering many years. What is perhaps still more curious—at first glance at least—is that this should be so.

As editor of the *Correspondance inédite de Buffon*, the naturalist's great-grandnephew would have us believe that Jean-Jacques first came to the attention of his illustrious ancestor towards the end of 1736.[1] This the editor deduces from the fact that in that year Buffon writes of Rousseau to a friend. M. Nadault de Buffon's scholarship, here as in a number of other instances, is far from impeccable, and even a cursory reading of the letter shows that the reference is, rather, to the poet Jean-Baptiste Rousseau, born in 1671, hence easily old enough to be Jean-Jacques's grandfather. Nor are we to learn from Buffon himself when he first became aware of the younger and, by far, more famous of the two Rousseaus.

But Jean-Jacques was to be more explicit as to the time of their first meeting. It has been said, and with considerable justification, that from the early 1740's to 1754 it was in Paris that Rousseau's ideas were to mature and his character to crystallize;[2] it was also a time when he frequented some of the most brilliant salons of his day. In the fall of 1742 the two first met in the drawing room of the beautiful and wealthy Mme Dupin. In his *Confessions* Rousseau relates that poor Jean-Jacques could not but cut a sorry figure in this exclusive circle where gathered only great personages, men of letters, dukes, ambassadors, and knights of the blue ribbon. One of their number was Buffon, who, at the age of 35, was a member of the Académie des Sciences and recently appointed superintendent of the Jardin du Roi. Completely at ease, faultlessly dressed, a model of the social amenities, he was the very epitome of the elegant eighteenth-century French gallant and gentleman. Moreover, he was well on his way toward achieving the position that Paul Hazard was to assign to him when he wrote that Buffon may not have been the greatest scientific genius of his day, but he was certainly the most typical.[3] There would seem to be little reason, then, for Jean-Jacques to be drawn either personally or intellectually to this accomplished personage of the *haute bourgeoisie* who would before

---

[1] Henri Nadault de Buffon, ed., *Correspondance inédite de Buffon* (Paris, 1860), I, 220; twenty-five years later, in a revised and enlarged edition of his ancestor's correspondence, Nadault de Buffon compounded instead of rectifying the error. In fact, he expanded his remarks by categorically stating that Buffon had voted for both of Rousseau's Discourses in the prize competitions of the Dijon Academy: J.-L. Lanessan, ed., *Œuvres complètes de Buffon* (Paris, 1884-85), XIII, 28. It is most unlikely, however, that this comparatively unknown text was responsible for the legend which sprang up during the bicentennial year of 1912.

[2] Alexandre Choulguine, " Les Origines de l'esprit national moderne et Jean-Jacques Rousseau," *Annales de la Société Jean-Jacques Rousseau* (1937), XXVI, 88.

[3] *La Pensée européenne au XVIIIe siècle; de Montesquieu à Lessing* (Paris, 1946), I, 189.

long be a titled member of the nobility. Was he not, to all intents and purposes, strikingly representative of those whom Rousseau was shortly to protest against so violently in his First Discourse, one of those " qui forment ce troupeau qu'on appelle société," where " sans cesse la politesse exige, la bienséance ordonne," and especially where " tous les esprits semblent avoir été jetés dans un même moule ? " On the intellectual level Buffon was already generally esteemed as a philosopher and scientist. We know the opinion Rousseau expressed concerning the species in the same essay: " illustres philosophes," " troupeau de charlatans criant chacun de son côté sur une place publique."

Apart from the retrospective reference for the year 1742 in the *Confessions*, we do not find Rousseau again mentioning Buffon until 1753, while Buffon's silence on Jean-Jacques will encompass a still longer period. There is every reason to believe, however, that each was becoming increasingly aware of the other in the intervening years. In July 1749 the publication of the first three volumes of the Natural History, including *L'Histoire naturelle de l'homme*, brought their author immediately to the attention of the reading public. It is a known fact that shortly after the appearance of these three volumes Rousseau was visiting his then closest friend, Diderot, every other day during the latter's imprisonment at Vincennes. As Professor Havens has pointed out,[1] it is unlikely that Diderot did not speak to Jean-Jacques of Buffon's newly exposed ideas. This seems even more probable because it was a period when Diderot assiduously read and took voluminous notes on Buffon. He hoped, upon his release, that the prison's governor would return these notes to him so that he could pass them on to Buffon for a second edition already in preparation. These were also months when Rousseau was at work on the First Discourse which, the following year, was to erupt even more dramatically on the public than had the first volumes of Buffon. Whether any of the latter's ideas were to be reflected in the *Premier Discours* will be discussed later.

There is no direct mention of the natural historian in the First Discourse, but that Buffon had unqualifiedly won Rousseau's respect by 1753 is quite apparent. It is then that Jean-Jacques wrote, but never sent, an extremely sharp letter to the literary critic, Elie Fréron. Standing out from among the numerous sarcasms directed at the editor of the *Année Littéraire* was Rousseau's declaration that if all men were such as Buffon, he would indeed be glad for them to cultivate the sciences—then only would the human race be a society of the wise (*C.G.*, II, 58).

That same year Rousseau published his play, *Narcisse*, with a Preface he considered one of the best of his writings. It was another blast at contemporary philosophers and men of letters in general, whom he called vain as well as cowardly. Still, he admitted, there were a few sublime geniuses who towered above the rest: " ... c'est à eux seuls qu'il convient, pour le bien de tous, de s'exercer à l'étude, et cette exception même confirme la règle " (H., V, 108). Buffon must have been one of these because soon

---

[1] George R. Havens, ed., *Jean-Jacques Rousseau: Discours sur les Sciences et les Arts* (New York, 1946), 177.

thereafter, Rousseau, setting to work on his *Discours sur l'inégalité*, marked the author of the *Histoire naturelle* for distinction in a note to the very first line of the essay's Preface. " Dès mon premier pas," he writes, " je m'appuie avec confiance sur une de ces autorités respectables pour les philosophes, parce qu'elles viennent d'une raison solide et sublime qu'eux seuls savent trouver et sentir " (H., I, 127).[1]

Coming from Jean-Jacques, this constituted exceedingly high praise, and before long he was dining alone with Buffon in Paris (*C.G.*, II, 119). But in 1756 Rousseau left the capital not to return until near the end of his troubled life. During the ensuing years of tempestuous creation and frenzied roaming, he attempted to keep abreast of each successive tome of the *Histoire naturelle* as soon as it appeared. In letters from Switzerland and England to booksellers in Paris and Amsterdam—Duchesne and Guy, Panckouke and Rey—he pleaded for Buffon's latest volume or volumes.[2] But there was a significant gap in his set. He succeded in filling it only in 1764 after two years of striving. Rousseau's frustration may well be understood, for the tome was, as he wrote in 1763, the one " qui me fait le plus besoin, étant celui où il est question de moi " (*C.G.*, XI, 51).

It was in 1764, also, that the personal relationships between Buffon and Rousseau were to be renewed, though indirectly and through intermediaries. In the fall of that year Rousseau learned from his faithful friend, the wealthy Swiss botanist, Du Peyrou, that Buffon had inquired about him through his fellow scientist, Daubenton (*C.G.*, XI, 24-25). This would seem to be little more than a roundabout *politesse* from the Sage of Montbard reaching the recipient in a very indirect manner. But Rousseau, now harassed from so many sides, was strangely moved, and in his reply to Du Peyrou he seized the occasion to declare that one of his regrets was not to have been able to see Buffon more often in the past, since his own thoughts and writings would have profited by it.[3] This is no less than an extraordinary admission on the part of the overly sensitive Jean-Jacques, for not long before he had procured the volume of the *Histoire naturelle* in which he had been singled out for criticism (F., II, 566). But, far from bearing malice, Rousseau not only played the rôle of a penitent schoolboy before his master, he commended him as he had few other contemporaries. For it is in this letter, almost entirely devoted to singing Buffon's praises,

---

[1] Rousseau then proceeds to quote the entire opening paragraph of Buffon's anthropology, *Histoire naturelle de l'homme*. Here, by way of introduction to his subject, the naturalist advises that it is within himself that man must seek, discover, and finally understand his true nature (Flourens, II, 1). *Œuvres complètes de Buffon* (*avec la nomenclature linnéenne et la classification de Cuvier*) *revues sur l'édition in-4 de l'Imprimerie Royale et annotées par M. Flourens* (Paris, 1853-55) will be the source of reference in the *Histoire naturelle*, as it is far more readily available than the comparatively rare *Editio Princeps*: the Flourens edition will hereafter be referred to as " F."

[2] Among the references in the *Correspondance générale* to procurement of volumes or plates of the *Histoire naturelle* are the following: V, 545; IX, 161; X, 317; XI, 1, 15, 36, 83, 148, 151, 169, 178, 184, 250; XIII, 345; XV, 173; XX, 95.

[3] " Un de mes regrets est de n'avoir pas été à portée de le voir davantage et de profiter de ses obligeantes invitations; je sens combien ma tête et mes écrits auroient gagné dans son commerce " (*C.G.*, XI, 25).

that we find the following often quoted passage: " Ses écrits m'instruiront et me plairont toute ma vie. Je lui crois des égaux parmi ses contemporains en qualité de penseur et de philosophe; mais en qualité d'écrivain je ne lui en connois point: c'est la plus belle plume de son siècle; et je ne doute point que ce ne soit là le jugement de la posterité " (*C.G.*, XII, 25).

This was a time when the sense of persecution weighed heavily on Rousseau. In 1762, the Parlement de Paris had publicly burned both *Le Contrat social* and *Emile*, and ordered the seizure of their author. He had fled to Môtiers in Switzerland, hoping to move on to Geneva, when he learned that there too the books had been condemned and his person subject to arrest. He had no home of his own and, even worse, he no longer held the title of which he had once been so proud: that of *Citoyen de Genève*. Again he learned—this time through Panckoucke, the bookseller and mathematician in Paris—that Buffon had inquired about him (*C.G.*, XII, 154). Once more Rousseau, deeply touched, expressed his respect and esteem for Buffon, while explaining to Panckoucke that he was not writing the naturalist directly because " il y a des âmes dont la bienveillance mutuelle n'a pas besoin d'une correspondance expresse pour se nourrir " (*C.G.*, XII, 156).

It was Buffon who wrote Jean-Jacques a word of encouragement at a moment when the latter had almost reached the breaking point. The letter has been lost, but we know something of its contents because of Rousseau's letter to Du Peyrou asking him to reply in his stead. Du Peyrou was instructed to inform Buffon of how profoundly moved he was by the latter's interest during this period of horrible crisis; but unable to comprehend Buffon's advice not to antagonize Voltaire, and seeking inspiration in the naturalist's own description of the tiger in the *Histoire naturelle*, he made the following striking comparison: " M. de Buffon veut-il que je fléchisse ce tigre altéré de mon sang? il sait bien que rien n'apaise ni ne fléchit jamais la fureur des tigres. Si je rampois devant Voltaire, il en triompheroit sans doute, mais il ne m'en égorgeroit pas moins " (*C.G.* XII, 272).[1]

A week later, Rousseau wrote again to Du Peyrou stating that the *Lettres de la Montagne* had been burned at Geneva with Voltaire playing the part of " l'Inquisiteur." He wished M. de Buffon to be assured that he had done nothing to provoke Voltaire's hatred—and, in truth, Jean-Jacques never was to see any justification for this very real enmity. He added that he himself, as always, had the highest esteem for M. de Buffon, and was very flattered by his offer of the *Histoire naturelle* as a present, but that the work was much too precious to him not to have a set already (*C.G.*, XII, 325).

---

[1] Buffon depicts the lion as cruel through necessity, whereas, " Le tigre... quoique rassasié de chair, semble toujours être altéré de sang; sa fureur n'a d'autres intervalles que ceux du temps qu'il faut pour dresser des embûches; il saisit et déchire une nouvelle proie avec la même rage qu'il vient d'exercer, et non pas d'assouvir, en dévorant la première;... Il n'a pour tout instinct qu'une rage constante, une fureur aveugle qui ne connaît, qui ne distingue rien " (F., III, 55).

When, a few months later, Buffon learned of Rousseau's hasty departure from Môtiers, he again took to his pen. This is, as has already been pointed out, the only existent letter between the two, and it is a little masterpiece of gentle irony and intelligent sympathy. One example of the irony: " J'ai vu avec douleur que vos prêtres sont encore plus intolérants, plus féroces que les nôtres," and then the well-effected conclusion: " Je vous aime, monsieur, je vous admire et je vous plains de tout mon cœur " (C.G., XII, 196).

With the manuscript of the *Confessions* completed, his persecutions now but a nightmare of the past, and his agitated heart finally at comparative peace, Rousseau, with eight more years to live, headed north towards Paris in the spring of 1770. Each step along the route was a personal triumph and he found life good. Wishing to visit Buffon, he stopped off at Montbard. In his correspondence he tells of the " accueil le plus obligeant " there extended him (C.G., XIX, 344). But it has been left to others to relate again and again how, upon arriving at Buffon's *cabinet d'étude*, he dropped to his knees to kiss the threshold in homage to a great man.[1] The following year, through the intermediary of Panckoucke, he was again offered the *Histoire naturelle* as a present, and this time he accepted (C.G., XX, 95). Nor did Buffon's attempted good offices stop there. In a letter written to his friend and collaborator, Guéneau de Montbeillard (5 décembre 1771), we read the curt and, at first glance, enigmatic sentence: " Je pense absolument comme vous au sujet de Jean-Jacques, et j'écrirai en conséquence à Panckoucke." The story of the concerted and thoughtful gesture which followed has often been distorted in the retelling; it would be well, then, to turn to Mme. Necker for the original account of the affair: " M. de Buffon pouvoit faire avoir mille écus de rente à Rousseau: Panckoucke les lui donnoit d'une nouvelle édition de ses œuvres: Rousseau parut d'abord enchanté; le lendemain il arrive tout changé, et, dans une profonde indignation contre M. de Buffon: Vous m'avez séduit, s'écria-t-il; non, il ne sera pas dit dans la postérité que Jean-Jacques a vendu ses pensées; on peut vendre le travail de ses doigts, copier de la musique pour nourrir sa femme, mais jamais le fruit de sa tête." [2]

From all current evidence, it would seem that Buffon, who was so often impelled by personal interest in his dealings with others, always acted towards Rousseau sympathetically and unselfishly. After Jean-Jacques's death, however, the *Confessions* were available for all to read. Given Buffon's disciplined nature, his overwhelming sense of propriety, it is not difficult to believe what has been reported as his final judgment: " Je l'aimais assez; mais lorsque j'ai vu ses *Confessions*, j'ai cessé de l'estimer. Son âme m'a révolté, et il m'est arrivé pour Jean-Jacques le contraire de ce qui arrive ordinairement: après sa mort, j'ai commencé à le mésestimer." [3]

---

[1] Hérault de Séchelles claims to have had this story—already so well-known in the eighteenth century—verified by Buffon himself: *Voyage à Monbar* [sic] (Paris, an X), 15.

[2] *Nouveaux Mélanges, extraits des manuscrits de M^me Necker* (Paris, an X), I, 164.

[3] Hérault de Séchelles, 27.

It is quite evident, from this account of their personal relations, that Rousseau's long-standing esteem for Buffon is noteworthy. A number of reasons for this attitude immediately come to mind: Buffon's own continued courage, and even audacity, in the face of threatened censorship: his mode of life, dignified, independent, and semi-withdrawn following his brilliant initial successes. Then too, he was, in Rousseau's expressed judgment, the greatest stylist of the age; and, above all, he was consistently willing to extend kindness and consideration " à ce pauvre proscrit," as Jean-Jacques described himself (*C.G.*, XII, 24).

To complete the picture, some attention should be given to the complex problem of their intellectual relationship as well. The extent of this influence will be properly understood, however, only when critical editions of Rousseau's works, beginning in 1755 with his *Discours sur l'origine de l'inégalité* and extending through *Emile*, receive the same competent treatment already afforded the *Discours sur les sciences et les arts*. It should be said at the outset that there seems no evidence of influence of Jean-Jacques's writings on those of Buffon, except in one instance, and then, as will soon be apparent, by way of reaction.

When the first three volumes of the *Histoire naturelle* appeared in 1749, they gained immediate acclaim with their striking attempt to join scientific fact with bold, philosophic speculation. Rousseau's original manuscript of the First Discourse, submitted to the Académie in 1750, has been lost along with his revised and expanded second manuscript. Before the date of publication, Rousseau had sufficient opportunity to know Buffon's first three volumes, either at first hand or through Diderot, and to revise his work in the light of his readings or discussions with his friend.[1] The fact remains there is no specific proof that he utilized Buffon as a source during the composition of the First Discourse. Still, it is a fact that Rousseau opened the " Première Partie " of his essay with a daring, majestic sweep which ignored the account of man's origin in Genesis and stressed his rise from primeval nature. In this he was following, wittingly or not, in the footsteps of Buffon for, on a still more imposing scale, with equal eloquence and even more audacity, his predecessor had depicted a whole evolving universe, with unorthodox references to man, in which the aroused Jansenists of the *Nouvelles Ecclésiastiques* and the Faculté de Théologie of the Sorbonne were scandalized to find no evidence of belief in any particular act of creation. The thought immediately arises that here Rousseau found more than fleeting inspiration for the development of his own early speculations on evolving man in a changing universe.[2] But until

---

[1] Furthermore, as Buffon states in the foreword to the sixth volume (1756) of the *Histoire naturelle*, the first volume was printed in 1746 and the second in 1747, though their date of publication was held up to coincide with volume three in 1749. There should therefore have been ample opportunity for many persons to become well acquainted with the contents of the first two volumes considerably in advance of their official appearance.

[2] Nor has anyone expressed this rapport between the ideas of Buffon and those of Jean-Jacques Rousseau on the subject more succinctly than Gustave Lanson. Without mentioning by name any work of Rousseau, Lanson writes: " A Buffon, qu'il admira

more tangible evidence comes to light, Buffon's influence on Rousseau's ideas at this stage must remain nothing more than a tantalizing possibility.

Rousseau is probably best known to the layman for his doctrines on the natural goodness of man. Now it is true that only a few passages of the First Discourse stress man's natural state, free from the vices of civilization. But this concept will play an important part in the Second Discourse, and it was Buffon who, in 1749, declared for all to read that perhaps " la vertu appartient à l'homme sauvage plus qu'à l'homme civilisé, et... le vice n'a pris naissance que dans la société " (F., II, 201). But we shall see that, four years later, he was to take Jean-Jacques to task for adopting precisely the same supposition. Still this represents scant evidence that Rousseau had been drawing upon the work of Buffon for confirmation, guidance, or inspiration.

Of greater interest to us in the present study are those instances where Rousseau openly calls on Buffon's authority in support of his own arguments and, by so doing, furnishes irrefutable proof of influence. They are most strikingly in evidence in the *Discours sur l'inégalité;* and, as we have already seen, the first of these occurs at the very beginning of the essay.[1] Again, while discussing the natural fertility of the earth's surface, Rousseau mentions Buffon by name and quotes from the first volume of the *Histoire naturelle* (F., I, 127-128) in support of his argument (H., I, 85, and note 4, 129). Once more, in pondering the question of life expectancy among men and animals, the author cites Buffon for corroboration (H., I, 87, and note 7, 132).

Among the passages of the naturalist which Jean-Jacques quotes in the essay, only this one, drawn from the article on the " Horse " (F., I, 396), need detain us here, for it throws new light on the Rousseau-Buffon relationship. " Du Cheval " is in volume IV of the original in-quarto edition published in 1755—in other words, in sufficient time for Rousseau to have read the book before submitting the 1755 essay for the Académie de Dijon prize competition. By calling our attention to the article in question, Rousseau admits being familiar with the volume in which it appeared. Furthermore, other ideas found in this fourth volume are developed in the Second Discourse, though Jean-Jacques does not state that they stemmed from Buffon. But critics have been puzzled by the fact that Rousseau desperately sought the fourth volume in the 1760's, because, as he stated, it was the one missing from his set and, even more important, " étant celui où il est question de moi." A careful study of the complicated history of the various Buffon editions reveals, however, that Rousseau already owned the contents of the fourth volume, but in one of the duo-decimo editions. The conclusion seems inescapable that during his years of wandering Rousseau was hopelessly confused by the sundry editions of the *His-*

---

toujours profondément, il a demandé les notions capables de préciser, de soutenir son hypothèse de l'homme naturel, et l'idée de la lente évolution par laquelle l'univers et les êtres qu'il porte se transforment." *Histoire de la littérature française*, 12th ed. (Paris, 1912), 787.

[1] See p. 40, footnote 1.

*toire naturelle* then pouring from the presses. It is the seventh in-quarto volume, which appeared in 1758, that was lacking, and which he was able to acquire only in 1764. It is, moreover, the only volume in Buffon's works where he discusses Rousseau, referring to him as " un Philosophe, l'un des plus fiers censeurs de notre humanité," one who maintains that early man, free of vice, has been corrupted by society (F., II, 566). It is, as we have pointed out, the hypothesis Buffon himself suggested in 1749— before Jean-Jacques composed either of his two famous essays. In fact, we may now conclude that Rousseau possessed all that was included in the six in-quarto volumes of the *Histoire naturelle* well before the publication of such significant works, for instance, as *La Nouvelle Héloïse*, *Le Contrat social*, and *Emile*.

But to return to Rousseau's Second Discourse. The specific references to Buffon mentioned above are merely a part of the evidence indicating how carefully his work had been read and how extensively his ideas had been utilized. In an often neglected but highly competent study, " Recherches sur les sources du *Discours de l'inégalité*," Jean Morel has proved the early volumes of the *Histoire naturelle* to have been a primary source of the " information scientifique " scattered throughout the Second Discourse.[1] Rather than repeat those aspects so ably handled by Morel, it would seem more fruitful in the present instance to pause over two matters treated in the Discourse where Buffon's rôle as inspirer of Rousseau has been neglected in research to date.

The first of these is related to the remarkable Note 10 of the Second Discourse (H., I, 138-144), the long appendix on men and apes that has led some to view Rousseau as anticipating Charles Darwin by at least a century In this respect we read: " Le brillant esprit qui entrevit le premier le remarquable mécanisme de la sélection naturelle est, je crois, Jean-Jacques Rousseau." [2] It will be recalled that in Note 10 Rousseau advanced the thesis that man and certain higher apes might well be of the same species. A score of years later, Lord Monboddo, bearing in mind this same note, as well as Buffon's remarks in the fourteenth volume (1776), first edition, of the *Histoire naturelle*, where the " Nomenclature des singes " was taken up in general and the " orang-outang " discussed in particular, was perhaps the first to point out clearly the difference of opinion between these two distinguished eighteenth-century writers regarding man's relation to the great apes. Following a summary of Buffon's text, Lord Monboddo declared: " It is from these facts that we are to judge, whether or not the Orang Outang belongs to our species. Mr. Buffon has decided that he does not. Mr. Rousseau inclines to a different opinion." [3]

---

[1] *Annales de la Société J.-J. Rousseau*, 1909, 179 ff.

[2] Alfred Giard, *Controverses transformistes* (Paris, 1904), 19. This theory is further developed by Edmond Perrier in *Lamarck* (Paris, 1925), 21-22, where we are told that Darwin could indeed have been inspired by the *Discours sur l'inégalité*. More prudent, Arthur O. Lovejoy prefers to consider Rousseau as an evolutionist in the anthropological and sociological sense rather than in the biological. See his " Monboddo and Rousseau," *Essays in the History of Ideas* (Baltimore, 1948), 40 and 51.

[3] *Of the Origin and Progress of Language*, 2nd ed. (Edinburgh, 1774), I, 290.

This is certainly a correct conclusion, and one that has ever since been corroborated by scholars. In particular, Buffon's statement, " ... si l'on ne devait juger que par la forme, l'espèce du singe pourrait être prise pour une variété dans l'espèce humaine," immediately followed by his conclusion that " ... quelque ressemblance qu'il y ait donc entre l'Hottentot et le singe, l'intervalle qui les sépare est immense," is a passage that has been quoted many times as proof of Buffon's definitive position on the subject. And it has often been one point of departure in that continuing debate on whether Buffon could properly be considered an evolutionist in his own right.[1]

In the present study, chronology is important, and of greatest concern is Rousseau's 1755 interpretation of Buffon's ideas on men and apes, and whether or not he utilized these ideas in the Second Discourse. A careful reading of Note 10 suggests that, in its conception, Rousseau relied heavily on the article entitled " Histoire de l'âne " in what was originally the fourth volume of the *Histoire naturelle*. Among the daring hypotheses that the reader of 1753 was able to discover here was the assertion that if the ass were to be considered of the same line as the horse, then one could also add that the ape was of the same family as man, and furthermore that both man and ape had the same origin. In fact, all animals may have descended through eons of time from a single source. This was indeed bold speculation for the day, and two paragraphs further on Buffon hastens to add: " Mais non: il est certain, par la révélation, que tous les animaux ont également participé à la grâce de la création " (F., II, 414). We are immediately reminded of the words of the naturalist's friend Diderot, written the following year: " Si la foi ne nous apprenait que les animaux sont sortis des mains du créateur tels que nous les voyons, et s'il était permis d'avoir la moindre incertitude sur leur commencement et sur leur fin, le philosophe abandonné à ses conjectures ne pourrait-il pas soupçonner que l'animalité avait de toute éternité ses éléments particuliers, épars et confondus dans la masse de la matière; ... La Religion nous

---

[1] Monboddo's thesis of conflicting views between Buffon and Rousseau has been elaborated on competently by Professor Lovejoy in his " Monboddo and Rousseau," and especially by Professor Hester Hastings in *Man and Beast in French Throught of the Eighteenth Century* (Baltimore, 1936), 113-132. Curiously enough, both studies completely ignore a work which, in its own way, is as important to the topic the writers are treating as is Edward Tyson's *Orang-Outang, sive Homo Sylvestris* (1699). I am referring to Benoît de Maillet's far more imaginative, though much less scientific work, *Telliamed ou entretiens d'un philosophe indien avec un missionnaire françois sur la diminution de la mer, la formation de la terre, l'origine de l'homme, etc. Mis en ordre sur les mémoires de feu M. de...* Par J. A. Guer, Avocat (Amsterdam, 1748); see especially II, 171-183. A selective bibliography on Buffon's theory of evolution would be too long to enumerate here. However, an early and still valuable study is Arthur O. Lovejoy's " Buffon and the Problem of Species," *Popular Science Monthly*, LXXIX (1911), 464-473 and 554-567. Two of the most important contributions to the debate in recent years are Paul Ostoya's *Les Théories de l'évolution* (Paris, 1951), 47-57, and J. B. Wilkie's thoughtful article, " The Idea of Evolution in the Writings of Buffon," *Annals of Science*, XII (1956), 48-62, 212-227, 255-266. Finally, attention might profitably be drawn to Lester Crocker's chapter, " Diderot and Eighteenth-Century French Transformism," in *The Forerunners of Darwin*, ed. Bentley Glass (Baltimore, 1959).

épargne bien des écarts et bien des travaux." [1] There is little difficulty in discerning Diderot's ironical intent. Nor was there reason for Rousseau to think otherwise about Buffon's declaration, " Il est certain, par la révélation." After all, the 1753 volume of the *Histoire naturelle* opened with an exchange of letters between the " Députés et Syndic de la Faculté de Théologie " and Buffon, where the naturalist laid to rest the Sorbonne's alarms with an explanation that he was later to qualify as " sotte " and " absurde." [2] And in his *Discours* of 1755, where Jean-Jacques wrote, " Commençons par écarter tous les faits, car ils ne touchent point à la question " (H., I, 83), it is evident that these " faits " included the story of Creation as related in the Scriptures. In other words, Rousseau was using a subterfuge common enough in the eighteenth century, and one he had seen utilized in Diderot's *Pensées* as well as in the work to which the latter was indebted, Buffon's *Histoire naturelle*.[3]

Still, the hypothesis Buffon both advanced and retracted, on the relationship between men and apes, is not in itself convincing proof that the article, *L'Ane*, had served as a major source of inspiration for Rousseau's speculations in Note 10. Among Jean-Jacques's and Buffon's contemporaries, De Maillet, Linnaeus, Maupertuis, La Mettrie, and others had pondered the subject and hinted at consanguinity before 1755 or even 1753. But there is another theory put forth in *L'Ane* which is both striking and original with Buffon. It is his new definition of species based on the problem of hybridism and the limits that cross breeding imposes upon fertility. Stated simply, it is the contention that if two animals interbreed with the result that their offspring cannot do so likewise, the parents are not of the same species (F., II, 415-416). The naturalist specifically refers to the horse and the ass. But it was Rousseau who, having profited from Buffon's observations, prudently arrived at the following conclusion: " Il y aurait pourtant un moyen par lequel, si l'orang-outang ou d'autres étaient de l'espèce humaine, les observateurs les plus grossiers pourraient s'en assurer même avec démonstration: mais outre qu'une seule génération ne suffirait pas pour cette expérience, elle doit passer pour impraticable, parce qu'il faudrait que ce qui n'est qu'une supposition fût démontré

---

[1] *Œuvres complètes*, Assézat-Tourneux (Paris, 1875-77), *Pensées sur l'interprétation de la nature*, II, 57-58.

[2] *Correspondance inédite de Buffon*, II, 68. Professor Jean Piveteau prefers to believe that Buffon's reference to revelation is entirely sincere (*Œuvres philosophiques de Buffon*, Paris, 1954, 355). Letters of Buffon throughout his career, however, show his ability to dissimulate, in the face of religious authoritarianism. In a letter to a friend, written in 1730, we find him confessing that he has made every effort to write in a style which would free him from what he called " les tracasseries théologiques." And a recently discovered letter pictures him as early as 1739 advising another friend to " prendre partout le ton ironique " in an essay which, if published undisguised, might cause its author serious difficulties. See Franck Bourdier and Yves François, " Lettres inédites de Buffon," in *Buffon*, ed., Roger Heim (Paris, 1952), 186.

[3] The most cursory reading of the *Pensées* reveals the extent of Diderot's debt to Buffon. Professor Aram Vartanian informs me that he plans to study this relation between Buffon and Diderot, a subject hardly yet touched upon.

vrai, avant que l'épreuve qui devrait constater le fait pût être tentée innocemment " (H., I, 142).

If further and still more tangible proof is needed that Buffon's writings remained uppermost in Rousseau's mind while composing Note 10, Jean-Jacques himself has furnished it in the conclusion of his six-page, closely printed Note. Therein, he observes that only men of Buffon's stature, having travelled to the farthest corners of the earth, could return with the truth about natural, moral, and political history. He then adds, " Je dis que quand de pareils observateurs affirmeront d'un tel animal que c'est un homme, et d'un autre que c'est une bête, il faudra les en croire " (H., I, 144).

The first volumes of the *Histoire naturelle* reveal, as we have already suggested, a second preoccupation of considerable moment: namely a study of sex as related to all living creatures. This subject will receive more than passing mention in the *Discours sur l'inégalité*, and in a number of Rousseau's later writings. The pages Buffon devoted to the sexual instinct and sexual customs among men and animals added much to the piquancy of the first four volumes, and, in no small measure, increased their popularity with an ever-growing reading public. " Descriptions téméraires pour l'époque," and " tirades quelque peu osées," as described by M. Roger Heim who concludes concerning Buffon, " Ainsi a-t-il écrit avec bienséance, dans une verve subtile, sur des sujets scabreux." [1] To this M. Franck Bourdier adds: " Les dames, nous disent les chroniqueurs de l'époque, mettaient l'ouvrage à leur chevet. C'était la première fois que l'on traitait ces délicats sujets de façon aussi scientifique dans un ouvrage pour les gens du monde." [2]

Among the many observations expressed by Buffon on the subject of love is one which is supposed to have deeply shocked Mme. de Pompadour: " Il n'y a que le physique de cette passion qui soit bon " (F., II, 352). As further clarified by the naturalist, man alone tortures himself in a thousand different ways by idealizing the love relationship. This thought may in turn have strongly impressed a Rousseau meditating from his own experiences. Without disclosing any source, he followed Buffon's reasoning almost literally, at once expanding on his predecessor's line of thought, now deviating ever so slightly, and finally returning to a simpler version of the argument. Even sentences or short phrases from Buffon's " Discours sur la nature des animaux—homo duplex " (1753) find a clear echo in Rousseau's *Discours* of 1755. Thus, on one hand, Buffon's development of the subject begins, " Distinguons donc, dans les passions de l'homme, le physique et le moral " (F., II, 350), and Rousseau repeats, " Commençons par

---

[1] *Buffon*, 10.

[2] " Principaux aspects de la vie et de l'œuvre de Buffon," in *Buffon*, 27. The second part of M. Bourdier's statement is, however, open to question. He has overlooked Nicolas Venette's *Tableau de l'amour dans l'état du mariage* (Amsterdam, 1687), also known as *De la Génération de l'homme*. This fascinating little work enjoyed 71 editions under the ancien régime, and was first called to my attention by Professors Gilbert Chinard and Jacques Roger. It manifestly prepared prospective readers of the *Histoire naturelle* for further analysis of " ces délicats sujets." Moreover, from internal evidence it seems most likely that Buffon, though not Rousseau, was thoroughly acquainted with Venette's quite remarkable manual on sex.

distinguer le moral du physique dans le sentiment de l'amour " (H., I, 101). Further on, Buffon wonders, " Mais les animaux sont-ils bornés aux seules passions que nous venons de décrire " (F., II, 352), and Jean-Jacques repeats: " Bornés au seul physique de l'amour... " (H., I, 101). Each in turn also expresses a bitter rhapsody on love. The ideas are the same, but, surprisingly, it is the natural historian, and not Jean-Jacques, who is extravagantly lyrical.

Buffon: " Amour ! désir inné ! âme de la nature ! principe inépuisable d'existence ! puissance souveraine qui peut tout et contre laquelle rien ne peut, par qui tout agit, tout respire et tout se renouvelle !... Amour ! pourquoi fais-tu l'état heureux de tous les êtres et le malheur de l'homme ? " (F., II, 351).

Rousseau: " Parmi les passions qui agitent le cœur de l'homme, il en est une ardente, impétueuse, qui rend un sexe nécessaire à l'autre: passion terrible qui brave tous les dangers, renverse tous les obstacles, et qui, dans ses fureurs, semblent propre à détruire le genre humain, qu'elle est destinée à conserver " (H., I, 101).

This is a theme that will be compellingly woven into *Emile*, the unfinished *Emile et Sophie*, and, especially, the *Nouvelle Héloïse* which is, first and foremost, the story of a couple suffering the anguish of human love—decidedly an example of, " No love, no novel." In Buffon's eyes, this latter work, he informed Mme. Necker, was the tale of a " babillard." As for his own interests *in rebus amoris*, they almost invariably took a more practical, down to earth, and even clinical turn. This approach was first strikingly apparent in " De la Puberté " and " De l'Age viril, " those sections of the *Histoire naturelle de l'Homme* wherein the reader of 1749 could find detailed information on sexual development and behavior traced from adolescence to adulthood. Here he offered physiological bases for the discussion of such topics as virginity, chastity, marriage, continence (including its dangers), even libertinage. All these themes were to appear in various subsequent works by Rousseau. Finally, we may note that in this eagerness to emulate Buffon as an authority on the physiology of sex, Jean-Jacques did not hesitate to appropriate his contemporary's words, phrases, and thoughts.

The same is equally true, and even more striking, in another domain, namely, the rearing of children. Mme Necker's statement in the *Nouveaux Mélanges* is well known: " M. de Buffon avait donné plusieurs préceptes d'éducation physique pareils à ceux qu'on trouve dans Emile. Je conseillois, disoit-il, et Rousseau a commandé " (II, 80). Neither Mme. Necker nor Buffon was overstating the circumstances. It is surprising, then, that André Ravier's detailed study of the history and doctrine of Jean-Jacques's famed pedagogical work does not once mention the author of the *Histoire naturelle*.[1] Rousseau himself has been more generous, and Buffon is quoted in the book a number of times, but not as often as the author of *Emile* would have us believe when he recognizes his debt in a footnote: " Voici

---

[1] André Ravier, *L'Education de l'homme nouveau; essai historique et critique sur le livre de l'Emile de J.-J. Rousseau* (Lyon, 1941), 2 vols.

encore une autre cause bien expliquée par un philosophe dont je cite souvent le livre, et dont les grandes vues m'instruisent encore plus souvent " (H., II, 104).

The eminent Rousseauist, Charles W. Hendel, is one of the few to have given some idea of the impact which certain of Buffon's theories had on Rousseau's treatise on pedagogy. Scattered throughout the second volume of *Jean-Jacques Rousseau, Moralist* (1934) are various references to the influence of *De l'Enfance*, a subsection of the 1749 edition of the *Histoire naturelle de l'Homme* (F., II, 9-27), on *Emile*. And indeed, we find in these opening pages of Buffon many topics that Rousseau will treat along parallel lines some twelve years later. These include infant mortality, dentition, sleep during infancy, tears as a language, the choice of wet nurses, the sense of touch in the learning process, speech development and habits, benefits of rural life for the growing child, the intricate problem of imagination and fear, the question of a tutor, and the famous principle in Buffon's, not Rousseau's words: an education " par laquelle on ne force pas la nature " (F., II, 27). The temptation is strong to compare passages from the two authors on each of the above subjects. But the purposes of the present study would, I believe, be sufficiently served if two extracts were quoted from Buffon, whose equivalents might be readily called to mind since they are among the most celebrated counsels in *Emile*, and among those closest to the heart of its author.

The first of these is the famous argument for nursing by the mother. Buffon opens the subject as follows: " Tout le monde sait combien il est important pour la santé des enfants de choisir de bonnes nourrices; il est absolument nécessaire qu'elles soient saines et qu'elles se portent bien.... Si les mères nourrissaient leurs enfants, il y a apparence qu'ils en seraient plus forts et plus vigoureux; le lait de leur mère doit leur convenir mieux que le lait d'une autre femme ...car on voit des enfants qui ne peuvent s'accommoder du lait de certaines femmes; ils maigrissent, ils deviennent languissants et malades " (F., II, 25). The second is that which condemns the use of swaddling clothes. This is a thought that Buffon had already expressed in no uncertain terms before all Europe listened to Jean-Jacques's impassioned plea on the same subject:

A peine l'enfant est-il sorti du sein de sa mère, on l'emmaillote, on le couche la tête fixe et les jambes allongées, les bras pendants à côté du corps, il est entouré de linges et de bandages de toute espèce qui ne lui permettent pas de changer de situation;.... Les peuples qui se contentent de couvrir ou de vêtir leurs enfants, sans les mettre au maillot, ne font-ils pas mieux que nous?... On ne peut pas éviter, en emmaillotant les enfants, de les gêner au point de leur faire ressentir de la douleur; les efforts qu'ils font pour se débarrasser sont plus capables de corrompre l'assemblage de leur corps que les mauvaises situations où ils pourraient se mettre eux-mêmes s'ils étaient en liberté " (F., II, 16).

There are, however, two aspects of Buffon's influence on *Emile* that are far more general than those just indicated. Professor Hendel has, moreover, shown awareness of both (*op. cit.*, 78, 79). The first is suggested by Rousseau's declaration in *Emile* concerning the work itself: " Ce devrait être l'histoire de mon espèce " (H., II, 387). In this study of man, Rousseau had the image of a natural being in the process of exhibiting its self-causative, abiding character. This is precisely the concept which Buffon had been applying to nature as a whole.

Still more illuminating is the second instance of a comprehensive influence of the *Histoire naturelle* on Rousseau's educational treatise. Although Buffon's monumental *Epoques de la nature* did not appear until 1778, in his earliest works almost thirty years before, he had demonstrated that both the changes in Nature and the development of the human being fell into defined stages. In *De l'Enfance* (1749) and especially in that part of the *Discours sur la nature des animaux* entitled *Homo duplex* (1753), we very clearly see this emphasis on the various steps in an individual's growth. There is no need to discuss here Rousseau's famous " quatre âges " which mark a child's progress from birth to maturity: the age of infancy, that of sensation, followed by that of reason, and, finally, the period when sentiment, or feeling, is achieved. What is less known, however, is the fact that each of these celebrated cycles had already been duly treated, although in a less systematic fashion, in Buffon's first writings. For instance, we may recall that Rousseau stresses the helplessness characteristic of the infant in the first stage. But it was Buffon who, in 1749, developed this subject more fully with these words, whose very rhythm evokes Jean-Jacques's emphatic style:

" Si quelque chose est capable de nous donner une idée de notre faiblesse, c'est l'état où nous nous trouvons immédiatement après la naissance: incapable de faire encore aucun usage de ses organes et de se servir de ses sens, l'enfant qui naît a besoin de secours de toute espèce, c'est une image de misère et de douleur; il est dans ces premiers temps plus faible qu'aucun des animaux; sa vie incertaine et chancelante paraît devoir finir à chaque instant; il ne peut se soutenir ni se mouvoir; à peine a-t-il la force nécessaire pour exister et pour annoncer par des gémissements les souffrances qu'il éprouve, comme si la nature voulait l'avertir qu'il est né pour souffrir, et qu'il ne vient prendre place dans l'espèce humaine que pour en partager les infirmités et les peines " (F., II, 9-10).

Rousseau's age of sensation, filled with physical activity, can also be traced to Buffon, who affirms that " le principe matériel domine... dans l'enfance," and then proceeds to describe in colorful detail the various motor activities of the child (F., II, 346). Like Rousseau after him, Buffon now analyzes " le temps où la faculté raisonnable domine," which he succeeds in describing masterfully (F., II, 347). Finally, Buffon shows the same awareness as Rousseau of a fourth stage during which the adolescent, turning his gaze inward, so to speak, examines his emotional and moral self. Both authors are concerned with transcending values, but whereas Rousseau passionately seeks " la lumière intérieure " (H., II, 239), Buffon speaks objectively in terms of " le principe spirituel " (F., II, 348).

As we have seen, a careful reading of both the second *Discours* and *Emile* bears evidence of Buffon's influence in the development of Rousseau's thought. *Rapprochements* in other works could also be shown, and the *Lettre sur les spectacles*, the *Nouvelle Héloïse*, the *Contrat social*, and Rousseau's *Correspondance générale* all point to the varying degrees of an intellectual relationship as well as the personal bond of sympathetic understanding that existed between these two eminent contemporaries. There is, however, no evidence of plagiarism, although that of influence is incontestable. Like most important thinkers, Buffon, who had read widely, drew upon many sources—Aristotle, Lucretius, Descartes, Bacon, Leibniz, and Newton, to name a few—to evolve his own philosophic contribution. Rousseau did likewise, but among his own careful readings must be listed the works of Buffon.

By way of conclusion, it might be pointed out that this examination of the nature of a relationship could well be made to extend beyond the life span of each author. When Rousseau, the son of a humble watchmaker, died in 1778, his title of *Citoyen de Genève* had been restored, and his place in history as a strange, provocative genius had already been established for posterity. Georges-Louis Leclerc, the great-grandson of a peasant—though this he would never have avowed—died just ten years later at the age of 81. He carried into death the distinction of membership in some dozen learned academies in the two hemispheres, while his copper coffinplate bore the resounding titles of " Comte de Buffon, Seigneur de Montbard, Marquis de Rougemont, Vicomte de Quincy, Seigneur de la Mairie, Les Harans, les Berges et autres lieux."

Both had premonitions of the coming Revolution with all its violence. But the turbulent years at the end of the century were kinder to Rousseau's memory than to that of Buffon. In 1794 Jean-Jacques's remains were borne in triumph to the Panthéon and there enshrined, while his widow received a governmental pension. Buffon's coffin was stripped of its lead covering which went to supply ammunition for the army, and his only legitimate son, a colonel in the Revolutionary forces, climbed the scaffold in 1793, and proudly proclaimed moments before his head fell: " Citoyens, je m'appelle Buffon." Rousseau's *Contrat social*, fulfilling the period's aspirations, became the Bible of government under both the Girondins and Robespierre. But when the Comité de Salut public endeavored to comply with a foreign potentate's wishes by sending him a set of the *Histoire naturelle*, none could be found that did not bear the words " De l'Imprimerie Royale." It was finally decided to present in its stead ten volumes of some obscure author of *Les Oiseaux coloriés*.

It might be argued that the emotionalist and the literary man won out during the Revolution, a moment of apotheosis for Rousseau, but not for the man of science. If so, such has not always been the case, and the growth of knowledge in the biological sciences was to make important use of Buffon's contributions. Not without prejudice, but certainly with sincerity and ample justification, Diderot had written late in life: " Je préférerais... quelques pages à choix de l'*Histoire naturelle*, à tous les ouvrages de Rousseau." [1]

---

[1] *Essai sur les règnes de Claude et de Néron*, III, 95.

Sainte-Beuve, looking back on the age, declared that Buffon was the belated survivor among the four great figures of the French eighteenth century—the other three being Montesquieu, Voltaire, and Rousseau—and " ferma pour ainsi dire ce siècle le jour de sa mort." [1] In addition, readers of the *Causeries du lundi* were informed that it was the naturalist " qui, à son époque, avait le plus de sens et de jugement " (XIV, 325). Moreover, since Sainte-Beuve's general appreciation, the picture of Buffon as the irreproachable stylist and man of letters has been steadily gaining ground. It is perhaps particularly noteworthy that Baudelaire, a keen judge of style, wrote in *Le Spleen de Paris*, " Je n'ai jamais rougi, même devant les jeunes écrivains de mon siècle, de mon admiration pour Buffon." [2] It will be remembered, on the other hand, that the author of the *Fleurs du mal* dismissed Rousseau as " Jean-Jacques—auteur sentimental et infâme " (p. 1193), a judgment which appears, however, excessively harsh. But what is more than a little curious is Buffon's re-emergence today as both a man of science and of letters. By the end of the nineteenth century, a new awareness of the naturalist's place in the history of scientific thought was in evidence, and Henry Fairfield Osborn was to write: " He may be said to have asked all the questions which were to be answered in the course of the succeeding century." [3] In the first half of the twentieth century, historians of science became increasingly aware of this new evaluation through the position maintained by Erik Nordenskiöld with such success in his *History of Biology*: " Buffon has played a fundamental part in the history of biology, not on account of the discoveries he made, but on account of the new ideas he produced.... Many of the ideas produced by Buffon have now been incorporated in the general knowledge of natural science.... His services ...must in all fairness be duly acknowledged; in the purely theoretical sphere he was the foremost biologist of the eighteenth century, the one who possessed the greatest wealth of ideas, of real benefit to subsequent ages and exerting an influence stretching far into the future." [4]

As recently as 1952, M. Roger Heim, Director of the *Muséum de l'Histoire naturelle*, wrote in his Preface to the latest book on Buffon: " Popularisant la nature en un siècle où Rousseau s'efforce de la faire aimer, son influence rejoint celle de Jean-Jacques en lui donnant d'autres motifs, puisés sur une autre forme de sentimentalité, purement esthétique, riche de vérité, rationaliste déjà, dirait-on aujourd'hui, en tout cas parfaitement et logiquement équilibrée." [5] And thus it has been left to the latest in a long line of Buffon's successors in the present Jardin des Plantes to link together again, with singular appropriateness, the names of Rousseau and Buffon.

---

[1] *Causeries du lundi* (Paris, n.d.), IV, 348.
[2] *Œuvres complètes*, ed., Y. G. Le Dantec (Paris, 1954), 358.
[3] *From the Greeks to Darwin* (New York, 1894), 138.
[4] *The History of Biology* (New York, 1936), 228-229.
[5] *Buffon*, 11.

# BUFFON'S PLACE IN THE ENLIGHTENMENT *

It is no easy matter to treat Georges Louis Leclerc, more familiarly known as the comte de Buffon. The difficulty involved is reflected in Buffon's own undertaking when he decided to write a history of natural science in fifteen volumes that would include nothing less than a theory of the solar system's coming into being, another on the evolution of the earth through seven vast epochs—*i. e.*, vast for the age—and then a history of all substance, organic or inorganic, that is bound up with the earth: man, quadrupeds, birds, fish, reptiles and a host of other creatures as well as the ever changing world of matter on, over, or in which they moved and had their being. Buffon's work was finally to comprise forty-four, not the originally planned fifteen volumes, and despite half a century of tireless effort in his eighty-year life, he did not live to see it completed.

The difficulties to which he exposed himself can, perhaps, best be illustrated by a true anecdote concerning the man and his work. While he was still alive, he experienced the signal honour of seeing a statue erected in acknowledgment of his accomplishments. It bore the inscription: NATURAM AMPLECTITUR OMNEM, "Il embrasse toute la nature." Beneath this inscription, so the story goes, a wag placed a sign bearing the old French proverb: "Celui qui trop embrasse, mal étreint." The moral is clear; in attempting to discuss Buffon, the historian of ideas is also apt to run the risk of "celui qui trop embrasse." But so far as the legend on the pedestal of Buffon's statue is concerned, authorities of the day, not wishing to have the witticism repeated, had the first Latin inscription replaced by the equally pompous, MAJESTATI NATURAE PAR INGENIUM. Both maxims, each in its way, illustrate the problems involved in presenting one such as Buffon. He himself attempted to accomplish too much, as revealed in the first maxim, and he had the almost superhuman task of living up to his reputation as depicted in the second. Such are the complexities that, so far, no satisfactory comprehensive study on the man and his work has yet been published in French,[1] and no volume at all has yet appeared in English.

---

* Reprinted from *Studies on Voltaire and the Eighteenth Century*, XXV, Transactions of the First International Congress on the Enlightenment (Geneva, 1963), 603-629. Permission to republish granted by Theodore Besterman.

[1] The appearance of Jacques Roger's *Epoques de la nature* (1963) is an outstanding contribution to the knowledge of Buffon and, at least partly, invalidates this statement.

Since his death as during his lifetime there has been a long chain of conflicting statements extending down to the present about Buffon and what he stands for. Thus, most recently, from the lochs and streams of Scotland there comes a sophisticated and charming book about otters entitled *Ring of Bright Water*. At one point, its author, Gavin Maxwell, says:

" But that garrulous eighteenth-century clown the Comte de Buffon, whose nineteen volumes had acquired a petulant flavour by his contemporary translator's insistence on the use of the English word ' pretend ' for the French *prétendre*, did not, on the whole, approve of otters. He was a whimsical man, much concerned with the curious, and credulous as to the existence of the most patently improbable creatures, which he himself tried assiduously to produce by arranging monstrous matings (after much experiment he was disappointedly forced to the conclusion that a bull and a mare ' could copulate neither with pleasure nor profit ') [1]; furthermore he appeared to attach some mystic significance to whether an animal could or could not be persuaded to eat honey. Otters, he found, could not."

What sort of a scientist, we may ask under the persistent prodding of Mr. Maxwell, is this!

And from the deserts of Arizona, Mr. Joseph Wood Krutch, in his delightful books on natural history, depicts many things including a Buffon a century behind the times in science, a living anachronism quite capable of adopting a view that even educated laymen of the day regarded as little more than a vulgar superstition. In one instance Mr. Krutch concludes: " Insofar as Buffon survives, it is as a belletrist, especially as a maker of full-dress phrases, a coiner of commonplaces." [2] What sort of a scientist is this indeed!

To give balance to the picture, there is George Gamow who, in his *Biography of the Earth*, states that Buffon's *Histoire naturelle* " is probably the most brilliant and comprehensive study of natural science ever written" (p. 9). Charles Singer in *A Short History of Scientific Ideas* speaks of " the remarkable insight of the accomplished Buffon " (p. 328), while Karl Walter Scheidt, former director of the Rassenbiologisches Institut of the Hanseatic University at Hamburg, declares that " it is Buffon's unchallenged service that he was the first great representative of a ' doctrine of epigenesis '; and in consideration of his theory of human race origins he can frankly be called the ' first anthropologist.' " [3]

This, I believe, is a fair sampling from present day non-specialists in Buffon who, for better or worse, have had their word to say before passing on to more compelling interests. Was it always so?

In the preface to *Back to Methuselah*, George Bernard Shaw tells how, as a boy in a Dublin bookstore with his father, he saw a pretentious gentle-

---

[1] Mr. Maxwell's wit and urbanity obviously exceed his familiarity with certain basic problems in the history of ideas.

[2] *Great American Nature Writers* (New York, 1950), 68-69.

[3] Quoted by Earl W. Count, *This Is Race* (New York, 1950), 360, from Scheidt's *Beiträge zur Geschichte der Anthropologie* (1924).

man who entered with an imperial air to demand the works of the French naturalist, "the celebrated Buffoon." Buffon was still so famous, Shaw informs us, that, despite his youth, he had immediately recognized the blunder of the egregious culture seeker. "Every literate child at that time," Shaw adds, "knew Buffon's Natural History as well as Aesop's Fables."

A little over a hundred years ago, Sainte-Beuve, the historical critic *par excellence* of his day—looking back into the preceding century—had no hesitation in calling Buffon, along with Voltaire, Montesquieu and Rousseau, one of the four great men of the age. Moreover, according to the author of the *Lundis*, since he outlived the other three, with his death Buffon had the added distinction of bringing the period of the Enlightenment to a close.

When Montesquieu died in 1755 Diderot alone, among men of letters, was present at the obsequies. Although the aged Voltaire had returned in triumph to Paris, when death came in 1778, his remains were propped upright in a carriage and stealthily removed from the city under the cover of darkness. Rousseau, who died two months later, was not to have his apotheosis until shortly after Robespierre's fall in 1794. The *Mercure de France* of 26 April 1789 reports, however, that upon Buffon's death a fortnight before, many of the most distinguished names of France were on hand to pay final respects to a great genius in the presence of 20,000 onlookers. And in England, the *Gentleman's Magazine*, in echo of French periodicals of the day, declared that the last of the great Frenchmen of the century was dead and that the "four bright lamps," Montesquieu, Voltaire, Rousseau and Buffon were now "totally extinguished."

It may be safely said, then, that Buffon received greater worldly honours not only when among the living but also upon his death than his three eminent predecessors. Nor are reasons hard to find why this was so.

For some time interest in man and the universe had been given increased impetus by the stress being placed on certain scientific approaches. Cartesian methodical doubt was fast demolishing many of the long respected positions supported by neo-Aristotelian authority, by the "science" of theology along with organized religion, and even by superstitions venerable with age. There were also the rational *a priori* ideas in the Cartesian tradition which themselves helped clear the air of outworn systems while offering new, often fruitful ones in their place; Descartes' own emphasis on matter in motion as a basic creative principle for the world of being might be considered one of these. Then too, there was an increasing insistence upon the somewhat narrower, experimental, *a posteriori* approach in the Baconian-Newtonian tradition that in the last half of the seventeenth century served as a guiding principle of the Royal Society of London, and was soon to sweep across the Channel to shake the very foundations of the newly-established *Académie des sciences* in Paris. Along with these intellectual drives came the sensationalism of John Locke which, with Voltaire's *Lettres philosophiques* in 1734, gave Frenchmen of a speculative turn of mind a fresh awareness of man *qua* man in relation to himself, his fellow-men, and the world within reach of his senses.

Buffon, born in 1707, reached manhood at a time when these ideological currents had reached new strength, not each by itself, but in conjunction one with the other. There will be in Buffon's own intellectual formation a fusion of all three, Cartesian rationalism, Baconian-Newtonian experimentalism, and Locke's sensationalism, which will mark in one way or another everything that he wrote. This is not surprising. These approaches, far from being mutually exclusive in the general advance of science, proved especially productive in the field of natural history. Far more than mathematics, or physics, or astronomy, natural history was interested in both science and life.

A young, ambitious Buffon had for some time been looking on all sides to see where he could use his intelligence, which he had in abundance, the better to seek fame and add to his already considerable fortune. Well-grounded in law, mathematics and botany, he nevertheless found the three fields already crowded with distinguished names. He decided to cast his lot elsewhere. When, in 1739, through skilful manœuvering and influence in high places he became curator of the *Jardin du roi*, he chose in irrevocable fashion the career of a natural scientist, and he chose exceedingly well.

It was a time when amateurs of science throughout western Europe, having tried their hand at such physical sciences as astronomy, physics, geology and chemistry in its most elementary form, became increasingly drawn to another, more dramatically varied science which, seemingly, could be grasped with greater facility and pleasure. Then too, it had a marked appeal for the acquisitive propensity so strong in squirrels, pack rats and *homo sapiens*. By the first half of the eighteenth century, members of the more prosperous upper classes were indulging to a degree before unheard of in the mania of collecting. In England and France, especially, private collections in natural history were springing up on all sides. There were collections of sea shells, minerals, fossils, and herbs. Members of the nobility often achieved added stature by keeping menageries, and the presence of a weary, moth-eaten lion, a South-American tapir or a small elephant gave a cachet lacking in the less exotic private zoos on great family estates.

Moreover the eighteenth century was one of the great ages for compendia, and the continuous flow of volumes of the *Histoire naturelle* from 1749 to the author's death some forty years later, was, with the possible exception of Diderot's *Encyclopédie*, the most striking compendium of the Enlightenment. Nor is it to be forgotten that Buffon was the first of his day to demonstrate that science and literature could be so closely and so appropriately wedded as to add brilliantly to the *éclat* of the writer and his work. And even today generally hard to please essayists in the field of natural history feel obliged to doff their hats to the magnificent " *style noble* " of some of Buffon's pages before passing on to attack with amused scorn the qualities of his science.

Lastly, Buffon succeeded in having his monumental work published with no initial cost to himself on the royal presses of the realm. This was one indication of his quite exceptional ability to turn almost everything of a materialistic nature to his own advantage. To be published by the

*Imprimerie royale* had another more consequential importance, however. It permitted the author to bring out his successive volumes on natural history exempt from censorship. As a result, with far more ease and much less anxiety than in the case of Montesquieu, Voltaire or Rousseau, he was able to publish startling theories and daring ideas that were clearly recognized as such under the very eyes of church and state.

For these reasons alone, then, it is easy to see why his multi-volumed *Histoire naturelle* was, along with the *Spectacle de la nature* of the *Abbé* Pluche, the most commonly owned work of the eighteenth century. It made passionately interesting reading for friend and foe alike, and in many quarters was indispensable, as shown by Rousseau, who refused the work as a gift of the author by saying that it was altogether too precious for him not to have a set already. Buffon who, as David Hume once remarked, looked more like a marshal of France than a writer, would be observed frequenting the leading salons of Paris and the provinces, seated in the various academies to which he had been duly elected, lording it over the large holdings of the *Jardin du roi* or strolling along the royal paths at Versailles. He was, one might say, as handsomely impressive and as ubiquitous as those luxuriously bound volumes of his natural history.

But there is a fact that has been given little emphasis either by his contemporaries or by posterity. It is that there was and still is far less known about Buffon the man and his work than was and is the case of his three illustrious compeers. Montesquieu's chief interests were those of a brilliant satirist of the contemporary scene, an amateur man of science whose experiments for the Academy of Bordeaux quickened his deterministic outlook in all things, and a magistrate less concerned with legal procedure than political philosophy. These interests found their culminating point in the most significant of a small corpus of works when the *Esprit des lois* appeared in 1748. Voltaire's correspondence was so prolific and so detailed, his published works so vast, his activities—social, cultural and intellectual—so highly publicized, that he was everywhere recognized as one of the prime movers, perhaps the unquestioned leader of the *philosophes*. A courageous and stubbornly blunt Rousseau made little effort throughout his anguished life to hide his basic thoughts and his sensitive feelings. What he said, wrote and did, was immediately exposed to an entire continent. Furthermore, of the quaternion it was he alone who set down confessions, *Confessions* the like of which had never before been known.

And Buffon? Was he a *philosophe*, or an *encyclopédiste*, or even a figure of the Enlightenment? Whether or not he was any of these has been and doubtless for some time to come will be both affirmed and denied. For the moment, his right to the title of Encyclopedist, by way of illustration, might be examined. Evidence of enmity in varying degrees toward Buffon has come down to us in sufficient quantities to establish a tradition. Condillac's case needs no comment, but there are indications that d'Alembert, Raynal, Condorcet and Voltaire, among others,[1] had no steadfast

---

[1] Albert Dastre's "Buffon et les critiques de l'*Histoire naturelle*," *Revue des deux mondes* (Jan. 1900), 202-217, although excellent as far as it goes, is no longer adequate as a study of eighteenth-century critical reaction.

love or admiration for the naturalist. He has, then, time and again, been depicted as one who was held in scorn by the Encyclopedic group of which he was no part. But it is also known that Diderot, having obtained his collaboration on the *Encyclopédie*, enthusiastically described Buffon's article " Nature," already received and soon to be published.[1] Since, in due course, an article, " Nature," did appear, Buffon is today often classified as a contributor to the Encyclopedia, and hence an *encyclopédiste*.[2] But is the article that made its appearance in Tome XI the one promised by Buffon? Or does the letter ' O ' with which it is signed indicate the author to be none other than d'Alembert?[3]

This uncertainty about Buffon's rôle as an *encyclopédiste*, hinging as it does on the possible authorship of the article " Nature," is part of a much larger pattern. There was the social and intellectual portrait, reasonably simple in its broader lines, that he himself wished to present to his age and to posterity. It was at once that of the *grand seigneur*, wise in the ways of his fellow men, and that of the dedicated man of science who, through his genius, could help the cause of progress as few before had been able to do.

But Buffon was highly resourceful; he was, when necessary, devious and, moreover, skilled in the art of duplicity when the occasion warranted. And the occasion did warrant when fame and fortune were deeply involved and when that peace of mind indispensable for his continued work in natural science was at stake. In 1751 the Faculty of Theology of the Sorbonne was gravely alarmed that the first books of his *Natural History* seemed to run counter to Genesis; without hesitation Buffon published a statement declaring his veneration for holy writ and for the Sorbonne, and acknowledged that the Sorbonne was always right. A letter to a friend written the previous year stated that he had taken every precaution to avoid theological bickering which he dreaded far more than he did the criticisms of physicists and mathematicians.[4] And in another letter, some thirty years later, he confessed little concern when his most recent writings again aroused the theologians; he foresaw nothing more serious than the possibility of having to sign an explanation as absurd and as stupid as the first had been.[5] It was rarely, however, that he revealed himself as inti-

---

[1] In the *Avertissement des éditeurs*, Vol. II, of the *Encyclopédie*, Diderot says: " Nous ne pouvons trop nous hâter de publier que M. de Buffon nous a donné pour un des volumes qui suivront celui-ci l'article *Nature*; article d'autant plus important qu'il a pour objet un terme assez vague, souvent employé, mais bien peu défini, dont les philosophes n'abusent que trop et qui demande pour être élevé et présenté sous ses différentes faces, toute la sagacité, la justesse et l'élévation que M. de Buffon fait paraître dans les sujets qu'il traite."

[2] Cf. Jacques Proust's monumental *Diderot et l'Encyclopédie* (Paris 1962), 459, 518.

[3] Such is, in fact, the opinion of Lucien Plantefol: " NATURE est signé de l'O majuscule, bien fait pour être le monogramme aussi bien d'un géomètre parfait que de Jean Le Rond d'Alembert," " Les Sciences naturelles dans l'*Encyclopédie*," *Annales de l'université de Paris* (oct. 1952), 172.

[4] To the *Abbé* Le Blanc; Henri de Nadault de Buffon, ed. *Correspondance inédite de Buffon* (Paris, 1860), I, 47.

[5] To Guéneau de Montbéliard (II, 68).

mately as this in his letters. They were usually what he wanted them to be, flat, dull business and legal documents. We know that various *philosophes* corresponded with him, though their letters have not come down to us. His general practice was to destroy correspondence received as soon as it no longer held any practical value, and he apparently expected recipients of his own letters to do the same. He knew when to be reticent and when to speak. It was a lesson which, as an old man, he tried to teach the young Hérault de Séchelles, advising him never to clash openly with the powers that be as had Diderot, Voltaire and Helvétius.[1] The lesson profited the budding journalist little; the impulsive anticleric, though a revolutionary, lost his head on the scaffold. But Buffon, who, moreover, was aware of the approaching revolution, could show magnificent impartiality by cautioning equal prudence on the part of a man of the cloth. Thus the *Abbé* Jean Louis Soulavie was to relate to Benjamin Franklin the word of caution he too had received from the intendant of the King's gardens: " I refer," he told Franklin in 1781, " to the philosophers, who long for a revolution, and are preparing one against religion. I refer particularly to Buffon, who said to me in December 1778, that this revolution would direct its first efforts against the French clergy, and who advised me to take care of myself." [2] Does this statement imply that Buffon was among those *philosophes* preparing a revolution against religion? Is this in keeping with what we know of Buffon? But what do we know of him?

An aura of mystery still hangs over this wily Burgundian whose very friends were quite incapable of portraying him convincingly. So much of the information we have comes from anecdotes of his old age, or what his enemies had to say, or from legend and fable always quick to take over when facts are missing. This obscurity—often more willful and far more subtle on the naturalist's part than with any other outstanding figures of the Enlightenment—continues to encourage supposition and conjecture. Buffon himself once said: " Sur la scène du monde, je m'avance masqué." [3]

---

[1] See Hérault de Séchelles, *Voyage à Montbar* (Paris, an IX).

[2] Jean-Louis Soulavie, *Historical and Political Memoirs of the Reign of Lewis XVI* (London, 1802), V, 166-167.

[3] The *philosophes* did, of course, often attempt to conceal their true sentiments by producing their more dangerous works under the cloak of anonymity or through the use of pseudonyms. Buffon practiced neither method and yet, I think, could be considered more than any of his contemporaries to have gone through life wearing a mask. But the mask metaphor was not an uncommon one during the Enlightenment, as the following exchange strikingly indicates. In reply to Voltaire's observation that the world at large is but a poor masquerade, the Jesuit, Saverio Bettinelli, replies on 15 January 1760: " Mais ce qui vous réjouira le plus c'est la mascarade des Philosophes. Buffon se fait écolier de la Sorbonne, Montesquieu désavouë les Lettres Persannes, et ment avec décence, comme dit d'Alembert, qui de son côté combat logiquement en Catholique contre les Protestans; Rousseau s'enterre pour faire du bruit, et veût être lu des hommes qu'il déchire; Diderot ne respire que les beaux sentimens dans ses comédies — jusques à la Beaumelle est dévot pour Me de Maintenon. Tous ces grands génies sans préjugéz prennent un masque et en changent souvent; ce sont les plus grands Comédiens que j'ai vû à Paris " (Best. 7979). In his reply of 24 March 1760, Voltaire defends the English against an accusation of hypocrisy by Bettinelli, then goes on to defend the French of his day: " Comme les Français ne sont qu'à demi libres, ils ne sont encor hardis qu'à

It is this figurative mask that has so frequently hidden the real Buffon from his contemporaries and from posterity alike. I have tried to explain elsewhere how this reliance upon a mask was determined by his relation to the age.[1]

With few exceptions, the aims and achievements of the century's most daring thinkers came into unremitting conflict, under Louis XV, with disintegrating yet oppressive authority in civil and ecclesiastical matters alike. Voltaire, Diderot, d'Holbach and Rousseau were, among others, insurgents against the imposed traditions. But if Buffon's part has remained ambiguous it is, I feel, that on the one hand his independence of thought and his well-concealed cooperation with the *philosophes*[2] belong to the current of the Enlightenment, while on the other hand his personal conduct, social position, and official functions may be identified with the interests of the privileged aristocracy and an intolerant authoritarianism. Only by attempting to handle with uncommon judgment and tact all controversial issues could Buffon hope to maintain that delicate equilibrium which enabled him to pursue his aims among the opposing forces of the day. And his aims were manifest: to increase his already considerable fortune, to hold on to the many honours acquired through the years, and, above all, to carry on peacefully his monumental work in natural history. Only by pursuing this latter task could he expect to fulfil one of the ideals of the Enlightenment—man's partial liberation from and conquest of the forces of nature.

Because of his mask, or if you will, despite his attempt to maintain this delicate equilibrium, there are those who have proven with ease that here was an exemplary Roman Catholic as well as one of the pillars of the *ancien régime*. Others, equally convincing, have revealed him to be a deist, an agnostic and even, quite baldly, a materialistic atheist.[3] There are those who have agreed with Rousseau that his was the finest pen of the century, and others with d'Alembert that he was high-flown and verbose in all he wrote, while his celebrated dictum, " Le style c'est l'homme même," is still subject to contrary interpretations. Buffon's giant enterprise, a universal natural history, is either looked upon as essentially the work of a single man, or as the combined efforts of a far-flung network of corre-

---

demi; il est vrai que Buffon, Montesquieu, Helvétius etc[a] ont donné des rétractations; mais il est encor plus vrai qu'ils y ont été forcés, et que ces rétractations n'ont été regardées que comme des condescendances qu'on a pour des frénétiques; le public sçait à quoi s'en tenir: tout le monde n'a pas le même goust pour être brulé comme Jean Hus et Jérôme de Prague; les sages en Angleterre ne sont point persécutés, et les sages en France élludent la persécution " (Best. 8078).

[1] " Buffon and Rousseau: aspects of a relationship," *PMLA*, LXXV (June 1960), 184-196.

[2] See, for example, Jacques Roger, " Diderot et Buffon en 1749," *Diderot Studies* (Geneva, 1963), IV.

[3] Conflicting views on this aspect of Buffon are, and from the beginning have been, legion, and among the founding fathers of the new republic across the sea, John Adams, unlike Benjamin Franklin and Thomas Jefferson, found the Frenchman too materialistic and irreligious for his taste. See Edwin T. Martin, *Thomas Jefferson, Scientist* (New York, 1952), 133.

spondents abroad and a team of collaborators at home. His science can and should be reduced to a single principle,[1] or it combined those of Descartes, Newton, Leibniz, Spinoza and Locke. He was a writing-desk scientist who, in full court dress with decorations gleaming, limited himself to penning grandiose theories, or he was an indefatigable experimenter in physics, comparative anatomy, optics and silviculture at a time when experimental science [2] was at last coming into its own. These are some of the discrepancies that are repeatedly voiced by commentators on Buffon. These contradictions blur still further his rôle in the Enlightenment.

There is a far more uncertain domain, though, where well-meaning but misguided biographers have blindly chosen between contrary accounts, or have accepted supposed facts on conjectural grounds, or have even been guilty of repeating stories that are blatantly apocryphal. These have to do exclusively with presumed factual knowledge of Buffon's life. A few examples from many should suffice. Biographers have, for instance, furnished us with three distinct versions of young Buffon's grand tour with the Duke of Kingston and the latter's tutor, a pipe-smoking German by the name of Hinckman[n] or Dr. Nathan Hickman, an Englishman and fellow of the Royal Society of London.[3] Buffon had—depending on the source consulted—one, two or three serious duels.[4] In the first of these he wounded or killed an Englishman, or a French or Croatian army officer, and over a girl or a game of cards. When in England he was wounded in a duel by the cousin of either Lord Grandisson or the Duke of Kingston. Or did he go to England at all? The question is of importance in the history of Anglo-French relations. Until recently it has been answered in the affirmative and often in some detail. Among the handful refusing evidence of any such trip or trips is Stephen F. Milliken, who has presented a most plausible explanation of how another legend concerning Buffon may have been born.

---

[1] Aram Vartanian would hold that Buffon's system could be reduced to Cartesian matter in movement, *Diderot and Descartes* (Princeton, 1953), while Robert Wohl would affirm that it stems from the Newtonian principle of attraction, " Buffon and his project for a new science," *Isis*, LI (1960), 186-199.

[2] Two recent articles of considerable importance have cast added light on Buffon in the field of experimental science. They are W. E. Knowles Middleton's " Archimedes, Kircher, Buffon and the burning-mirrors," *Isis* (1961), 533-543, and Lesley Hanks's " Buffon et les fusées volantes," *Revue d'histoire des sciences* (June 1961), 137-154. In the same issue of the latter periodical, letters newly discovered by Françoise Weil, " La correspondance de Buffon-Cramer " (97-136), give further evidence of the young Buffon's very real gift for mathematics.

[3] Credit must go to Harcourt Brown for shedding new light on the Hinckman[n]-Hickman problem (" Buffon and the Royal Society of London," *Studies and Essays in the History of Science and Learning Offered... to George Sarton*, New York, 1947), and to Stephen F. Milliken for adding to Professor Brown's information in a forthcoming book tentatively entitled *Buffon and the British*. See also Weil, *op. cit.*

[4] In his 1860 edition of the *Correspondance inédite de Buffon*, Nadault de Buffon informs us that his illustrious ancestor had one duel (see I, 4), but by 1885, in his notes to the *Correspondance Générale*, the duels have increased from one to three (see J.-L. Lanessan edition of the *Œuvres complètes de Buffon*, XIII, 6, n. 1, and XIV, n. 1).

It is characteristic that the naturalist himself made no attempt to put order into the different accounts of his *gestae* already current during his lifetime. There is, in fact, much reason to believe that he was not averse to adding a few touches to an already confusing picture.[1] It was quite in keeping with his determination to remain *masqué*. Buffon the careerist was a man with a mask, a man capable of bland retractions, a writer able to couch his ideas in a disconcertingly ambiguous style, a thinker who was most willing to be traditional where it did not interfere with his deepest convictions. The wearing of such a mask was frankly disconcerting to a d'Alembert, a Condorcet, a Roland, a Marmontel, and even at times a Voltaire—all men of the Enlightenment—and a recurring term they applied to Buffon in conversation, correspondence and memoirs, was that of "charlatan." Not so for a Montesquieu, a Diderot, a Rousseau and somewhat later, a French revolutionist, for Mirabeau was to feel justified in saying: " M. de Buffon est le plus grand homme de ce siècle et de bien d'autres." Montesquieu, Diderot, Rousseau and Mirabeau were less concerned with the man wearing the mask than with the man behind it. For them here was an arresting mind, one qualified to give startling new values to science and the philosophy of science:—in a word, the mind of a man of the Enlightenment.

It would be impossible within the scope of the present inquiry to go into all of Buffon's scientific interests, some of which, to be sure, were merely corollary to what significantly and perhaps permanently contributed to man's general knowledge and to that of science in particular. But there are certain terms in the history of science and that of ideas with which his name—rightly or wrongly—has been closely associated. One of these is that of "evolution." This has been so, though in ambiguous terms, ever since Erasmus Darwin, in part inspired by an acquaintance with the *Histoire naturelle*, worked out an explanation of organic life according to fairly elementary evolutionary principles in his *Zoonomia* at the end of the eighteenth century. The association of Buffon's name with evolution took on increased emphasis, though, when Erasmus' famous grandson, Charles, in the " historical sketch " which prefaced the second edition of the *Origin of Species*, declared: " Passing over allusions to the subject in the classical writers, the first author who in modern times has treated it [transformism] in a scientific spirit was Buffon." What factors in Buffon's thought led Darwin and Samuel Butler, for instance, to see in the French naturalist the first writer of modern times to treat transformism in a scientific spirit? And again, what are these same factors that have since led others to reject him completely as an evolutionist?

---

[1] This is occasionally apparent in his correspondence, but becomes plainly evident with a careful reading of the *Notice sur la vie privée de m. le comte de Buffon par le r. p. Ignace Bougot, capucin, desservant de la paroisse de Buffon*. The good, simple Capuchin, endowed with unshakable credulity, is the inexhaustible source of a number of stories some of which were fed to him by the protagonist himself. It has been generally overlooked that father Bougot's *relation* is available in its entirety in the Lanessan edition of the *Œuvres complètes de Buffon*, XIV, 405-412.

By evolutionist is invariably meant, it appears, an enlightened forerunner of Darwinism.

The first three volumes of the *Histoire naturelle* which appeared in 1749—including the *Théorie de la terre* completed some four years before when Buffon was 38—themselves give a good indication of the affinities and divergencies of his science and philosophy when compared with the general intellectual climate of the time. His method was that of induction, and in this respect he was in agreement with the prevalent scientific spirit of the age which stressed the importance of observation. Not satisfied with considering observation or description an end in itself, however, he wished to synthesize his facts and observations and those of others in an effort to arrive at some comprehensive truth or truths. This attempt of his to understand facts and observations and, if possible, push them to their extreme consequences itself distinguished him from his contemporaries in general. For Buffon, then, seemingly isolated facts could serve as a point of departure for comparison and unification into a system of general laws. Newton, whose picture hung over his desk at Montbard, had reduced the mechanical aspects of the universe to a unifying system of law. Buffon gives every indication of wishing to extend Newton's principles to the world of living matter as well.

But before applying Newton's system to the organic world, he wished to use it as a point of departure for his own speculation concerning Newton's clockwork universe. This universe was for Newton and the majority of his disciples conclusive proof offered by science of the existence of a supreme being, for a great clock implied a great clockmaker who had set all in motion. Buffon strongly felt, like Bacon before him, that science and theology should be separated. Having taken for granted the Newtonian law of attraction in the movement of heavenly bodies, Buffon began speculating where attraction left off. He theorized that there was a no less general force of impulsion, or centrifugal motion, that, along with gravitation, was responsible for the planets' perpetual rotation in fixed orbits around the sun. Through brilliant scientific speculation he then proceeded to explain the planets' movements in such a way that half a century later he drew the praise of Laplace who held him to be the only one who, since Newton's discoveries, had attempted to go back to the origin of the planets and their satellites. Buffon, then—unlike Newton and his followers in general—was very much concerned with the "how" of what to him was patently an evolving universe. His hypotheses on the subject, early in the *Théorie de la terre* and late in the great *Epoques de la nature*, gave a physical account of the world which completely rejected supernatural explanations. From the beginning he made it clear that he would advance theories based on natural causes alone. Thus our solar system may have resulted from a stray comet's glancing blow at the molten matter of the sun. The impact hurled torrents of formless liquid into space with a spinning motion; from this were formed incandescent masses that, turning on their axes, slowly cooled in orbit around the celestial body from which they had originated. Hundreds of years later, the slow, inexorable action of the seas over the face of the earth may well have produced mountains, valleys and other irregularities that were to emerge with the receding waters. And marine deposits would be left behind that, with time, would become fossilized as testimony to the irresistible change that was the order of the universe.[1]

In the *Epoques*, with his thinking influenced by Leibniz's *Protogaea*, Buffon bent his efforts especially towards establishing a chronology of cosmic evolution. A little over a century before, Ireland's archbishop, James Ussher (1581-1656), had offered the date, 4004 B.C. as that primordial moment when the universe had come into being, and it was a date widely accepted in the eighteenth century. To be sure, science had, for some time, been taking liberties with the account in Genesis for their cosmogonic computations. "By and large," to quote from a recent scholar,[2] " man's notions of the Earth's origins and history remained comfortably within the limits of what could be taken for a drama presided over by a Divinity. Even Newton had tried to fit the Earth's age somehow into the Christian chronology. If with Copernicus, the Earth had been displaced in space from the center of the universe, it remained nonetheless true that up until the eighteenth century it had not yet been removed from the temporal center of things, thus perpetuating in natural science an anthropocentric and teleological conception of man's place in the universe."

It was with Buffon that this temporal anthropocentrism began to vanish. According to his conjectures, Jupiter, for example, had taken at least three times as long to cool to the touch as had the earth. Authoritatively precise figures were arrived at as he continued to carry out experiments on small metal balls first heated to the point of incandescence to compute

---

[1] All this was scandalous to contemporary theologians and scientists alike, and the Abbé de Lignac in his *Lettres à un Amériquain* (1751), encouraged by no less a figure than Réaumur, expressed deep concern over Buffon's explanations based solely on the materialist conception of matter in motion obeying the laws of chance. Strong protests were heard in the philosophic camp as well, and, in his summary of the first three volumes of the *Histoire naturelle*, Raynal declared, in the *Nouvelles littéraires* of Grimm's *Correspondance littéraire* (I, 336-337), that the work " réussit médiocrement chez les gens instruits," and concluded that " M. de Buffon voit très-bien les faits, et médiocrement les choses métaphisiques." Nor could Voltaire's philosophy conceive of the terrestrial globe coming into being, evolving through successive stages, and destined, ultimately, to sink into icy oblivion; to do so, as he pointed out in *Les Singularités de la nature* and elsewhere, was to be guilty of playing god with mere words. Cf. Otis Fellows, " Voltaire and Buffon: Clash and conciliation," *Symposium IX* (1955), 222-235. And Marmontel summed up not only his own opinion of Buffon, but that of such *encyclopédistes* as d'Alembert, Condorcet and Roland, when he wrote in his *Mémoires*: " Gâté par l'adulation et placé par la multitude dans la classe de nos grands hommes, il avait le chagrin de voir que les mathématiciens, les chimistes, les astronomes ne lui accordaient qu'un rang très inférieur parmi eux; que les naturalistes eux-mêmes étaient peu disposés à le mettre à leur tête, et que parmi les gens de lettres, il n'obtenait que le mince éloge d'écrivain élégant et de grand coloriste." Montesquieu, on the other hand, while admitting that a considerable number of French scientists were opposed to Buffon, states, " Pour moi, qui y trouve de belles choses, j'attendrai avec tranquillité et modestie la décision des savants étrangers," and adds: " Je n'ai pourtant vu personne à qui je n'aie entendu dire qu'il y avait beaucoup d'utilité à le lire " (letter to Monseigneur Ceruti). As recent studies have been quick to show, Diderot was one of those who read Buffon with great profit; cf. Roger, *op. cit.*, and Jean Mayer, *Diderot, homme de science* (Rennes, 1959).

[2] Aram Vartanian; from a manuscript in the present writer's possession.

the time needed for the cooling of planetary bodies. These mathematically-controlled experiments, related to a reading public unaccustomed to thinking in terms of hundreds of centuries, represented no doubt a certain amount of window-dressing.[1] His published calculation of the earth's age as some 80,000 years instead of the traditional 6000 was in itself a generous concession to the prevailing spirit of the day; in his unpublished manuscripts at the *Muséum national d'histoire naturelle* he deals with figures that run into the millions. But even those appearing in the *Histoire naturelle* introduced to eighteenth-century Europe a new concept of geological time where nature is in a perpetual state of change. " Nature is," Buffon states in the *Epoques*, " very different today from what it was at the beginning and from what it became as time passed." And he concludes: " Nature has successively taken different forms; the skies themselves have varied, and all things in the physical universe, like those of the moral world, are in continual movement of successive variations."[2]

Buffon was the only ranking French scientist of his day who had tried to write a cosmogony. And, in fact, his explanations involving the development of the physical universe from unorganized matter to its present state were submitted in much more detail and with a far greater sweep of geologic time than had ever before been the case. In short, he offered a concept of inorganic evolution that staggered the imagination of the eighteenth-century layman and stimulated the thinking of as eminent a scientist as Laplace. Newton's mechanical principle of attraction had been applied to dead matter; could the world of living matter, which was in such great abundance, be subject to a like obedience to law? Buffon's attempts to answer this question render complex and varied whatever opinions he may have had that animals and plants have developed by a process of gradual, continuous change from previously existing forms.

Life he held to be a physical—not a metaphysical—characteristic of matter, and one to be found in the animal and vegetable kingdoms between which there is no distinct line of demarcation. Furthermore, the varieties of organic life often revealed such fine gradations that there were times when it was difficult indeed to speak of species; and Linnaeus's attempts at classification were gross and arbitrary. In the early pages of the *Histoire naturelle* especially, Buffon was not impressed by any unity in nature's plan, being struck, rather, by its variety as well as the multiplicity of means at its disposal. Somewhat later he was to suggest a rule of thumb definition regarding species that proved to be convenient and useful. Two creatures could be held as belonging to the same species if the products of their mating could, in turn, produce offspring. This led him to the conviction

---

[1] Such is, for instance, the plausible conclusion of Francis C. Haber, *The Age of the world: Moses to Darwin* (Baltimore, 1959), 118.

[2] " ... si nous l'embrassons dans toute son étendue, nous ne pourrons douter qu'elle ne soit aujourd'hui très-différente de ce qu'elle était au commencement et de ce qu'elle est devenue dans la succession du temps.... La nature s'est trouvée dans différents états; la surface de la terre a pris successivement des formes différentes; les cieux même ont varié, et toutes les choses de l'univers physique sont, comme celles du monde moral, dans un mouvement continuel de variations successives," *Œuvres complètes*, IX, 456.

—contrary to that of Voltaire, for one—that all mankind was of one species. Having, with time, spread over the surface of the globe, it had, however, undergone various changes through the influence of climate, food, mode of living, disease and the mixture of dissimilar individuals. These same influences were, of course, equally capable of modifying not only all animals but plants as well.

At the very center of this, Buffon insisted, was the power of reproduction, a vital force of nature worthy of the most careful study. In his investigations and speculations he was, to be sure, sorely hampered by the fact that genes had not yet been discovered, and that chemistry was still in a most elementary state. His over-all approach to the question was, nevertheless, strikingly modern in that he began his inquiry with the most primitive forms of reproduction and worked his way up the ladder of life. Tremblay's earth-shaking discovery of the phenomena of division and regeneration among polyps fitted in well with what Buffon knew from early experience in tree-grafting or growing a tree from a single branch. And it strengthened his conviction that no explanation of the workings of nature could be found through final causes, but would have to be sought in certain concrete influences evident in the physical universe alone.

This led him, along with the English priest, John Needham, to support the theory of epigenesis in the face of such formidable opposition as that of Malpighi, Swammerdam, Leibniz and, later, Bonnet, Haller, Spallanzani, along with a host of others who advocated the far more metaphysical and less scientifically sound theory of generation, preformation or *emboîtement*.[1] But it also led to Buffon's and Needham's belief in spontaneous generation, a concept ridiculed by leading contemporaries and twentieth-century " nature writers " alike. It is too often forgotten that Buffon's acceptance of spontaneous generation was a further example of his attempts to find other than supernatural explanations for the processes of life.[2]

As a trained mathematician he tried to take into account all the problems related to generation and to find terms at once specific and logical. In his attempts to explain how living matter organized itself, he created the term *molécule organique*—perhaps inspired by Leibniz's monad—to apply to the innumerable organic particles that, he was convinced, constituted living matter, just as the atom theory explained substance of inorganic matter. But the organizing principle might best be explained, he reasoned, by what could be called—for want of a better term—*moules intérieurs*.

---

[1] Naturalism identified itself with epigenesis as a theory of generation, while those who wished to reconcile a finalistic theology with natural science held to *emboîtement des germes* in preformation of organism in the egg. Much more than the fate of a scientific hypothesis was involved in this quarrel between Buffon and his critics on the subject of reproduction. The difference was fundamentally between two types of philosophy, a naturalistic and a spiritualistic one.

[2] For much the same reasons Fontenelle had found the Cartesian theory of vortices to be far closer to the reality of matter in motion than Newton's laws of attraction where it was necessary to hold that some invisible, seemingly supranatural force operated across vast stretches of space. Both Fontenelle and Buffon subscribed to that aspect of the Enlightenment which appealed to reason guided by common sense; vortices and spontaneous generation, in their judgment, fitted such a pattern.

These inner moulds, let it be presumed, have an active power that shapes the organic molecules, thus controlling the different parts of an organism including its nutrition, development and reproduction, whether the entity be animal or vegetable. These inner moulds, entirely imperceptible except for their effects, have been variously interpreted by students of Buffon's thought as " mechanisms in Nature " (Wohl, p. 192), the " organizing activity " of nature (Haber, p. 142), and " the constant form of every living creature." [1] Buffon was fully aware that he was merely presenting a possibility, but one more possibility that allowed him to avoid acceptance of a supernatural act of creation.

The terms *molécule organique* and *moule intérieur* had the disadvantage of being catching phrases, easily subject to ridicule, and, at the same time, terms suggesting something precise for what still remained vague. Diderot, for example, could and did express much the same thoughts, all the while utilizing obscure, indeterminate expressions that successfully covered important areas of ignorance. Moreover, and the fact has been repeatedly forgotten in considering Buffon's theories, organic molecules and inner moulds were merely tentative suggestions or suppositions designed to lend support to the less popular but far more scientific theory of epigenesis. Moreover, epigenesis, not preformation, may lead to a theory of evolution.

Those who have seen Buffon as a forerunner of Lamarck and Darwin have had little difficulty in finding short passages scattered throughout the *Histoire naturelle* suggesting that he was an early advocate of organic evolution. In the article, " De l'âne," in 1753, he tendered the hypothesis that all animals may have originally stemmed from a single source (*Œuvres*, II, 414). He forthwith denied such a possibility in the name of divine truth; the hypothesis had nonetheless been advanced. By 1766, however, in the article, " De la dégénération des animaux," he repeatedly gives minor and even major examples of variations in animals belonging to the same general family. And in *Epoques*, some twelve years later, he states categorically that nature accepts successive alterations, lends herself to new combinations, in fact, to mutations [the word is Buffon's] of matter and form (*Œuvres*, IX, 456). Recent scholarship has been little impressed by this transformist terminology, and the point is often made that theories embracing spontaneous generation or the *moule intérieur* exclude all possibility of a concept of evolution (Wohl, p. 196). On the other hand, if Buffon did recognize any variation in species, it was merely in the form of a degeneration.[2] In the face of such prevailing judgments, we might cite the judicious conclusion of Mr. J.S. Wilkie in his excellent monograph, " The most reasonable interpretation of Buffon's conservatism in the application of the idea of evolution seems to be, then, that the causes of evolutionary

---

[1] Erik Nordenskiöld, *The History of Biology* (New York, 1936), 226.

[2] This latter position is that taken by Paul Ostoya, *Les Théories de l'évolution* (Paris, 1951), 52, and Jean Piveteau, " Introduction à l'œuvre philosophique de Buffon," in *Œuvres philosophiques de Buffon, Corpus général des philosophes français* (Paris, 1954), xxxiii-xxxiv.

change which his mind had really assimilated did not appear to him adequate to explain anything beyond rather minor and superficial changes." [1]

What are we to conclude from this? If we accept it at face value, we see that the direction of Buffon's ideas pointed in the general direction of evolution; but he carried so much excess baggage in the way of cumbersome subsidiary theories—organic molecules, inner moulds, spontaneous generation, the rigid fixity of species or no species at all, merely gradations—that the concept never fully entered his understanding.

On the other hand, there is still so much we do not know about evolution, and the secrets of one of its fundamental aspects—as the Nobel laureates in medicine for 1962 have demonstrated—are only now beginning to be unlocked. What Wilkie, Ostoya, Piveteau and Wohl have really proved is that Buffon had very little to do with Darwinian evolution. But there is, conceivably, a whole current of transformism outside of the Darwinian and, indeed, quite opposed to it. It would, moreover, be a current stemming—at least in part—from Buffon. For him the phenomenon of man was not an accident of nature but inherent in matter and energy. Life itself is a quality of matter, and in this light the theory of *moules intérieurs* is not so ridiculous as it first appears.[2]

Buffon's point of view and that of Lamarck rejected the rôle of blind chance. In both, we find an absence of the accidental so apparent in Buffon's contemporary, Diderot. The neo-Lamarckian position with its abnegation of sheer chance is in decided contradistinction to the neo-Darwinian position, and we recall Samuel Butler's horror over Darwin's assumption that there was no order or purpose in the universe. Lamarck's purposive evolution may, after all, derive directly from Buffon despite today's prevalent belief that the two are as far apart as the vitalistic and mechanistic approaches can be.

---

[1] " The Idea of Evolution in the Writings of Buffon," *Annals of Science* (September, 1956), 220.

[2] Nor carrying this to the individual, whether man or animal, is it completely absurd if we realize that Buffon was obliged to fall back on terms of his own devising, where science had not yet advanced to the state where it needed an expanded terminology. He was one of the first to perceive the *données* of the problem of heredity. The *moule intérieur* was a convenient term for an area of general ignorance. But Buffon saw, contrary to general belief, that the elements of heredity had to come from both parents and, as it were, in pieces—the father's nose, the mother's eyes; they come together in the mother's womb. That this should take place through the forces of attraction, a mechanistic principle, rather than one based on chemistry, should surprise no one aware of the high repute in which Newtonian physics was held and the low status enjoyed by chemistry in the eighteenth century. On the other hand the award of the 1962 Nobel prize in medicine went to three scientists who have depicted heredity as a pattern of nucleotides. In doing so, they have demonstrated that the secret of heredity and of mutation resides in the architecture of the molecule of deoxyribonucleic acid (DNA) within each living organism. This represents the complex and subtle mechanism by which each biological species reproduces itself generation after generation. For want of a better term, this recently discovered principle has been named the " coil of life " which determines what each creature shall be. The functions of Buffon's " inner mould " and the new Nobel laureates' " coil of life " are far from dissimilar even if one is motivated by mechanistic and the other by chemical principles. But did Buffon, after all, limit himself to a mechanistic principle or did he too find a chemical affinity in the field of attraction? That is the opinion of Ernst Bloch, " Das chemische Affinitätsproblem," *Isis* (1926), 119-157.

And one of the twentieth-century disciples of Buffon's thinking may well be Pierre Teilhard de Chardin, who tells us in *Le Phénomène humain* (1955) that the causes we see around us go back to generalized laws. The quality inherent in Buffon's matter—the active power of his " inner moulds "—may be nothing less than a scientific expression of what *Père* Teilhard insists upon, in metaphysical terms, as the inwardness of things. Correlated with this, certainly, is another concept. Has every evolutionary change brought divergence as illustrated, for example, by the vast number of sub-species in Darwin's observations? In the introduction to the English translation of *Père* Teilhard's work—*The Phenomenon of Man*—Sir Julian Huxley, referring to the Jesuit Father and distinguished palaeontologist, says: " He usually uses *convergence* to denote the tendency of mankind, during its evolution, to superpose centripetal on centrifugal trends, so as to prevent centrifugal differentiation from leading to fragmentation, and eventually to incorporate the results of differentiation in an organized and unified pattern " (p. 14). As for Buffon, his theory of the races of man would imply that in mankind, at least, the process of divergence has come to a halt, and the overlying principle of change in man is that of convergence—except for the rare human monsters called to our attention in *Addition à l'histoire de l'homme* (*Œuvres*, II, 307). If there are other currents of evolution than those in *The Descent of Man*, then Buffon may reenter the history of ideas as a far more significant personality than the pompous intendant of the King's garden who has come down to us as fumbling on the threshold of Darwinism.

His first memoirs on problems of mathematics and physics were published in the *Histoire de l'Académie royale des sciences* in 1733. The fifth volume of his *Histoire naturelle des minéraux* appeared the year of his death in 1788. Buffon devoted the fifty-five years of his life that lay between to making scientific inquiries on a large range of subjects. During a considerable part of this time he worked on the *Histoire naturelle*. It is doubtless possible to call his monumental work " a courtly natural history," and himself " an official court writer " who depicted " the order of nature " as " identical with the order of the Bourbon society." Indeed, it has been done (Krutch, 69-70). To do so, however, is to depict him as one satisfied with the status quo in the history of ideas, a natural scientist static in his thinking, an intellectual *retardataire* when the French Enlightenment was at its height.

Such a picture is, of course, false. Though certain essentials in his thinking were to remain constant throughout the years, there may be observed a decided evolution in Buffon's thought. Jacques Roger tells us in his notable *Les Sciences de la Vie dans la pensée française du XVIII$^e$ siècle* (p. 599): " Il n'est pas possible de dire que Buffon a cessé d'être philosophe pour devenir naturaliste entre le quatrième tome de l'*Histoire naturelle* et le premier tome du *Supplément*. Mais il est vrai que la réflexion s'enracine davantage dans la réalité scientifique. Ce sont les faits qui suggèrent les idées, et la pensée de Buffon va s'enrichir et se nuancer à mesure qu'elle découvrira de nouveaux objets. Mais c'est surtout en suivant ses voies propres qu'elle va se développer, se préciser et se compléter, jusqu'à résoudre enfin d'une manière originale les problèmes qu'elle soulevait en 1749."

In reply to Immanuel Kant's query, *Was ist Aufklärung?* there has been, within the past decade, an increasing tendency to turn to Buffon for at least a partial answer. Recent scholarship in France especially has been intent upon showing how, on the one hand, he was able profit by scientific discoveries and new ideas in evolving his views on man and the universe, and how, on the other, he often outstripped his fellow-*philosophes* in attempting to join scientific fact with bold, philosophic speculation. Moreover, his views frequently inspired others—a Diderot, a Lamarck, a Laplace, a Cuvier, even a Darwin—to push his inquiries to fruitful conclusions.

As a final word, it might be appropriate to stress the point that a great and fervent ideal animated the labours of Buffon. This ideal was that natural science might rightfully be accessible to all enlightened and interested minds. This did not mean the type of " scientific popularization " which had already begun to make noticeable progress in the eighteenth century and was to become so current that today it is almost the only medium of communication between science and the curiosity of an intelligent public. Buffon's work was not intended to be a vulgarisation of such a kind which would announce to the uninitiated—*ex cathedra*—the dogmas, conclusions and formulae of the sciences without revealing the reasons, evidences and ideological bases on which they rested. Buffon's goal was to make intelligible to a person capable of thinking straight, some of the most technical, abstruse and difficult matters pertaining to the science of his day. This explains in part why no late eighteenth-century library of consequence in western Europe would have been without the *Histoire naturelle*. Buffon's readers saw in his work the opportunity of assimilating into their thoughts and attitudes on man and the world, the body of existing natural science just as they were able to do in the field of the arts and the humanities. This led them to believe, along with Buffon himself, that man through the assimilation of knowledge, including that of the natural universe in which he lived, could realize his own destiny by becoming master of the world around him.

# THE THEME OF GENIUS IN DIDEROT'S
## *NEVEU DE RAMEAU* *

It has become an academic commonplace to note in Diderot's life and works (and especially in the *Neveu de Rameau*) two distinct natures in unremitting conflict one with the other. One of these, Daniel Mornet and others point out, is that of the deterministic materialist who holds the individual to be but a helpless link in the chain of universal necessity. The second, some critics aver, is that side of Diderot in which enthusiasm for humanity, love of science and preoccupation with ethics, help the eighteenth-century " philosophe " strive toward his ideal—mankind improved through intelligent effort. This dichotomy in Diderot's character has seemed so apparent in the *Neveu* that scholars have not hesitated from the first to see in the dialogue between LUI and MOI a sustained dialectic where Diderot's two natures inexorably move on to an insoluble dilemma. It has even been hinted that the essential theme of the work is little more than a pre-Freudian clash between the id and the ego.

No doubt speculation will persist for some time to come on this enticing, but perhaps no less theoretical key to the true significance of the *Neveu de Rameau*. In the meantime, the dialogue suggests other and equally provocative subjects of investigation for the unravelling of its perplexing intricacies. Among these is the problem of talent and genius that pervades its pages and offers the added attraction of a theme which, by the utmost consequence of the debate, suggests an essential agreement between MOI and LUI; the latter, in the long view, may well overshadow an impression of veritable collisions between two adverse points of view. If such is the case, a study of this theme might well throw more light on the purpose of the *Neveu de Rameau* and upon the complex figure of Diderot himself.

The intent of the present investigation would, I think, be better served were Buffon's theory of the *homo duplex* here set aside, and Diderot's character considered in another light. In Diderot's personality there are in evidence two elements, one of which derives from the other, and which, in some measure, explain the seeming contradictions in the writer's preoccupation with the great problems of existence and its detailed manifestations. One of these is an excessive sensibility which makes of him a man of intense enthusiasm but one with a social conscience. The other is an insatiable

---

* Reprinted from *Diderot Studies II* (1952), 168-199.

curiosity which stems from the first element—a curiosity which drives him to ponder on Nature in all its immensity and seeming contradictions, to examine all its problems, to seek, if not to find, all the answers to the question of existence. Sensitive as he was to the great currents of the age and to his own personal triumphs, vicissitudes and aspirations, Diderot inevitably—by his very temperament—was keenly aware of and drawn by that strange phenomenon of the occasional man of genius as distinguished from the all too common man of talent.

There is, unfortunately, no adequate study concerning the conception of genius in the French seventeenth century, and there is nothing reliably comprehensive on the subject in the eighteenth. It is easily apparent, however, that up to the Revolution the view was widely held that a man of genius was but a man of superior talent or an exceptional, perhaps highly disciplined " homme d'esprit." When in 1758 Voltaire, in *Le Pauvre Diable*, taunts Fréron with " Tu n'as point d'aile, et tu veux voler ! " this special warp is quite incidental to the general pattern of argument he weaves six years later in the article " Génie " of his *Dictionnaire philosophique* where he poses the rhetorical question: " Mais au fond le génie est-il autre chose que le talent ? " And Buffon, on his election to the Académie Française at the age of forty-six, is able to maintain in his celebrated *Discours sur le style* (and with the respectful approval of his peers) that genius is substantially the organizing power of the mind. A logical terminus for such assessments is the dictum attributed to Buffon by Hérault de Séchelles late in the century: " Le génie n'est qu'une plus grande aptitude à la patience."

Until proved otherwise, it may be assumed that such a point of view represents a simplified and misunderstood Cartesianism. That is to say a Cartesianism which, in the eighteenth century, strove for sustained clarity and logic of expression, but largely ignored two sources of creative inspiration, feeling and imagination.

The seventeenth century was far from being so dogmatic, although modern scholars are not agreed on the emphasis which was then given to such seemingly non-rational factors as genius. In *La Formation de la doctrine classique*, René Bray draws upon evidence to prove that the entire century held genius to be the prime requisite of the creative artist.[1] On the other hand, the dominant impression afforded by Daniel Mornet in his *Histoire de la littérature française classique* is that, though the age paid lip service to genius, it did so under duress and in the face of rational discipline.[2]

In both cases, however, we find but the vaguest inferences as to how genius was understood by writers of the seventeenth century. At least until a more exhaustive study has been made, the conclusion we are no doubt compelled to accept is that genius was held to be an indefinable intuition, and that it was a concern of the man of letters to extract for his own profit, and by the process of deduction, all that this intuition contained.

---

[1] Chapter II, " Le Poète, le génie, l'art et la science," especially 85-90.

[2] See, in particular, Part I, Chapter I, " Les Doctrines."

It is precisely in connection with Diderot, however, that the whole question has recently been given new and generative perspectives. Already in 1939, Professor Herbert Dieckmann had insisted upon our seizing the permanency in the development of Diderot's thought in general in order to strip his " inconsistencies " of their finality and thus more readily grasp his true significance in the history of ideas.[1] Two years later, in " Diderot's Conception of Genius," [2] we find Mr. Dieckmann's own highly rewarding application of such a procedure as he painstakingly traces Diderot's " act of thought " which had led him to consciousness of the problem of " the genius." The study, in part an analysis and classification of the various reflections of Diderot on the nature of genius, is the first to accentuate the implications derived from situating him historically in the development of the concept.

Among the inquiries to which Mr. Dieckmann's contribution has opened the way are Miss Eleanor Walker's " Towards an Understanding of Diderot's Esthetic Theory," [3] and Professor Margaret Gilman's " The Poet according to Diderot." [4] Miss Walker resolves what in the past had been viewed as a conflict between the empirical and intuitive tendencies of Diderot's mind by emphasizing the psychosomatic bases for his insights into the act of artistic creation. Carrying this contingency still further, Miss Gilman has been particularly successful in showing the impossibility of committing Diderot to a frozen esthetic of the creative processes and of genius. And she has ably demonstrated that Diderot's ideas on the point in question were neither static nor consistently contradictory within the framework of his thinking, but rather, dynamic and evolutionary. Following Miss Gilman in what is perhaps the most tellingly comprehensive work to date on this aspect of the " philosophe," M. Yvon Belaval has, in turn, insisted upon the evolutionary character of Diderot's understanding of creative genius. But in so doing, M. Belaval has given marked stress to the constancy with which Diderot's continually reaffirmed conception of omnipresent Nature is deeply rooted in this and all other problems within his broad range of interests.[5]

Considerable work in Europe and America has already been done to situate Diderot in the history of esthetics. Each of the four critics mentioned above has, however, by studying the question of Diderot and creative expression, emphatically contributed to an expanded comprehension of the complexities involved and to a more explicit understanding of their implications. Still, it has been only incidentally that scholars have implemented their studies of the problem by referring to the *Neveu de Rameau*; and even in analyses of the Satire itself, where the maze of themes has been unravelled with the greatest care, that of genius has received but scant attention.

---

[1] " Zur Interpretation Diderots," *Romanische Forschungen*, LIII (1939), 47-82.

[2] *Journal of the History of Ideas*, II (1941), 151-182.

[3] *Romanic Review*, XXXV (1944), 277-87.

[4] *Romanic Review*, XXXVII (1946), 37-54.

[5] *L'Esthétique sans paradoxe de Diderot* (Paris, Gallimard, 1950).

Professor Leo Spitzer is one of those who have more recently touched upon the problem only to brush it aside almost immediately. In "The Style of Diderot,"[1] Mr. Spitzer, who finds serious shortcomings in Daniel Mornet's "La Véritable Signification du *Neveu de Rameau*,"[2] nevertheless arrives at much the same conclusion in the field of esthetics as has M. Mornet in that of ethics. According to Mr. Spitzer: "It could be said that, in this dialogue, Diderot the philosopher is instituting a trial against his own artistic sensitivity, with all its expressive, impersonating, pantomimic, caricaturing, satirical elements" (p. 154). Or again, Mr. Spitzer prefers to see the *Neveu de Rameau* as a "parody of the nephew which was a parody of [Diderot] himself" (p. 167).

However difficult it might be to refute these affirmations, the fact remains that the implications of such an interpretation are, in part, misleading. It is yet to be proved convincingly that Diderot unmistakably identifies his own creative temperament with that of Jean-François as depicted in the dialogue. Few will deny, however, that the Satire represents one more instance of Diderot's remarkable ability for self-projection into the situation of another—a talent already so clearly manifest in *La Religieuse*. But Diderot's own admonition in 1758 might well apply in some measure to *Le Neveu* itself: in *De la poésie dramatique* he tells us: " Pourquoi chercher l'auteur dans ses personnages? Qu'a de commun Racine avec *Athalie*, Molière avec *Le Tartuffe*? Ce sont des hommes de génie qui ont su fouiller au fond de nos entrailles, et en arracher le trait qui nous frappe " (A.-T., VII, 363).

At the same time it is readily apparent that, in the composition of the dialogue, Diderot has been concerned with his own preoccupations as well as fired by his own creative impulse. The springtide of his exuberance and of his individuality have withdrawn, leaving him a man edging the fifties. It is a moment of pause following the death of his father, the increased anxieties attached to the Encyclopedia, and the attacks of his enemies, where occasional resignation mingles with a gentle but pervasive melancholy. Even his love for Sophie has reached that point where he can write: " Ma tendresse sera d'une couleur brune qui ne sied pas mal à ce sentiment."[3] It is a time when, before plunging with renewed vigor, as a man and writer, back into the turbulent mainstream of the century, Diderot returns to the dialogue form where two opposing characters, two different talents are nevertheless in a temporarily analogous situation—that of self-evaluation and retrospection. In consequence, the author's personal aspirations, judgments and failures have become an indissoluble part of the whole. But it is also a period which M. Pierre Mesnard in convincing manner[4] has shown to represent a decisive term in Diderot's life, where he evolves a unified view of his existence. This, in turn, has allowed him to define

---

[1] *Linguistics and Literary History* (Princeton, 1948).
[2] *Revue des Deux-Mondes*, 7th per. XL (1927), 881-908.
[3] *Lettres à Sophie Volland*, éd. A. Babelon, 2ᵉ éd. (Paris, 1938), I, 125.
[4] " Sophie Volland et la maturité de Diderot," *Revue des Sciences Humaines*, Nouv. Sér., fasc. 53 (1949), 15.

himself in relation to others, and to have greater self-assurance in passing judgment on his fellow beings. And nowhere in the *Neveu*, perhaps, are these tendencies more in evidence than in the pages devoted to the theme of talent and genius.

With regard to this question, then, there seems less justification in professing the Satire to be a polemic of Diderot's directed against himself than an exploration and demonstration, through the dialectic of conversation, of a concern which was to be of cardinal interest throughout his life—that of man and the creative impulse. The Nephew, who willingly and wilfully stands exposed before the spectacle of his frustration and failure, serves, in the vortex of dialectic, as a point of reference in an attempt to understand the creative processes of the mind, whether fulfilled, thwarted or impotent. Moreover, in choosing a protagonist who has sacrificed integrity for expediency, talent for easy living, Diderot has found a measure whereby he may more readily assess not only his own theories on creative genius, but the distance which, after all, separates him from the total bankruptcy of the scoundrelly and yet pathetically eccentric outcast who confronts him. Specifically, it is a picture of one phase of eighteenth-century life seen from a particular angle but alive with ironic implications as the two interlocutors in their late forties reach, almost simultaneously, crucial points in their careers. Indeed, it is a time when the individual tensions of both are complex and sensitive to their respective situations. Each, in his own way, has felt the destroying pressures of the age.

The encounter itself, presumably authentic, must have occurred in 1760 sometime after the Parisian theatre-goers had been introduced to Palissot's notoriously contentious comedy, *Les Philosophes*. There now seems little reason to doubt Rudolf Schlösser's exacting scholarship which concludes that the Satire is a unified product of the year 1761, the essentials of which have remained unchanged; this despite interpolations and minor revisions extending to 1775.[1]

The process of accretion and amplification, then, which Diderot carried on in subsequent reworkings did little more than expand what was already, in its first draft, a masterpiece. Here, an associative mind at its best, the wealth of ideas and the rich train of thought on a wide variety of subjects make one hesitate to choose a dominant theme. Nor, perhaps, is there one, unless it be the complexity of life in eighteenth-century France where the ever-present past and living actuality of two personalities meet with the consequences of existence. Indeed, Diderot might well have said about *Rameau* what Gide was to confess concerning one of his own works: "Je me persuade que l'idée même de ce livre est absurde, et j'en viens à ne plus comprendre du tout ce que je veux. Il n'y a pas, à proprement parler, un seul centre à ce livre, autour de quoi viennent converger tous mes efforts."[2] But if, as upon careful consideration seems to be the case, it is in the Nephew's presence, rather than the preponderance of any single

---

[1] *Rameaus Neffe. Studien und Untersuchungen zur Einführung in Goethes Übersetzung des Diderotschen Dialogs* (Berlin, 1900), 11-25.

[2] *Journal des Faux-Monnayeurs* (Paris, 1927), 49.

topic, that the unity of the work is discernible, it is essential to determine why this should be so. What turns in the lives of each led up to the explosion that is the *Neveu de Rameau*?

Although he had already been imprisoned for three months in 1749 for intellectual indiscretions such as the *Lettre sur les aveugles*, it was in the decade to follow that Diderot was to undergo the most critical period of his life—one of infinite incident and endless uncertainty. While the author of *Candide* and he who had written the *Nouvelle Héloïse* continued to be objects of European acclaim, Diderot still remained relatively in the shadows. He was devoting the greater part of the energy and enthusiasm of his mature years to directing the collective enterprise which was the Encyclopedia. The realization gave him pause and there were moments when he wondered whether all this time and effort could not have been put to better use in bringing forth what was in him to say. It is not surprising that he should be moved by such preoccupations for, throughout his life and writings, the creative impulse was one of those subjects to which he would most frequently return. Constantly alert to its manifestation in others, equally often he scrutinized himself questioningly. Whether, in reply to Helvétius, he recalled his schooldays when effortlessly he had snatched the laurels from a diligently studious and ambitious classmate (A.-T., II, 340), his mid-life when he so often weighed the possibility of his acceptance by posterity, or his later years, when he again wondered whether the tyranny of genius would be forever foreign to him (A.-T., II, 341), the prepossession remained steadfast. But in 1758 responsibility for the Encyclopedia hung like a great chain about his neck. It was a moment when d'Alembert's defection was an imminent possibility and the failure of the *Fils naturel* an accepted reality. Furthermore, the clamorous assaults of such " anti-philosophes " as Chaumeix, Moreau and Palissot were reaching a feverish pitch in their increasing effectiveness. With the future of the Encyclopedia seriously jeopardized, Diderot's courage and self-reliance were sorely tried. It was then he wrote Voltaire:

" Mon cher maître, j'ai la quarantaine passée; je suis las de tracasseries. Je crie, depuis le matin jusqu'au soir. Le repos, le repos, et il n'y a guère de jour que je ne sois tenté d'aller vivre obscur et mourir tranquille au fond de ma province. Il vient un temps où toutes les cendres sont mêlées. Alors, que m'importera d'avoir été Voltaire ou Diderot, et que ce soient vos trois syllabes ou les trois miennes qui restent " [A.-T., XIX, 452].

The following year was equally inauspicious. On the basis of testimony by Chaumeix, the *Conseil d'Etat* withdrew the Encyclopedia's privilege of sale which preceded by a few months its condemnation at Rome. Falsely accused as the author of a flagrant satire, *Mémoire pour Abraham Chaumeix*, Diderot hesitated between standing fast and fleeing. In addition, 1759 was the year when d'Alembert's withdrawal from the Encyclopedia became an accomplished fact.

Despite these vicissitudes, Diderot continued to block out literary projects which were fermenting in his head. But in a letter to Grimm on

July 18, he nevertheless confessed to no longer having the requisite drive to realize the plans of a creative writer. A moment of profound despondency to be sure. There was also the reproof of his contemporaries, however, that, though he was eminently capable of composing isolated little pieces of considerable merit, he had produced no significantly important work complete in itself. Although the year which produced Palissot's *Philosophes* was likewise the one in which Diderot was to compose *La Religieuse*, he himself had had little tangible assurance till then of his ability to write a sustained masterpiece.

Literary historians have followed Goethe's lead in viewing the success of *Les Philosophes* and the failure of *Le Père de famille* early the following year as the chief motivation of the *Neveu de Rameau*. Diderot must certainly have been smarting in the knowledge that all Paris had been discussing Palissot's vicious portrait of him as Dortidius. And, in return, far from mere good-natured persiflage, the *Neveu* was to contain some of the most violent, personal invective of the age. In this light, it is cumulatively a severe ethical indictment of a social class whose pernicious luxury fosters all that is mediocre in arts and letters while attempting to tread under foot the sensitivities, tastes and creative faculties of the superior man. Moreover, the poor reception afforded his experimental *drame bourgeois* posed the problem whether to accept the evaluations of the majority of his fellow critics, or to place himself in the *avant garde* of new trends and new appreciations which might or might not mark the future. There is more than a suggestion of personal preoccupation—as well as consideration for Richardson's literary fate—that drove him at this time to write: " Malheur à l'homme de génie qui franchit les barrières que l'usage et le temps ont prescrites aux productions des arts, et qui foule aux pieds le protocole et ses formules ! il s'écoulera de longues années après sa mort, avant que la justice qu'il mérite lui soit rendue " [A.-T., V, 216].

Whatever the importance of these considerations may be, the fact remains that Diderot's choice of the moment and the protagonist seems both fortuitous and deliberate. A world of tragi-comic catastrophe and consequence has closed around the bohemian nephew of the great Jean-Philippe Rameau. Neither an imposter nor a charlatan, though an eccentric who, moreover, had thought it to his advantage to prostitute his gifts as a musician and degrade himself as a man by deceit and flattery, he represents an ideal selection for the LUI of the dialogue. Indeed, Diderot virtually begins his Satire by telling us that his interest is occasionally drawn by monstrous and vertiginous nonconformists such as the Nephew. The reason is that their character, in violent contrast with that of normal people, breaks the routine of conventional thinking, restores the natural individuality of those present and, most important of all, allows the discerning to ascertain more easily the truth. This is reminiscent of Fontenelle's admonition in the *Origines des Fables*: " ... étudions l'esprit humain dans une de ses plus étranges productions: c'est là bien souvent qu'il se donne le mieux à connaître." Diderot here finds the opportunity to study the creative urge—an essential factor of genius—in one of its strangest distortions. The Nephew provides a grotesque approach to the serious problem of the nature of genius: its moments of inspiration and insight, its attendant aberrations and defeats.

The psychological situation of the dialogue is slightly suggestive of that in a Racinian tragedy. The scene has been well set in advance. Before the *Neveu de Rameau* begins, the past has led up to a moment of crisis in the life of Jean-François. The early fifties had seen him endowed with a famous name, more than ordinary musical gifts and a hot thirst for renown. His talents were, upon occasion, applauded in homes of the eminent, and among his music pupils were a number of distinguished ladies. In 1757, striving to outrival the late Couperin and follow in the footsteps of his own illustrious uncle, he had published his *Nouvelles pièces de clavecin*. And at least three of the compositions were played in the Concert du Louvre. Success and even fame seemed within his grasp.

But with the passage of a handful of years, when the dialogue catches up the Nephew on a particular afternoon in the Café de la Régence, his feelings of rejection and insecurity are dramatically acute. Diderot has seized him in the complete distintegration of his aspirations when, realistically facing his frustraton and failure, he defiantly defends a *modus vivendi* which he cannot but accept. His sources of creative invention in musical composition have long since dried up. His charmingly delectable wife has already died, which has cut off one possible road—though a highly questionable one—to prosperity. Moreover, his unbridled tongue has only too recently made him an outcast from the society of parasites and hangers-on around the board of the wealthy Bertin. He is now cut off from those most able to appreciate his peculiar talents and distorted loyalties. He has reached a point where, though a man of wit and musical attainment, he is willing to take an inventory of himself and the world about him. A strange, vehement creature, in turn harshly cynical, spiritually despondent or engagingly insolent, he stands unabashed before Diderot in all his nakedness.

Such is the LUI who confronts the author at a time when Diderot, no longer young, is singularly preoccupied with serious self-questioning. And the Nephew's presence will provide the catalyzer to set him writing with remarkable ease and vitality a work for his own satisfaction and that of posterity. The confrontation, moreover, has another, equally significant interest. Hegel and others have looked down upon the rôle of MOI as almost passive and colorless before the miming, strutting, posturing and declaiming LUI. To be sure, we may safely say that the Diderot-MOI of the dialogue is pre-eminently the circumspect, the attentive, the well-nigh dispassionate observer. Does Diderot attach any consequence to this rôle? In 1765 he most emphatically will, and we read in the *Essai sur la peinture*: " Les hommes froids, sévères et tranquilles observateurs de la nature, connaissent souvent mieux les cordes délicates qu'il faut pincer; ils font des enthousiastes sans l'être; c'est l'homme et l'animal " [A.-T., X, 520). This concept of the superior man, the great creative intelligence, will frequently reappear under Diderot's pen to find a final expression in the *Paradoxe sur le comédien*: " Dans la grande comédie, la comédie du monde, celle à laquelle j'en reviens toujours, toutes les âmes chaudes occupent le théâtre; tous les hommes de génie sont au parterre" (A.-T., VIII, 368).[1] But the MOI of the *Neveu* comes surprisingly close to achieving that detachment of the transcendent mind acclaimed in the above passage. It would appear then that, already in 1761, Diderot has represented in practice what is to be so positively advocated in the *Paradoxe*. The calm reason, imperturbability, intellectual poise and self-possession of the " philosophe " stand in marked contrast to the vacillation, impetuosity and turbulence of the Nephew. Whether or not Diderot ascribes any of these latter characteristics to himself, by his very choice of interlocutors he has succeeded in enlarging his field of consciousness. The dialectic to follow will be neither an elaborate game of pretense nor an exercise in self-deception, but the occasion for the writer to express his doubts, voice his uncertainties and rationalize the conflicting forces within him. Circumstances may well have caused Diderot to ponder whether he himself merely represents the Nephew plus a balanced critical sense or, perhaps, something more enduring. The moment to examine, both as an external observer and out of personal experience, and possibly more completely to understand the creative processes, whether fulfilled, thwarted or impotent, seems to be at hand.

In a dialogue that is both swift and engaging, the significance which is to be given genius is obvious as early as the first paragraphs. Once the amenities between the two interlocutors have been dismissed, the spontaneity and naturalness of discussion are remarkably preserved with the nearest subject at hand—chess-players at the Régence. As we are carried away on the stream of conversational speculation, it is readily apparent that the focus of the first ten pages of the dialogue itself is primarily on the serious question of the nature of genius, viewed from a variety of angles. Moreover, the subject will remain with the participants to the closing pages, now sharing the limelight, or again, receding into the background. In one way or another, then, its presence is felt almost continually throughout the dialogue, whether independently or in relation to other factors. This is in fact so evident, that a structural analysis of the topic reveals that it could itself represent the unified matter of a dialogue apart.

With the relative merits of the ever-present chess-players as a point of departure, Diderot-MOI and Rameau-LUI fall into complete and immediate agreement that mediocrity must be dismissed, but that those who are really great should be spared. To this, MOI adds that a vast number of men are obliged to practice the various arts for a man of genius to emerge. Abandoning his earlier position, LUI quickly warms to an attack on men of genius for, like his uncle, they are monomaniacs to the exclusion of all else. Though they should no doubt be emulated in this respect, they are, in contradistinction, unnecessary; furthermore, they are thoroughly detestable.

---

[1] Leo Spitzer may well be justified in calling sympathetic attention to Herbert Dieckmann's assertion that the *Paradoxe* is clearly " a polemic of Diderot's against himself, an antagonism between his extremely sensitive and his rationalistic tendencies " (*op. cit.*, 182, note 28), but Miss Gilman is more strikingly so in noting that the *Paradoxe* is a manifesto which represents the peak in Diderot's esthetic evolution (*loc. cit.*).

MOI observes that he had known LUI when the latter had been in despair, because he himself was only commonplace, and chides him on his inconsistency. MOI finds the Nephew's point that men of genius are peculiar well taken, but declares that they are worthy of our reverence, even if man-made laws may do them injustice.

MOI then states that the genius of Rameau the Elder is still doubtful while Racine's genius is unquestioned though, like LUI's uncle, the great playwright had been far from praiseworthy as a man. It is at this juncture that Diderot develops the tree metaphor—the striking figure where the man of genius is likened to a majestic tree which saps the strength of other trees around, and smothers the plants growing at its roots. Yet its top reaches to the clouds and its fruit is exquisite, while its widespread branches offer shade to past, present and future generations of men. Such is the nature of the sublime poet, Racine.

To the Nephew's comment that, were Nature powerful as she is wise, such men would be both great and good, Diderot-MOI objects that the general order of things would then be subverted. As preoccupations become more personal, however, both agree LUI to be mediocre, and the Nephew finally owns he would prefer being a genius since he is resentful of his mediocrity as well as envious of the superior man. Conjointly, he confesses how much he would like to have written two of his uncle's compositions for, capable of those, he would have been capable of others. He would, in consequence, have become a distinguished celebrity with all the advantages such a position offered. But, he continues, not only is he a nonentity, he is ignorant, stupid, mad, impudent and lazy as well.

LUI then explains the deplorable state in which Diderot finds him as a result of his expulsion from Bertin's table and home. This is followed by a fleeting moment of pride in past accomplishment when the mercurial Nephew speaks of his harpsichord pieces which, though neglected by his contemporaries, may well be esteemed by posterity above all others. Upon reflection, however, he again concludes that, up to the present, he has made no progress toward artistic or material success. In consequence, he feels nothing but remorse and self-contempt for the waste of those gifts which he recognizes Heaven to have bestowed upon him.

Refusing to commit himself as to where the responsibility lies, Diderot pities LUI for the abject state into which he was born or has fallen. In a spasm of seeming self-justification, the Nephew almost immediately illustrates the discipline and torture, for the sake of musical dexterity, to which he has subjected his fingers throughout the years. This leads him into his initial pantomime of the virtuoso, first as a violinist, then as a harpsichordist. The physical and emotional exertion he has thus undergone affords him a momentary feeling of artistic completion.

The mood is of short duration as the Nephew launches into a defence of his depraved literary and moral standards in the name of an inexorable materialism. This time MOI concludes that LUI is indeed to be pitied for his inability to conceive that one may rise above his fate. By way of reply the Nephew asserts that Rameau must remain what he is.

Having indicated the price a parasite must pay for his position in society, LUI inadvertently offers a definition of genius when, in mock admiration of Bertin's mistress, Mlle. Hus, he says of her accomplishments: " Sans étude, par la seule force de l'instinct, par la seule lumière naturelle: cela tient du prodige." But the admiration becomes sincere when he relates the story of Bouret's monstrous deception at the expense of his dog and the Lord Chancellor all to prove that men of genius read little, do much and are self-made. Indeed, such rare men as these—for Caesar, among others, is included—are a force of Nature. Nor should MOI forget that, in this respect, the Nephew too is worthy of attention, for: " Je suis rare dans mon espèce, oui, très rare." And LUI embarks on his theme of the genius represented by sublimity in wickedness, though he does not hesitate to place natural monsters like Bouret and the Renegade of Avignon above himself in the rank of great rascals. He is, nevertheless, anxious to force MOI to admit the superiority and originality of his own degradation over that of most of his contemporaries.

It is now that the great scene of musical mime is gradually but inevitably prepared. In defining song, the Nephew elaborates the theory that every musical art has its model in Nature. As Lui warms to his subject by illustrating his theory vocally and with appropriate gestures, MOI, in anticipatory delight, sees that his interlocutor is losing his head. It is soon apparent that the Nephew has passed into a state of mental abberation and ecstasy " près de la folie." In fact we learn from MOI that he does go completely out of his mind as his inspired impersonation of operatic presentation reaches its climax. Only then, bewildered and dazed, does he swim back to normalcy. In his own words, he is beaten and broken. Nor is this unusual, this unbridled enthusiasm; as the Nephew confesses: " Cela m'arrive presque tous les jours, sans que je sache pourquoi."

Having fully recovered from his moment of violently rampant inspiration, and with thirst of body and mind temporarily slaked, he freely admits that, through heredity and environment, he has always followed his penchants—including that for the vicious. Moreover, he refuses to deplore the fact, since those who fight against their natures are moral hybrids unequivocally indicative of the commonplace and worthy only of contempt. So it is once again that LUI rejects the tag of personal mediocrity to accept that of genius in baseness: a great scoundrel is a great scoundrel. Nonfulfillment in musical creativity, but perfection in infamy.

Pondering these conclusions, MOI points out that the wretched fiddler the Nephew acknowledges himself to be, could nevertheless have made his fortune in Paris through his appreciation of music. So far as LUI's character is concerned, however, MOI is moved to agree that he is indeed sometimes profound in his depravity.

When, on the other hand, the Nephew expresses a longing for his interlocutor's gifts, MOI brushes aside the compliment and broaches one of the most intrinsic of the themes of inquiry in the dialogue: Why, with his ability to appreciate, reproduce and communicate to others his enthusiasm for the finest passages of great composers, has the younger Rameau been powerless to compose anything worthwhile himself? By way of reply the Nephew points to the heavens crying out, "Et l'astre! l'astre!" for Fate, or Nature, had not wished it so. And yet, "Il me semble qu'il y a pourtant là quelque chose," tapping his forehead by way of emphasis and adding: "Je sens, oui, je sens." This leads him to confide that he had once been strongly persuaded of his creative genius, but alone and with pen in hand nothing would come forth.

Having now forgotten his ill-fated star and the patrilineal curse, he blames all on his environment: "Mais le moyen de sentir, de s'élever, de penser, de peindre fortement en fréquentant avec des gens tels que ceux qu'il faut voir pour vivre." As he depicts his creative urge victim of an enforced parasitism, it becomes ever more apparent that excuses are not wanting to explain his failure in the world of music. When MOI suggests that it would be more fruitful to shut oneself up in an attic the better to search one's artistic soul, LUI protests that he does not have the needed courage. Nor does he care to sacrifice his happiness to an uncertain success. Besides, the very name of Rameau he bears is a handicap. Then too, talent is not transmitted from father to son like a title of nobility.

By way of reply, MOI observes that such things should not be taken for granted and that, in LUI's place, he would have made an effort. The Nephew retorts that, since the age of fifteen, he has longed to do something to excite universal admiration; but he has found it impossible to create great works, and he recounts the tyranny of past vicissitudes by way of proof. In close keeping with Helvétius' thesis of a fatalism which obliges individual man to be a helpless victim of external forces and circumstances, LUI reaches the conclusion that, "De maudites circonstances nous mènent, et nous mènent mal."

As the dialogue reaches its close, however, the Nephew's moods continue to alternate between artistic exuberance and depression. Responsibility for his creative frustration is in turn laid to the door of an unhappy environment and inflexible heredity, while Fate has decreed that he be a musician. LUI here offers his illustration of inborn genius—the miller's apprentice who will never hear any other sound but the machinery's cliquet, but who might have in other circumstances composed the finest songs. When MOI proposes that whatever man undertakes, he is destined to it by Nature, the Nephew observes that she has made some strange blunders— furthermore the question of the rôle which Nature destines to individuals is complicated by such everyday experiences as hunger. In response, MOI points out that, though of necessity material things have a price, the Nephew is paying too dearly for them; he is, as a result, playing his base pantomime as he has always done and always will do. LUI disagrees on the cost, but agrees that he will continue to carry on as in the past. His only legitimate regret is the loss of his wife whose charms would have more easily helped him to obtain the wealth and position he so ardently desires. His farewell flourish shows him to be impenitent and even satisfied provided that such a life endure another two score years.

It is on this note that terminates a discussion of the problem of talent and the creative urge in French eighteenth-century society between Rameau-LUI, the artistic failure, and Diderot-MOI, who is perhaps no more than an equivocal success. It is also on this note that the *Neveu de Rameau* comes to an end.

We emerge from the dialogue with a strong sense of the folly and frustration of a life which is hopelessly unregenerate; yet the conversational resourcefulness and impudent candor of the Nephew have held the reader's attention to the end. The foregoing summary, although incomplete, should be sufficient to recall to the student of Diderot a vast array of references in his other works which would lend support to the arguments and examples proffered by the two participants in the colloquy. To present these references in any considerable measure offers the danger of reducing the inquiry to a game depending largely upon the shuffling of *fiches* and should, perhaps, be avoided. Moreover, consideration of the nature of Diderot's dialectical method seems called for before any attempt is made towards critical examination of particular points.

Critics such as Pierre Mesnard, Jean Fabre and Milton Seiden have insisted that MOI and LUI are not emotionally identical. There seems little reason to deny such a judgment, and, as we follow the dialogue, it becomes clear that the theme of talent and genius is being filtered through two temperaments, examined on two planes, even though, as some would maintain, the characters of the dialogue are but divergent manifestations of Diderot himself.

The oscillation, so apparent in *Le Neveu*, appears at first glance nothing less than vacillation and even contradiction on the part of the author. To so conclude, however, is to understand imperfectly Diderot's choice of the dialogue form in some of his most serious investigations.

The opportunity to present two sides of a problem, or even to multiply the points of view, is certainly the most valid reason for Diderot's preferred literary form in such major works as the *Entretiens*, the *Rêve de d'Alembert*, the *Paradoxe sur le comédien* and, more unexpectedly perhaps, in *Jacques le fataliste* and the *Neveu de Rameau*. In the above colloquies, whatever the problem may be, Diderot strongly gives the impression that it is his intention to hold it in the light and turn it around slowly before concluding with a conception which is not simple, which he does not wish to be homogeneous, and the synthesis of which he often leaves to the reader. It is as though he has taken his cue from Shaftesbury who had already written in *The Moralists: a Philosophical Rhapsody:* " Each understands and thinks the best he can for his own purpose: He *for Himself*; I for another *Self*. And who, I beseech you, for *the Whole*? " [1]

Reduced to its simplest terms, the *Neveu* appears as a series of discussions through the medium of a retrograde artist cursed with an illustrious family name and a philosopher of considerable intellectual prominence. Before scrutinizing Diderot's dialectical procedure and its consequences in such a framework, however, a closer examination of LUI as a personality is essential.

As a study in character, the dialogue is first and foremost the portrait of a fellow who, for inconsistency, has not his peer. We are already warned

---

[1] *Characteristicks*, II, *an Inquiry concerning Virtue and Merit* ([n.p.] 1699).

of this in the Horatian epigraph which introduces the Satire: " Born under the malignant influence of change." [1]

Like Montaigne, Diderot was ever intrigued by man's nature, " divers et ondoyant," and as late as the *Eléments de physiologie* (1774-1780) he persisted that, " Le plus constant est celui qui change le moins " [A.-T., IX, 423). Thus, as the dialogue unfolds, we see the Nephew moved in turn by pride and self-contempt, hope and dejection, faith in what he has already accomplished creatively but acceptance of its insignificance, and first satisfaction then dejection in recognizing that the mark of genius is not upon him. So too, we see him catering to his innate hedonism, while regretting it with his instinct as an artist. Nor in any way does Diderot seem to violate the dictum in Horace's *Ars Poetica:* " ... let the first impression be preserved to the end, and let his nature be consistent."

In no small degree, this consistency lies in Diderot's brilliantly sustained portrayal of the Nephew's constantly shifting dispositions; but it is to be noted that LUI's vacillations almost invariably derive from the diverse manifestations of the problem of genius. By way of illustration, it will be recalled that Diderot-MOI is specifically referring to a ramification of the question of genius when, in swift rebuke, he tells Rameau-LUI: " Vous ne serez jamais heureux si le pour et le contre vous affligent également; il faudrait prendre son parti, et y demeurer attaché " (A.-T., V, 393).

If the Nephew is shown to be, in part, victim of his own vacillation, during the course of the dialogue there are many indications as to why this should be so. But it is not thus that the recognized man of genius is constituted, and in the *Neveu de Rameau*, as well as elsewhere, Diderot shows the genius as one who, bent upon expressing his inner urge, ignores all other considerations in striving for its achievement.[2] In contrast, Jean-François emerges as one who has neither the stability of character nor the steady conviction required for even moderate success in art or, for that matter, in life itself.

This portrait, and indeed the dialogue as a whole, furnish an impact attesting to times of frustration and social decay, as well as of self-inquiry. By viewing the Satire from the middle distance of the interested reader, however, one is forcibly and immediately struck by the fact that, so far as society and the creative urge of the individual are concerned, this is not a study of extreme oppositeness.

Of the two protagonists, the approach of MOI is, in general, philosophically reflective with occasional overtones of practical reality. The Nephew, faced by the stubborn facts of his artistic, social and moral bankruptcy, is himself prone to indulge in philosophical speculation which, as we have seen in the summary, is not always in disagreement with that of

---

[1] According to Professor Gilbert Highet, such is in spirit a faithful rendering of the line: " Vertumnis quotquot sunt, natus iniquis " (Horat., *Lib. II, Serm. VII*).

[2] Cf. the following from *Satire I, sur les Caractères et les Mots de Caractère, de Profession, etc.*: " L'homme qui est tout entier à son métier, s'il a du génie, devient un prodige; s'il n'en a point, une application opiniâtre l'élève au-dessus de la médiocrité " (A.-T., VII, 309).

his opponent. And yet, as often as not, LUI seems to represent a deliberate though convincingly realistic foil to MOI's often speculative assumptions. It is the Nephew who continually contaminates the philosophic argument relative to genius, and to its less lofty corollary, the artist striving for expression in society. Concerned as he is with his personal preoccupations and experiences, time and again he twists the question at issue by getting down to particular cases and their application to his own situation. A striking example of this is offered early in the dialogue when Jean-François attempts to build a philosophical position against the *homme de génie* opposed to that of Diderot-MOI. Having defended his hatred for men of genius, LUI finds himself forced to admire them as well. He, too, would like to receive the plaudits of the multitude, to write music that would move the souls of men. But whereas MOI, in this part of the discussion, has been examining genius on something of an abstract, theoretical level, LUI distorts the philosophic argument in order to consider genius at the concrete, functional level where it may be measured by the success, prompt and tangible, of the artist's endeavors. Still, as he confesses, whatever admiration he himself may have for genius must be fleeting and quickly replaced by a rationalized hatred, the better to endure his own mediocrity (A.-T., V, 393-398).

That the Nephew has become a mediocrity is agreed to by both; they are also largely in accord as to why he is not a genius, or far less, a composer of talent. The problem in reverse, with little specific reference to the *Neveu de Rameau*, has been analyzed by Professor Dieckmann and others, particularly in relation to the two *Réfutations* of Helvétius, the *Rêve de d'Alembert*, the *Eléments de physiologie* and the *Paradoxe sur le comédien*. Many of the pertinent themes elaborated in such works of Diderot also play an important part in the inversive development of *Le Neveu*. They need be merely touched upon here.

Of these, the principal one and that upon which the others depend, is the primordial rôle assumed by Nature in fashioning the man of genius: " ... c'est la nature qui forme ces hommes rares-là," exclaims the Nephew (A.-T., V, 436). Or again, while admitting that Nature smiled when she created Leo, Vinci, Pergolesi and Duni, he confesses: " Quand elle fagota [le] neveu elle fit la grimace, et puis la grimace, et puis la grimace encore " (A.-T., V, 475). MOI willingly concurs, but finds that, despite the Nephew's lack of inborn genius as a musician, he was nevertheless destined for a musical career, for: " A quoi que ce soit que l'homme s'applique, la nature l'y destinait " (A.-T., V. 481). It is a point of view which is Diderot's own,[1] and upon which the two interlocutors are in fundamental agreement, a point of view, moreover, which a century later will be strikingly restated by Carlyle writing on Cagliostro: " Nature was pleased to produce such a man, even so, not otherwise."

The pattern of the Nephew's identity, responding to the compulsions of an individual nervous system with its extreme emotional mobility, is

---

[1] Cf. *Le Rêve de d'Alembert:* " Je suis donc tel, parce qu'il a fallu que je fusse tel " (A.-T., II, 138).

in evidence throughout the dialogue. In matters of the mind and emotions he is unrestrained, yielding himself without hesitation to chance impressions and random recurrence of mental activity. To the threat of anarchy, no stringent self-discipline is opposed. LUI himself speaks of " une fibre qui ne m'a point été donnée " (A.-T., V, 468) and of the " molécule paternelle... cette maudite molécule première " (A.-T., V, 469). The exceptionally gifted uncle, the talented but erratic father and Jean-François as well, from what we already know of them and from what Diderot reveals, suggest that the name of Rameau carried with it a mental taint, a tendency toward abnormally intense personalities. The causal elements here fixing the Nephew's failure as a creative artist are clearly neuro-biological and strongly foreshadow speculations on psychosomatic determinants to be found notably in the *Rêve*.[1]

But genius, itself a product of Nature, is something inherent in, or a rare product of organized matter as such, for Diderot's well-known theories on deterministic transformism seem to find specific application to the problem at hand. MOI's observation that, " C'est qu'il faut qu'il y ait un grand nombre d'hommes qui s'appliquent pour faire sortir l'homme de génie " (A.-T., V. 391) is not far removed from the terminology of an eighteenth-century biologist explaining the natural processes through which a species of a lower order evolves to attain a higher one or even a definitive structural form.[2] MOI and LUI see eye to eye on this as well as on the concept of genius as a monstrous form of human species, differing in kind from the normal, and thus an anomaly and a deviant in its time. As we have already seen, however,[3] the Nephew, sooner or later, feels impelled to obscure the philosophical argument by insisting upon his own position as a monster in society.

This leads us to a final topic illustrative of the dialectic here joined. Jean-François' faults do not lie solely in the stars, and the two interlocutors are well aware of it. In so far as *Le Neveu* is a social satire, it represents some of the most bitter invective directed against a single group—in this instance, Bertin's anti-philosophic set—written in the French eighteenth-century.

Though not endowed with genius, how could LUI at least have realized his unquestioned talents as a musician? Mr. E. M. Forster offers a twentieth-century answer not unlike that suggested in *Satire II*: " The clique is a valuable social device, which only a fanatic would condemn; it can protect and encourage the artist. It is the artist's duty, if he wants to be in a clique, to choose a good one, and to take care it doesn't make him bumptious,

---

[1] Cf. especially A.-T., II, 169-173.

[2] An idea constantly evoked in *Le Rêve* and which may be fruitfully compared with La Mettrie's assertion: " Par quelle infinité de combinaisons il a fallu que la matière ait passé, avant que d'arriver à celle-là seule, de laquelle pouvait résulter un animal parfait ! " *Système d'Epicure*, *Œuvres philosophiques de M. de la Mettrie*, nouv. éd. (Amsterdam, 1774), III, 222-223.

[3] *Supra*, 82; Cf. A.-T., V, 457.

sterile or silly.[1] MOI and LUI both make it plain that not only has the latter become an irresponsible parasite on society, but that the society he had specifically chosen for his physical and intellectual subsistence is among the least suited for the cultivation of higher artistic expression. The Nephew's association with " de mauvaises gens " has quite defiled any natural aptitude he may have had for creativity, just as it has so patently encouraged his disposition for moral inertia. He has become a victim of the predatory patronage of the Bertin-Hus-Palissot coterie which saps and vitiates the talent of men it encompasses. In such a milieu, the Nephew's artistic inspiration has been crushed and he has accepted the fatal tendency to take refuge along perverse paths to cynicism, frustration and ultimate disaster.

They are not the trials of a man of genius however much they may be those of a man of talent. As MOI suggests in *Le Neveu* and Diderot categorically states in the *Salon de 1765*, " Le génie travaille en enrageant et mourant de faim " (A.-T., V, 477; X, 250). The excuses which LUI offers for his own impotence as an artist are but a pale reflection, a mimicry of society's conspiracy against the truly great man—a conspiracy touched upon in *Le Neveu* (A.-T., V, 394) but which the Encyclopedia article " Eclectisme " had already noted in such great detail in 1755. Poverty along with the injustice and short-sightedness of others are the principal components:

" ... l'indigence qui jette un homme de génie du côté opposé à celui où la nature l'appelait; les récompenses mal placées qui l'indignent et lui font tomber la plume des mains; l'indifférence du gouvernement qui dans son calcul politique fait entrer pour infiniment moins qu'il ne vaut l'éclat que la nation reçoit des lettres et des arts utiles, ne sait sacrifier une somme aux tentatives d'un homme de génie qui meurt avec ses projets dans sa tête, sans qu'on puisse conjecturer si la nature réparera jamais cette perte... " [A.-T., XIV, 348].

Yet it is on this theme of man in society that the tension of the dialogue's dialectic shows Diderot's deep understanding of the dynamics and contradictions of the artist in eighteenth-century France. The Nephew's excuses have their validity too, for some measure of security—economic as well as emotional—is a necessary condition for a life seeking its full measure of creative expression. What emerges from this phase of the dialectic is that which lies between the gift of talent, or even genius, and what is made of this gift which is not always within the artist's control. The pure abstraction, by stress of circumstances, is sheared to the necessities of living. If the Nephew is not completely relieved of blame for his failure, he nevertheless offers a practical example, deliberately posited, of the compromise that philosophical equanimity and philosophical probity must make with everyday experience.

---

[1] " *La Raison d'Etre* of Criticism," *Music and Criticism, a Symposium*, ed. Richard F. French, Harvard University Press (Cambridge, 1948), 32.

Such an interpretation of the dialectic in the *Neveu de Rameau* gives a justification, I believe hitherto unstressed, for the ethical and pragmatic side of the work, at least so far as the relationship of the creative artist to the world in general is concerned. So viewed, it is not a study in extreme oppositeness, but rather a question of perspective, for Diderot-MOI is not too much the pure philosopher and LUI not the excessiveness of weak flesh. It would doubtless be pressing too far to state it is not the difference but the likeness which alone should be emphasized between the protagonists in respect to the problem we are examining. Nevertheless it is in their mutual attraction rather than repulsion that, within the central area of life itself, we find added pertinence in the theme of talent and genius here treated by Diderot.

All that is lacking for a well-spent discussion of this theme which has often been maintained on an abstract level is a concrete example of the artist at work. Specific examples we have so far considered have been of a negative nature. They do not evince either the man of talent or the genius in action, but rather the inertia forced on the individual—in this instance the Nephew—through the exigencies of life itself. Consequently, these illustrations concern themselves with the destruction of natural artistic interests by social, economic and biological pressure. But to complete the picture would seem to call for one or more positive examples: the dynamic illustration of the artist in the throes of inspiration.

This we are accorded through two notable scenes of musical pantomime. The first, in which the Nephew works out the shadowy and insubstantial fulfilment of his desire to be a great instrumental virtuoso (A.-T., V, 409-411), offers a striking example of Diderot's own vivid intensity as a writer and his interest in depicting scenes of pantomime. Still, there is no attempt here to realize fully the possibilities of a scene suggesting what Wordsworth would call the " spontaneous overflow of powerful feeling." It need not detain us longer.

But in the second and final musical pantomime (A.-T., V, 463-67) we are aware of having reached the climactic scene of the dialogue, the setting for which has been prepared, not through blind drift, but with consummate care and skill almost from the outset of the dialogue. Its representation is fundamental to our discussion—and for two reasons.

The first of these is the vital demonstration which this crucial point of the composition calls us to witness: the imagination fired by enthusiasm as the artist seeks the effectuation of the creative urge. We are reminded of T.S. Eliot's phrase relative to genius, " expert beyond experience," as the Nephew's musical intuition, deriving from the well-filled mind and partly acquired by long habit, offers a revelation that we have not before realized. And Professor Mornet is indeed justified in referring to " un de ses rares accès de génie," [1] as LUI's inspired pantomime reaches its highest pitch:

" Il pleurait, il riait, il soupirait, il regardait ou attendri, ou tranquille, ou furieux; c'était une femme qui se pâme de douleur, c'était un malheureux

---
[1] *Le Neveu de Rameau*, Les Cours de Lettres (Paris, 1947-1948), Fascicule III, 215.

livré à tout son désespoir; un temple qui s'élève; des oiseaux qui se taisent au soleil couchant; des eaux ou qui murmurent dans un lieu solitaire et frais, ou qui descendent en torrent du haut des montagnes; un orage, une tempête, la plainte de ceux qui vont périr, mêlée au sifflement des vents, au fracas du tonnerre. C'était la nuit avec ses ténèbres, c'était l'ombre et le silence, car le silence même se peint par des sons. Sa tête était tout à fait perdue [A.-T., V, 464-465]."

In a moment of inspired enthusiasm the Nephew, as middleman between MOI's or Diderot's own ideas as a philosopher and the public's reception of these ideas, has epitomized—though in satiric dress—the genius in action. This appears all the more true when we view the scene as an acutely living illustration, though touched with travesty, of the very mysterious process which leads up to the finished work and which Diderot briefly outlines elsewhere. In the familiar *Second Entretien* of *Dorval et Moi* we read:

" L'imagination s'échauffe; la passion s'émeut. On est successivement étonné, attendri, indigné, courroucé. Sans l'enthousiasme ou l'idée véritable ne se présente point, ou si, par hasard on la rencontre, on ne peut la poursuivre. Le poète sent le moment de l'enthousiasme; c'est après qu'il a médité. Il s'annonce en lui par un frémissement qui part de sa poitrine et qui passe d'une manière délicieuse et rapide, jusqu'aux extrémités de son corps. Bientôt, ce n'est plus un frémissement; c'est une chaleur forte et permanente qui l'embrasse, qui le fait haleter, qui le consume, qui le tue; mais qui donne l'âme, la vie à tout ce qu'il touche. Si cette chaleur s'accroissait encore, les spectres se multiplieraient devant lui. Sa passion s'élèverait presque au degré de sa fureur. Il ne connaîtrait de soulagement qu'à verser au dehors un torrent d'idées qui se pressent, se heurtent et se chassent " [A.-T., VII, 103].

In the scene from *Le Neveu* we see in operation the faculty of excitation necessary to create. The demonstration is complete when we are told of the effects of this inspired moment on the artist: " Epuisé de fatigue, tel qu'un homme qui sort d'un profond sommeil ou d'une longue distraction, il resta immobile, stupide, étonné, il tournait ses regards autour de lui comme un homme égaré qui cherche à reconnaître le lieu où il se trouve... " (A.-T., V, 465). Here again Diderot is closely following the second part of *Dorval et Moi* when Dorval, emerging from his ecstasy " comme un homme qui sortirait d'un sommeil profond " asks, " Qu'ai-je dit? Qu'avais-je à vous dire? Je ne m'en souviens plus." The *Eléments de physiologie* will offer us the clearest of statements as to what has taken place before our own eyes in both *Le Neveu* and *Dorval et Moi*: " Une idée singulière qui se présente, un rapport bizarre qui distrait, et voilà la tête perdue. On revient de là comme d'un rêve. On demande à ses auditeurs: Où en étais-je? Que disais-je? " Diderot continues: " Point de penseurs profonds, point d'imaginations ardentes, qui ne soient sujets à des catalepsies momentanées " (A.-T., IX, 423).

Yet the great artist must experience original vision and communicate it. What had Rameau's Nephew hoped to do in his celebrated scene? Through mime and voice he had been absorbed in conjuring up the dancers, singers and instrumentalists of an imposing orchestra in order to interpret musically the beauty and mysteries of Nature. Having perceived the methods, both conscious and unconscious, he has used, we may well ask whether he succeeded in his objective, and if only partly so, where he failed. This leads us to the second reason for giving such stress to the scene in the development of our inquiry.

Through the medium of the Nephew, Diderot has presented us with a brilliant pantomime of the inspired artist, but it is still only pantomime. LUI's feeling for music, developed through his past experience in connection with it, remains unchanged. This past interest had, we know, once led him to hope he was capable of such lofty creative expression in music that he would, one day, reap the rewards of recognized genius. Instead, we are witness to one type of artistic temper in a final stage of evolution. Quite uninhibited—there are those who have leveled the same charge against Diderot—the Nephew is obviously incapable of guarding that order and proportion essential to full realization of the creative mind. He unabashedly reveals himself as one into whose consciousness rush all sorts of ideas and reactions which, with equal abandon, he pours out to those around him. As Mr. I. A. Richards would say, his emotions are too easily stirred, too light on the trigger. For such a mind, impervious as it is to discipline and restraint, so completely a victim of emotional susceptibility, its strivings for artistic expression might easily lead to creative inertia or even chaos with attendant frustration. For as Wordsworth asserts:

> The Gods approve
> The depth, and not the tumult, of the soul.

It is precisely of this that the great scene of musical pantomime gives such a striking demonstration. We see that the Nephew has much of the same technique and many of the symptoms of genius without genius itself. But his emotional instability, his imagination-run-riot, his exaltation in excess of the circumstances, form a frame of reference which explains, to a large extent, why the positive illustration of the creative urge concludes in utter disorganization and failure of expression. The pantomime emerges as a hideous mockery of genius, as an eloquent but devastating symbol of total frustration, and the passersby, the chess-players and MOI himself, at first held in its spell, roar with laughter as they awaken to the fact that all this verges on the ludicrous.

Moreover, the distance between the dream and its realization cannot be bridged with fleeting pantomime, and the Nephew is well aware that he is capable only of miming his artistic aspirations and not of achieving them. Aristotle has stated that music is the most imitative of arts, and it is quite apparent to MOI and LUI alike that the Nephew's musical pantomime is but an imitation of an imitation. Some years later, in *La Réfutation de l'Homme*, Diderot will make a definitive distinction between the man of genius and the imitator: " Le génie attire fortement à lui tout ce qui se trouve dans la sphère de son activité, qui s'en exalte sans mesure. L'imitateur n'attire point, il est attiré; il s'aimante par le contact avec l'aimant, mais il n'est pas l'aimant " (A.-T., II, 411).

But the Nephew has pegged the ultimate in his artistic expression and his talent to the form for which he is most palpably suited—pantomime with all its ephemeral imitativeness. Once again permanency of artistic expression has eluded his grasp and as the momentary inspiration is shortly consumed in its own profusion, like des Esseintes in Huysmans' *A Rebours*, he stands with " sa fièvre d'inconnu, son idéal inassouvi, son besoin d'échapper à l'horrible réalité de l'existence, à franchir les confins de la pensée, à tâtonner sans jamais arriver à une certitude, dans les brumes des au delà de l'art ! " In the end, there is nothing left but for Diderot-MOI to dismiss him simply and scathingly: " Vous dansez, vous avez dansé et vous continuerez de danser la vile pantomime " (A.-T., V, 486).

From beginning to end, in the most general as well as the most specific sense of the term, the *Neveu de Rameau* remains a satire. And through the variety of his satirical means, Diderot has shown a new comprehension of the complexity of human nature whether represented by an individual *per se*, by a social being in eighteenth-century France, or by man in general.

In what is particularly pertinent to our investigation, we have seen two personages each confronted by the other's presence when both have experienced periods of prolonged frustration, each in his own way and for his own reasons. The Nephew had long since abandoned the road which led to his early aspirations. Had Diderot taken the wrong road as well and, if so, could something still be salvaged? Or was his case different? The encounter and discussion with Rameau's Nephew, or perhaps to be more exact, the actual composition of the dialogue has offered Diderot the opportunity once again to take bearings and to reopen for himself the whole question of talent and genius.

The social élite of Europe, who were Grimm's subscribers, were able to read from time to time in the *Correspondance Littéraire* of the fifties of the remarkable genius that was Diderot's.[1] There was, however, when *Le Neveu* was written, and there continued to be hesitation in Diderot's mind concerning the quality of his creative gifts and the best means at his disposal to give them the most satisfactory expression. On the other hand, whether through coquetry or conviction, throughout his life he was sporadically to reject the epithet of genius. A typical instance, late in life, may be found when, upon his return from the court and highly flattering interest of Catherine of Russia, he paused at Hamburg. There he addressed in the third person a letter to one of the city's illustrious citizens, Emmanuel Bach, which ends as follows: " La seule observation qu'il me permettra

---

[1] It was certainly Grimm, for instance, who wrote in the November 1, 1755 issue of the *Correspondance Littéraire*: " Jamais deux génies ne se sont ressemblés comme celui de Bacon et de M. Diderot. La même profondeur, la même étendue, la même abondance d'idées et de vues, la même sublimité d'imagination, la même pénétration, la même sagacité, et quelquefois la même obscurité pour leurs contemporains respectifs, et surtout pour ceux qui ont la vue faible."

de lui faire, c'est que j'ai plus de réputation que de fortune, conformité malheureuse qui m'est commune avec la plupart des hommes de génie sans y avoir le même titre." [1]

The conviction immediately suggests itself, however, that in 1761 Diderot had, in some way, found himself in the *Neveu de Rameau* and, in so doing, had developed a self-assurance and had unloosened creative individual energies which were to extend at least through the *Salon de 1767* and the *Rêve de d'Alembert*. One of his contemporaries, Ecouchard Lebrun, wrote in an ode entitled " A Monsieur de Buffon sur ses détracteurs " the following lines:

> L'esprit est le dieu des instants,
> Le génie est le dieu des âges.

The Nephew of Rameau comes to life in the pages of Diderot's dialogue with his dazzling flashes of insight and wit, and thus embodies the very meaning of Lebrun's " esprit." But Diderot, in the heat of creative composition, has brought a fresh voice to the question of creative genius and a new example of its fulfillment.

---

[1] Maurice Tourneux, *Diderot et Catherine II* (Paris, Calmann Levy, 1899), 476.

# *JACQUES LE FATALISTE* REVISITED[*]

> "How does one write a novel? I mean how can anybody possibly stick to a story, if he's at all sensitive to the significance of things?"
>
> (John Barth, *The Floating Opera*)

There are those who say with increasing insistence that, in eighteenth-century France, it is in the novel rather than in the theatre or poetry that the true spirit of the era in all its manifestations is most clearly revealed. Generally speaking, the novel of the day is the contemporary chronicle, reflecting as it does the changing face of the age—its customs, its passions, its humanitarian dreams, its discussions of social and metaphysical questions. If an Anatole France saw in certain obscure eighteenth-century French novels a pageant of the life of the times with its typical dreams, realities and illusions, and imitated their spirit in *La Reine Pédauque* and other pastiches, present-day scholars have been gradually recognizing the same to be true of Diderot's novels.

Although, since the beginning of the nineteenth century, a number of critics have tried to set Diderot apart in the history of the French novel, he was, at least along the broader lines, adhering to certain fundamental French and even European traditions. He was, upon occasion, to use these traditions as a springboard for his own brilliant innovations. His first novel had been *Les Bijoux indiscrets* which, in many respects, was conventional enough among the licentious novels in the first half of the French Enlightenment. Down through the years it was generally referred to, but only in passing, with withering contempt. The Carlyles, the Barbey d'Aurevillys, the Saintsburys had their cutting say. Typically, an obscure British critic of the early twentieth century dismissed it as "a sort of literary garbage." Despite such unflattering views, this hastily written novel—the only one to be published during Diderot's lifetime—is redeemed, in part, by a few scattered pages which give promise of the intellectual ferment and refreshing originality that were to be characteristic of the author in subsequent works of fiction.

One of these was the forceful and poignant *La Religieuse*, completed in 1760. Only in the 1950's was it considered far more complex than had been thought to be the case when it was first published some twelve years

---
[*] Reprinted from *L'Esprit Créateur*, VIII (1968), 42-52.

after Diderot's death. That in itself is a long story. *Le Neveu de Rameau*, a dialogue, but also a novel to those who agree with the twentieth-century British critic and author, Walter Allen, who declares that " the novel in general is the most impure of art forms," was surely written in its first form in 1761. It was recognized by Goethe as a provocative masterpiece, and even Saintsbury, who approves of it in general, cheerfully tells us that it has " only touches of obscenity."

Diderot had also drawn up a galaxy of short stories which, themselves, marked a definite trend toward realism in French fiction, and little by little, he was arriving at the opinion of what good fiction should *not be*. By the time he had reached the age of sixty, he was ready to attempt a final realization of the novel as a literary genre according to his own tastes and abilities. Such a conception was to have little in common with the popular trends in French fiction he saw around him in the 1760's.

Earlier, Diderot had toyed with, only to abandon, the suggestive and symbolic allegorical tale then in vogue; nor did he seem to find inspiration for his own creative powers in the popular philosophical genre which reached its perfection in Voltaire's *Candide* (1759). By the time the impact of Rousseau's epistolary novel, *La Nouvelle Héloïse* (1761) had been felt on readers and novelists alike, Diderot knew his own mind in the field of fiction, and he inclined toward something else —something new and yet deeply rooted in the French spirit.

The old, the traditional to which he was to respond was the satirical, realistic genre with its lust for life, and its teeming variety, often presenting a vast spectacle of customs and mores in a given epoch. Its expression in French literature was most clearly exemplified in *Gargantua* and *Pantagruel*, in *Francion*, in *Le Roman comique*, and in *Gil Blas*, as the current passed from the sixteenth down into the eighteenth century. Rabelais, Sorel, Scarron, Le Sage—these were among the worthy representatives of a great tradition which in the Age of Enlightenment was in danger of being forgotten in the welter of new fictional genres rising to the fore. Diderot, by temperament and by talent, belonged to the older tradition. His mind worked through digression and association rather than through logical pattern, in the Baconian and experimental rather than in the Cartesian tradition. It is not implausible, then, that, surrounded by new fictional forms in France which left his inspiration fundamentally unrequited, he should with his restless and ever-alert mind, turn toward England. In Richardson, in Fielding, in Sterne, he found a new and refreshing departure from the eighteenth-century types of French fiction which had pushed the spontaneity and realism of even so relatively recent a novel as Le Sage's *Gil Blas* (1724-1735) into the background. And yet this newness in no small measure represented to Diderot qualities inherent in the earlier French literature to which he was attracted, qualities which led him to accept Sterne, for example, as the English Rabelais.

In 1762 Diderot published his short, eloquent essay in praise of Richardson, in which he cried out at one point, " O Richardson, Richardson, homme unique à mes yeux, tu seras ma lecture dans tous les temps ! " and concluded by declaring: " Le génie de Richardson a étouffé ce que j'en avais." Ten years later Diderot was to begin writing his longest novel, *Jacques le fataliste* which, among other things, was to reflect the humor and exploit an episode in Sterne's *Tristram Shandy*. And, like *Tristram Shandy*, the novel was to wander along with its chief characters seemingly at the mercy of the fates. "Digressions," exclaims Sterne somewhere, "incontestably, are the sunshine; they are the life, the soul of reading." And F. C. Green in his *Minuet* adds: "One has to read *Jacques le fataliste* to appreciate the justice of this remark."

Today's French anti-novel, more often than not with its anti-hero, and almost invariably with its anti-plot, has so often reminded recent critics of Diderot's last novel, that such avant-garde writers as Nathalie Sarraute, Michel Butor and Alain Robbe-Grillet, for instance, have been bluntly asked to what extent they have been influenced by *Jacques le fataliste*. All these exponents of the *nouveau roman* have, to be sure, denied any immediate or direct influence; any resemblances with Diderot's literary theories and practices were merely the result of *le hasard*. Chance, *le hasard*—there is a recurring term and concept in *Jacques*!

What is the plot or anti-plot of Diderot's novel? A rapid first reading of the book might not allow much more than the following summary. Jacques resembles a hero of Rabelais, chiefly through his love of the bottle; and he resembles a hero of Sterne mainly because of his sentimentality. The plot, presumably, is to deal with the love life of Jacques. After all, love is the main theme of eighteenth-century French fiction. But, in the present instance, we learn very little about it as it applies to Jacques; as Jacques and his master proceed with their journey on horseback, adventure after adventure, incident upon incident, break into the supposed narrative of Jacques' sentimental experiences. The episodes come in such fast succession that it is quite impossible to give an intelligible summary. A girl falls off a horse, an event which elicits mildly obscene, pseudo-philosophic bantering among those present; Jacques and his master meet bandits who are not bandits; there is more than one encounter with a funeral cortege, with nightmarish qualities and surrealistic overtones. At an inn the two voyagers hear stories including that of Madame de La Pommeraye, for years the best-known episode in the book. Once again en route, but where to?—Diderot has a ready reply for such a question, a reply echoed throughout the narrative; it runs something like this: "But for God's sake, author," the reader cries out petulantly, "where were they going?" "But for God's sake, reader, do you know where you are going? Does anyone ever know where he is really going?" The two travellers set out and again anecdotes, incidents, and digressions continue to pile up for the characters, the narrator or narrators and the reader. At the end of the novel Jacques is to marry his beloved Denise. He already wonders whether his master is not in love with Denise, but true to his philosophy, tells himself that if it is written by fate that his wife will be unfaithful, she will be, and if it is written she will not be unfaithful, she will not be, no matter what others may attempt. And with that Jacques falls asleep.

Upon reading the book Thomas Carlyle wrote in bewilderment and admiration, but with a certain perspicacity: "Like this there is nothing that we know of in the whole range of French literature." A full century later, George Saintsbury, lacking Carlyle's astuteness, fell into the trap set by Diderot. Saintsbury, a great admirer of the conventional, neatly-told narrative with its well-ordered plot, such as Madame Riccoboni knew how to compose, could not suppress his impatience with *Jacques*. His pen dripping with early twentieth-century academic sarcasm and pedantry, he declared: " It is comparatively of little moment that the main ostensible theme—the very unedifying account of the loves of Jacques and his master—is deliberately, tediously, inartistically interrupted and ' put off.' " Obviously Saintsbury was oblivious of or impervious to the judgment of the Goncourt brothers' statement, some years before, that with this work Diderot had ushered in the modern novel.

Full realization of the fact has been slow in coming, however. Charly Guyot, a Swiss critic and one of the leading European authorities on the history of French fiction, gives in the mid-twentieth century what is now the generally accepted explanation for this delay in recognition. Declaring that *Jacques* is a work full of the rarest, the most original fictional contrivances, Guyot adds that Diderot has long been—and perhaps still is—a victim of mischance.[1] There were, we are told, two glorious literary reputations: that of Voltaire and that of Rousseau. While Diderot, as general editor of the collective enterprise, the *Encyclopédie*, remained in semi-darkness, the author of *Candide* and the author of *La Nouvelle Héloïse* enjoyed European renown. His most personal works, Guyot concludes—those which were really to bring him fame—are posthumous.

It is now agreed that here is, as Cynthia Grenier has put it, a pungently witty quasi-novel of eighteenth-century mores and thought where one can find a fine blend of good, juicy, intellectual morsels to chew upon plus all the bawdy, detailed libertinage for which the period is duly celebrated. As in *Le Neveu de Rameau*, so in *Jacques*, we see Diderot's mind working through disgression and the association of ideas; and, as in the *Neveu*, so in the latter work, we are struck by the author's animation, his spirited dramatic dialogue, his irony and his oddities of mind. André Gide has called his own famous *Caves du Vatican* a *sotie*, that is to say a dramatic piece of a type particularly in vogue during the fourteenth and fifteenth centuries, in which all the characters are supposed to be more or less crazy. In recent years it has often been pointed out that *Jacques le fataliste* falls into the same category, that of the *sotie*.

By the middle of the twentieth century this particular novel had established itself for postcrity as a milestone in the evolution of the French novel. It included, as we have already suggested, 1. the old Gallic tradition; 2. superimposed English influences which, at times, had more than a little in common with the Rabelaisian and picaresque genres in France; 3. Diderot's own multi-faceted mind constantly striving for new goals in the fictional as well as in most of the other fields of expression.

Before touching upon *Jacques* in relation to modern esthetics of the novel, perhaps we could examine the question of whether there is a meta-

---

[1] *Jacques le fataliste*, avant-propos de Charly Guyot (Neuchâtel, 1946), 10.

physical or philosophical aim in the novel. There are those who say, for instance, that here Diderot is specifically studying the problem of human liberty, and that he wishes to demonstrate that everything in life is a linking of blind forces which man dominates only in his illusions. Others, more directly to the point, suggest that Jacques' fatalism is a literary counterpart of Diderot's determinism. There is no doubt but that Diderot liked to speculate on moral problems and that one which concerned itself with human destiny in its various forms was extremely popular in the eighteenth century. Voltaire will go into the subject in his philosophical tale, *Zadig, ou la destinée* relative to Christian doctrine and oriental fatalism; he will examine it in *Candide, ou l'optimisme* relative to Leibniz. In *Jacques le fataliste*, Diderot does so in relation to Spinoza or, more exactly, the protagonist's conception of the philosophy of Spinoza. Many twentieth-century readers, wishing to cut immediately to the bone, say that Jacques' attitude toward the problem is that of Diderot himself—that is, we are victims of the disenchantment and quixotic whimsy of a fate we do not control. I think that this problem is more involved, however, and that Jean Thomas is in error when he says in the *Humanisme de Diderot* that, through the adventures of his hero, Diderot depicts a fatalism more implacable than that of Spinoza to which Jacques constantly refers.

I should say that the novel is a satire against a number of things, and among them a brilliant satire on Spinoza's metaphysical determinism. In the unfolding of the narrative, in the diversity of the adventures which befall Jacques and his master, we find constantly brought up the same general comment on the inevitability of fate and man's need to be resigned to it. Through sheer monotony, then, Diderot forces upon the reader a realization that a formula which explains everything, explains nothing. Long before the end of the dialogue the absurdity of ascribing all events to destiny is made amply clear. For whatever man's destiny may be, his choice of action governed by the search for happiness in society—which constitutes his real moral problem—remains unaltered.

Perhaps more than a satire on Spinozistic fatalism, it is a satire against various views on fatalism. This is a point well made by J. Robert Loy in his excellent little book, *Diderot's Determined Fatalist* (1950). I believe, however, that the development below takes up certain aspects of the question that Mr. Loy has not touched upon. There are, I think, four positions in the novel: 1. that of Jacques the determined but pseudo-disciple of unrelenting Spinozism; 2. that of Jacques who, unconsciously by word and action, revolts against his adopted doctrine; 3. the position of the master, one of oscillation, of fluctuation; 4. that of the third person, the narrator, who addresses the reader and calls attention to the inconsistencies in the first three points of view.

Moreover, it seems to me that Jacques' theoretical position has through repetition and ironic treatment been reduced to an absurdity and his formula, " écrit là-haut," or, if you like, " written on the great scroll up yonder," has become a meaningless catch-all. In the final analysis, I think, he reveals his ill-defined fatalism under three forms: 1. as a mechanistic materialism whereby he sees the principles of cause and effect leading to an inevitable result in the future; 2. his religious fatalism in which he imagines the future incontrovertibly written in the heavens above (Diderot had been a great admirer of Milton's *Paradise Lost*); 3. his acceptance of the indisputable role of chance and caprice, perhaps the most dangerous sort of fatalism of all.

If *Jacques* is a satire of a number of things it is perhaps most strikingly a satire of the conventional romance or novel so popular in western Europe at the time. It was a point effectively made by Claude Roy in 1950 and emphasized ever since. Roy ingeniously observed: " Mais comme Pirandello a fait son théâtre en moquant le théâtre, Diderot a fait le chef-d'œuvre de ses romans (qui est *Jacques le fataliste*) avec un roman qui moque le roman, œuvre infiniment complexe, qui contient un roman, la critique de ce roman, et le roman de cette critique même." [1] More succinctly but less wittily, Yvon Belaval says the same thing when he states that *Jacques* is a story in which an analysis of the esthetics of narration constantly interferes with the narrative flow as the narrator places himself among his protagonists.[2]

And almost from the outset of the novel, the narrator does indeed put himself squarely among the leading characters. If he were a playwright, we would say that the author was calling out over the footlights to us in the audience when the occasion presented itself. And this is precisely what happened when the novel was with great success adapted for the Paris stage in 1962. Diderot himself was depicted on the stage, to the delight of the spectators, interrupting the action, arguing and discussing his characters and their adventures with the director. In the novel, however, even the reader is made to participate in the unfolding of the narrative. Diderot calls out to us from the stage-setting of the novel, he asks our advice, he makes us share his doubts, he wants to enjoy with us his esthetic theories, his literary hypotheses. Then, without pause, he returns to his characters and seems to have forgotten us, to reappear quite unexpectedly in order to carry on a dialogue with the reader. Early in the novel, we come to the incident of the girl falling off the doctor's horse, followed by quips of the personages, and by the philosophizing of Jacques. But enough of jests, enough of Jacques' metaphysical speculations; it is again time for the narrator to intervene ! What could not the adventure become in his hands, Diderot comments, if he took it into his head to tease us ? He could make the woman an important character—a niece of the neighboring village curate. He could stir up the peasants of the village. He could prepare all sorts of combats and love affairs. Diderot even suggests that, in her fall from the horse, the girl has revealed enough hidden charms to have Jacques, perhaps, fall in love a second time. But the reader presumably interjects to ask whether the author means that Jacques has already fallen in love with someone else. Precisely, says Diderot, and adds that all this should be cut short if the reader wants Jacques to get on with his love story. A love story ! As I have already intimated, the fact is important,

---
[1] *Europe* (Jan. 1950).
[2] *Jacques le fataliste* (Paris, 1953), 3 of " Notes."

for Diderot is very much of the opinion that the eighteenth-century stereotype of the novel—and as much could be said of the conventional novel in the nineteenth and twentieth centuries as well—is the love story!

Here and throughout, we see Diderot building on the traits of irony and digression, while wilfully introducing loose construction to his narrative. We see him refusing to build a novel—he prefers to let it take place. How easy it is to fabricate stories, he tells us on the second page of *Jacques le fataliste*. Another incident coming fast on the heels of the girl on horseback again illustrates Diderot's insistence that his story must take place. Jacques and his master have left an inn early in the morning, with some dozen brigands locked by Jacques in one room and their clothes in another. Suddenly our heroes notice they are being followed by a band of men. Jacques and his master view with trepidation the troop of horsemen, armed with sticks and pitchforks, bearing down upon them. But Diderot again intervenes. He sees that the reader may well expect some bloody action, some pistols shot off, some skulls cracked. But he adds: " Il ne tiendrait qu'à moi que tout cela n'arrivât; mais adieu la vérité de l'histoire, adieu le récit des amours de Jacques." Diderot concludes: " Nos deux voyageurs n'étaient point suivis: j'ignore ce qui se passa dans l'auberge après leur départ."

This last remark is, in itself, of interest. Why? It represents a new position on the author's part. In eighteenth-century fiction, as a rule, the author is one who has come across a collection of letters (*Les Lettres persanes*, *La Nouvelle Héloïse*, *Les Liaisons dangereuses*); or it is the manuscript of someone's *mémoires* (*La Vie de Marianne* and a quantity of other pseudo-memoirs of the day); or it is a story told to him (*Manon Lescaut*); or it is an autobiography (*Gil Blas*); or the narrator is omniscient, and is not only everywhere, but knows the innermost, unspoken thoughts of each character. Still Diderot, until the final pages, at least, assumes none of these positions.

In fact he declares in his own terms that he is writing an anti-novel: " Il est bien évident," he states, " que je ne fais pas un roman, puisque je néglige ce qu'un romancier ne manquerait pas d'employer. Celui qui prendrait ce que j'écris pour la vérité, serait peut-être moins dans l'erreur que celui qui le prendrait pour une fable."

It is already clear that one aspect of *Jacques le fataliste*, and a very important one, is Diderot's preoccupation with the esthetics of the novel as a literary genre. In chapter II he rejects a trick in narration that would have been typical of a novel by Prévost, and cries out: " ... cela aurait pué Cléveland à infecter... La vérité! La vérité!" And in his *Eloge de Richardson* (1761), we already find Diderot reproaching the conventional novel for numerous shortcomings. It sins through improbability, falseness, being over-plotted, replete with conventional characters and unnatural dialogue as well as miraculous dénouements. By novel, he goes on to say, the eighteenth century really means " un tissu d'événements chimériques et frivoles." Often there is much flowing of blood; we are carried off to distant lands where we risk being eaten by savages; we are imprisoned in secret places of debauchery; we get lost in realms of fantasy. And he concludes: "Non, je ne saurais digérer cela." In almost all of Diderot's short stories we find a preoccupation with the reality or truth of the story being told, and in his essay on Richardson, we find implicitly stated the threefold goals of the writer of fiction: 1. to seek the truth; 2. to make it credible; 3. to move the reader if possible. This preoccupation with realism is repeatedly underscored in the pages of *Jacques*. This realism, we might say, concerns the question of truthfulness towards reality as well as that of the illusion of reality. It seems to me we have a highly significant principle of esthetics here. Diderot appears to be saying that fictional writing is on the right path; it is carrying out its proper functions when it mirrors life. But when it intensifies and gives patterns to life it enhances the possibilities as a work of art.

Philippe Garcin, the French critic, one of many to be strongly drawn to *Jacques* during the past decade, himself suggests the view just mentioned, when he tells us that of all Diderot's writings, this is the one that most brilliantly emphasizes freedom of tone and inspiration, a freedom which always magnifies the meaning of important books. Then Garcin adds a statement that should, I think, be quoted in its entirety, for we sense that he is bewildered, delighted, shocked, dismayed and puzzled, like not a few of his fellow-critics of the mid-twentieth century. He tells us: "Ce roman qui n'est pas un roman ni d'ailleurs tout à fait le contraire d'un roman et qui ne s'explique pas seulement comme critique de tous les romans publiés jusqu'à lui (de tous les romans *possibles*), cette satire qui n'est pas vraiment gaie, cet essai qui n'est pas tellement sage, ce déversoir d'aphorismes insolents et d'anecdotes insolites constitue en somme le livre le plus louche de la littérature française au siècle des lumières."[1]

For Philippe Garcin and other European critics who have recently rediscovered *Jacques le fataliste*, we are, then, witnesses of a work which represents the liquidation, the pulverisation of the traditional rules of composition. But, according to these critics, *Jacques* has a very definite place in the esthetics of the novel as it insists on the significant detail, expressive pantomime, character portrayal palpitating with life and other traits leading to a broadening of the art of fiction.

Much more could be said on the esthetics of the novel in relation to *Jacques*. Much more could have been said about the novel so far as philosophy is concerned. The very title shows philosophical intention, and the master says to his servant: "Jacques, vous êtes une espèce de philosophe, convenez-en." One scholar finds Jacques more of a Leibnizian than a Spinozist. Present-day Marxists see in the dialogue between master and servant a sort of Hegelian dialectic, which, moreover, shows the proletariat on the march against the upper classes.

The third aspect of the novel, or, if you will, its third general theme (we have touched upon philosophy and esthetics) could well be that of ethics. Here there are far more questions than can be immediately answered. Diderot tells, and in detail, of Gousse; his noble gestures on one hand,

---

[1] *Critique* (1959), 204.

and his complete lack of principles on the other; Gousse, whose head has no more morality in it than that of a fish.

Is there any sort of ethics revealed or advocated in the book? How much is man totally a product of deterministic forces? How can a relativistic society set up a workable code of conduct? What about the place of the conformist and the nonconformist in society? And among the nonconformists, from the eccentric, through the perverse, the criminal, to the superman, or the monster, what are their places to be in society? What about social behavior in particular and in general? Madame de la Pommeraye has been called an iconoclast and even a monster. Why? And what about Père Hudson? Why would Diderot like us to speculate on the sort of child that would be the issue of Madame de la Pommeraye and Father Hudson?

Besides these three main aspects of the novel, the philosophical, the esthetic and the ethical, there are many other, lesser ones. And Carlyle seems justified in having said that he knew nothing like it in the whole range of French literature. But by way of conclusion, perhaps another critic, one of the best, although he is chiefly known as a poet of genius, might be called upon. Baudelaire! There is the tribute he paid to Diderot the novelist in his *Notices sur Edgar A. Poe.* And we read: " Aussi les romanciers forts sont-ils plus ou moins philosophes: Diderot, Laclos, Hoffmann, Goethe, Jean Paul, Maturin, Honoré de Balzac, Edgar A. Poe. Remarquez que j'en prends de toutes les couleurs et des plus contrastées. Cela est vrai de tous, même de Diderot, le plus hasardeux et le plus aventureux, qui s'appliqua, pour ainsi dire, à noter et à régler l'inspiration; et qui accepta d'abord, et puis de parti pris, utilisa sa nature enthousiaste, sanguine et tapageuse."

# METAPHYSICS AND THE *BIJOUX INDISCRETS*: DIDEROT'S DEBT TO PRIOR *

> I dont pretend to Examine the Nature and Essence of this Mind of Ours, This Divine *particula aurae*, as a Divine or a Philosopher, but as a Stander by to take a little Notice of some of its Motions, the feats of Activity it plays, and the Sudden Escapes and Changes it often makes.
>
> (Matthew Prior, *Essay on Opinion*)

> C'est à l'expérience que j'en appellerai de ce fait; et je vais peut-être jeter les premiers fondements d'une métaphysique expérimentale.
>
> (Denis Diderot, *Les Bijoux indiscrets*)

It is a paradox of sorts but one which is perhaps readily understandable that of all Diderot's works the *Bijoux indiscrets* has enjoyed the most editions and the least respect. What today might be judged its mildly titillating obscenities have no doubt been responsible down through the years for the *Bijoux*'s popularity as well as, upon occasion, its devastatingly low repute.

The *Bijoux indiscrets* has been a controversial novel for over two centuries: a parallel for the conflicting opinions greeting its first publication may be seen in the mixed reaction of each successive generation of readers. Passing them in quick review we see that, among the author's contemporaries, there were those like the *Abbé* Raynal, the *Abbé* Voisenon and Pierre Clément of Geneva, who found little to admire in the work; style and content alike met with their disapproval. Either unaware that all art aspires towards the condition of music, or not considering the *Bijoux* art, these three early critics divorced form from content, and cared for neither. Furthermore, they were in agreement that what gifts Diderot had were not suited to the genre at hand.[1]

---

* Reprinted from *Studies on Voltaire and the Eighteenth Century*, LVI (1967), 509-540. Permission to republish granted by Theodore Besterman.

[1] According to Raynal, " *Les Bijoux indiscrets* sont obscurs, mal écrits, dans un mauvais ton grossier et d'un homme qui connaît mal le monde qu'il a voulu peindre. L'auteur est M. Diderot qui a les connaissances très-étendues et beaucoup d'esprit,

There were others more favourably inclined. Louis Charpentier paid *Les Bijoux* the tribute of an extensive review in which he deplored the reader's continual exposure to salacious scenes but expressed reluctant admiration for some of its qualities.[1] Though Lessing's wholehearted appreciation of the novel was limited to some three pages on the French theatre, he warned against dismissing the work in general as an unmitigated farce merely because of its impudence. A wise man, he noted, often says in jest what he will afterwards repeat in earnest.[2]

All of these reactions were comparatively mild. It was the aging La Harpe, onetime friend and disciple of the *philosophes* turned defender of religion and the public order who, at the end of the Enlightenment, attacked Diderot and *Les Bijoux* with a new vigour and ferocity.[3] By doing so, he set the tone of revulsion that has frequently marked critical hostility well into the twentieth century.

In the nineteenth, that high-principled Scotsman, Thomas Carlyle, called it " the beastliest of all dull novels, past, present or to come," [4]

---

mais qui n'est pas fait pour le genre dans lequel il vient de travailler, " *Correspondance littéraire*, I, 139-140. Voisenon, himself a writer of oriental tales and *romans galants*, charged Diderot with appropriating the principal device of the *Bijoux* from a gay little tale [the reference is to *Nocrion*, published anonymously, and attributed variously to Caylus and the *abbé* Vernis] and of doing little with it: " Diderot, destiné à être chef de secte, n'en fit qu'une histoire froide, longue et triste," *Anecdotes littéraires* (Paris, 1880), 168. Deploring the fact that the novel's author took so little advantage of the diverse situations he had had the wit to introduce, and complaining about the weakness of the details, the length, frequency and tediousness of the digressions, Clément concluded: " En général, il n'y a pas assez de chaleur dans l'exécution, de légèreté, de fine plaisanterie, de cette fleur de gaieté, de ces naïvetés heureuses, si nécessaires aux bons contes," *Les Cinq années littéraires* (Berlin, 1755), I, 22-23 (letter dated " Paris, 25 février 1748 ").

[1] " Il amuse par des traits ingénieux, et pique la curiosité par le plaisir d'une critique adroite; en-sorte qu'il a profité du goût du siècle pour arrêter davantage le Lecteur sur ces objets; il est vrai qu'il a usé d'une réserve qui mérite quelque considération.... On ne peut nier que ses bijoux ne disent quelquefois des choses fort sensées; mais elles sont enveloppées de tant d'expressions, et d'images sales et ciniques, que l'utilité n'entrera jamais en comparaison avec le danger auquel s'exposerait l'esprit le plus froid en les lisant," *Lettres critiques, sur divers écrits de nos jours, contraires à la religion et aux mœurs* (Londres, 1751), II, 20-22.

[2] Ein kluger Mann sagt öfters erst mit Lachen, was er hernach in Erneste wiederholen will," *Hamburgische Dramaturgie* (Stuttgart, 1886), II, 202 (Stuck 84, 19 Feb. 1768). Contemporary opinion in Germany seems not to have been outspoken, and Roland Mortier tells us: " Lessing s'en était servi, il est vrai, mais avec prudence, et sans trop insister sur la nature de l'ouvrage. Quant aux autres lecteurs, ils se sont bien gardés de nous faire part de leurs impressions et il semble que l'on se soit borné à citer le titre de l'ouvrage, qui plaisait par son caractère énigmatique et piquant, sans qu'on sût très exactement de quoi il s'agissait," " Diderot en Allemagne (1750-1850)," *Université de Bruxelles. Travaux de la Faculté de philosophie et lettres* (Paris, 1954), 420.

[3] Diderot, the writer, moralist and philosopher, should be deeply ashamed to have spawned a novel licentious from beginning to end, " sans imagination, sans intérêt, sans goût," a novel in which, moreover, a crudely garish orientalism does little to conceal slavish and repulsive adulation of Louis XV and his mistress, Mme. de Pompadour. *Cours de littérature ancienne et moderne* (Paris, 1826), XVIII, 5-7.

[4] In characteristic fashion, Carlyle continued: " If any mortal creature, even a reviewer, be again compelled to glance into that book, let him bathe himself in running water, put on a change of raiment, and be unclean until the even," " Diderot," *Critical and Miscellaneous essays*.

while Barbey d'Aurevilly, nineteenth-century Catholic and conservative critic, found only such words as " porcherie," " saloperie," and " polissonnerie " to describe a novel almost beneath contempt.[1]

Carrying on this tradition in the twentieth century, that eminent English literary critic, George Saintsbury, sententiously dubbed *Les Bijoux*, " the unspeakable one."[2] Still more recent scholars, however well-disposed they may have been towards Diderot, have, on the whole, found it difficult to speak favourably of the novel. R. Loyalty Cru states sadly that this early work of a renowned thinker " belonged to a sorry class of writings, licentious for mere indecency's sake, to which every age and country has more or less contributed."[3] John Palache finds the novel heavy and clumsy, with a central idea that is tiresomely crude although it is redeemed in some small measure by such passages as Mangogul's dream and the literary discussion.[4] For André Breton it is " une œuvre de pur dévergondage dont il n'y a pas à se souvenir."[5] André Billy, hearkening back to the eighteenth-century *abbés* mentioned above, admitted more kindly that " la galanterie n'est pas son fort."[6] Luppol dismisses the *Bijoux* as " une nouvelle assez scabreuse,"[7] while Franco Venturi finds the novel's style either artificial or coarse and the ideas, save those—as we shall see presently—concerning certain philosophic conceptions of Diderot, manifestly superficial.[8] Georges May is fundamentally in agreement that certain parts of the novel are less exceptional than is sometimes claimed, and maintains with considerable truth that the various chapters comprising its pages " n'intéressent plus guère que les amateurs de littérature érotique."[9]

It may be noted from these latter observations that a more serious side to *Les Bijoux*, however imperceptible, does in fact exist. It was, as we have seen, a point first illustrated by Lessing two centuries before when he was so strongly impressed by the " Entretien sur les lettres " (chap. XXXVIII), parts of which he was to adapt to his own purposes. Assézat gave added emphasis to this point of view, already touched upon by Naigeon.[10] Assézat even went so far as to suggest that it was the very form of the *Bijoux* that permitted Diderot to " faire prévenir à des courtisans, à

---

[1] *Goethe et Diderot* (Paris, 1913), 762-763.

[2] Almost as an afterthought, Saintsbury added: " It really would require a most unpleasant apprenticeship to scavenging in order to discover a dirtier and duller," *History of the Novel* (London, 1917-1919), I, 403.

[3] *Diderot as a Disciple of English Thought* (New York, 1913), 357.

[4] *Four Novelists of the Old Régime* (New York, 1926), 111.

[5] *Le Roman français au XVIIIe siècle* (Paris [1925]), 315.

[6] *Vie de Diderot* (Paris, 1932), 115.

[7] *Diderot* (Paris, 1936), 67.

[8] And he concludes: " Même les parties de ce roman que les contemporains ou les critiques ont voulu sauver d'une condamnation globale, à les considérer de plus près n'ont, en général, pas grande valeur," *Jeunesse de Diderot (1713-1753)* (Paris, 1939), 126.

[9] *Quatre visages de Diderot* (Paris, 1951), 160.

[10] " Je dirai donc que *les Bijoux indiscrets* ont un caractère et même un mérite qui les distingue de tous les ouvrages de ce genre," J. A. Naigeon, *Mémoires historiques et philosophiques sur la vie et les ouvrages de D. Diderot* (Paris, 1821), 37.

des femmes, à des jeunes gens, des idées dont ils n'auraient jamais eu connaissance " were they offered in less palatable form.[1] Like his fellow countryman, Lessing, Karl Rosenkranz was specific in stating what he preferred in the novel. For him " Le Rêve de Mangogul " (chap. XXXII) was nothing short of a minor masterpiece.[2] It was, to be sure, Diderot's own opinion that this was the best chapter in the book[3]; most readers would agree.

In our day, Marie Louise Dufrenoy, while denying any literary quality to the *partie galante* of the *Bijoux*, is in agreement with Lessing, Assézat and Rosenkranz that it has merits in other respects. The best of Diderot's talents, she tells us, emerges when he practices " l'art de romancer les inventions et les découvertes," with a bantering humour that recalls *Gulliver's Travels*. And, like Assézat, she sees in the *Bijoux* the *pillule dorée* that will no longer be needed when the *philosophe* is fully master of his ideas.[4] There is, then, in some quarters, the frequent reappearance of a theme, discreetly suggested and rarely insisted upon, that this libertine tale, a sin of Diderot's comparative youth, contains in germ ideas that he was to develop on later, less frivolous occasions.

We have attempted to pass briefly in review a few representative opinions of and reactions to *Les Bijoux* since the novel's publication in 1748. With the exception of fleeting comments by professional critics and a few academically-oriented articles, the work has for the most part been neglected except by the general reader. But it may be safely assumed that, sooner or later, for better or worse, the novel will—despite its low repute—become the object of an extensive study. Before such an eventuality, however, there should doubtless be more probings in depth than has so far been the case.

Despite protests to the contrary by Naigeon and, perhaps, by Diderot, there is—as has sometimes been suggested—the distinct possibility that neither was sincere in deploring the novel's existence.[5] One is hard put

---

[1] What are these grave questions, these important ideas Diderot wished to share with the reader? Assézat places them in three categories: " D'abord celle de la réforme du théâtre que Diderot allait tenter bientôt sur la scène même de la Comédie française; ensuite celle des idées philosophiques dont il allait donner, peu d'années après, une formule sévère dans l'*Interprétation de la nature*; enfin la critique des mœurs de l'époque, critique qui n'était pas sans portée, précisément parce qu'elle était moins fine et moins complaisante que celle du modèle que l'auteur avait choisi, Crébillon fils." See " Notice préliminaire," *Les Bijoux indiscrets*, in *Œuvres complètes de Diderot* (Paris, 1875), IV, 134. Hereafter this edition will be cited only by volume and page.

[2] " Dieser Traum der den Realismus Diderot's in seiner ganzen Jungendfrische malt, ist ein Meisterstück," *Diderots Leben und Werke* (Leipzig, 1860), I, 67.

[3] It will be recalled that Diderot introduces the chapter as follows: " Le meilleur peut-être, et le moins lu de ce livre " (*A.-T.* VII, 255).

[4] " En effet, Diderot a présenté, sous une forme badine, dans un conte parsemé d'allusions et orné de peintures volontairement vaporeuses, les idées qu'il devait développer plus tard dans ses œuvres sérieuses," *L'Orient romanesque en France 1704-1789* (Montréal, 1946), I, 113.

[5] In the *Mémoires* (37), Naigeon reports that Diderot later referred to the *Bijoux* as " une grande sottise." In his own edition of Diderot's works, Naigeon did not hesitate to publish the novel, and even included three scarcely edifying chapters not appearing in the original edition (XVI, *Vision de Mangogul*; XVIII, *Des Voyageurs*; XIX, *De la Figure des insulaires et de la toilette des femmes*).

to imagine an older though not necessarily wiser Diderot being embarrassed by its ribaldry and licentiousness. Well past middle life, in the *Rêve*—especially the *Suite*—in *Jacques*, in the *Supplément*, in his correspondence, he often adopted an approach as unconstrained as any displayed in the *Bijoux* of 1748. Was he chagrined by the paucity of ideas in this early novel? In 1775, as Roland Mortier has shown, the by now eminent Frenchman offered for republication several extracts of his philosophical works to a young German.[1] Among Diderot's contributions were two chapters from the *Bijoux*, the " Rêve de Mirzoza " and the " Voyage dans la région des hypothèses."

Today there would be general agreement that Diderot had done well to choose the " Voyage." The only parts of the novel that are noteworthy, Franco Venturi tells us, are those where the author's philosophical ideas are in evidence. The Italian scholar adds: " Sa polémique contre la conception abstraite de l'âme humaine, quelques observations sur l'amour platonique, l'éloge de l'expérience et les idées de l'écrivain sur les rêves sont des pages où s'exprime la partie la meilleure de Diderot. Ce sont quatre petits essais de ' métaphysique expérimentale,' d'après sa propre expression."[2]

The Venturi passage is itself of moment, and its interest is further heightened by that part having reference to the soul. This interest in the twenty-ninth chapter entitled " Les Ames," although the following chapter —" Suite à la conversation précédente "—should be but rarely is given consideration as well, is indicative of a new trend. It is only in the twentieth century that this little dialogue on the soul, its nature and its location, has been given a certain amount of serious attention. This attention has corresponded, though to a lesser extent, to the increased attention afforded Diderot. But he is not so much the brashly godless materialist the nineteenth century insisted upon. He is, rather, Diderot the *philosophe*, an enlightened example of one primarily interested in the life sciences with special emphasis on biological man with all the latitude that can be given the term.

Thus Jean Pommier is himself something of a pioneer when, in 1939, he makes constructive critical remarks on the *Bijoux*,[3] and even more so when he has a word to say on the two chapters in question. At the outset he, too, refers to and even cites Mirzoza's remark which, in the light of later Diderot criticism, is to become one of the most quoted lines in the *Bijoux*: " Je vais peut-être jeter les premiers fondements d'une métaphysique expérimentale." The ensuing discussion on the seat of the soul, with its possibly far-reaching conclusions, leads, Pommier suggests, directly to Condillac.

This reference to Condillac along with Diderot's own possibly flippant allusions to Descartes and the pineal gland, themselves almost lend an aura of respectability, even of consequence, to Mirzoza's metaphysics.

---

[1] Roland Mortier, " *Le Journal de Lecture* de F.-M. Leuchsenring (1775-1779) et de l'esprit ' philosophique, ' " *RLC* (1955), XXIX, 216.

[2] *Jeunesse de Diderot*, 128; Diderot's " expression " is in *A.-T.* IV, 245.

[3] *Diderot avant Vincennes*, 59-72.

And about the same time, but independently of Pommier, Venturi arrives at much the same conclusion. In his perceptive pages (128-130), he points out that Diderot's bias for fresh observation and personal experience animates the *philosophe's* notion of the relation between body and soul. He sees Diderot's world as one that is not receptive to systems in general and Descartes's rationalistic separation of the body from the soul in particular, a separation that elevates the soul as ratiocinative intellect to an isolated position that cannot account for the vital and sensual man Diderot sees in the *Bijoux* and will develop further in the *Lettre sur les aveugles* and the *Lettre sur les sourds et muets*. It is inconceivable to Diderot, as Venturi understands him, that the body, which apparently expresses the soul when walking, dancing, loving, at least as much as the intellect, should be disconnected from the soul. Thus the use of Diderot's comic conceit: ascending from the feet, the soul, far-ranging, nimble, journeys through an astonishing number of limbs and appendages. If, then, one were to attempt to discover the true seat of the soul, according to Venturi's Diderot, one would have to resort not to the rationalism of Descartes, but to biological empiricism: for the soul of the gambler, it is suggested, is located elsewhere than, say, the soul of the libertine. Based on distinctions, this kind of perception, a very human kind of perception, is the product of a mind that moves from experience only with the greatest reluctance.

In 1943 an erudite Marxist, under the name of Jonathan Kemp, finds chapter twenty-nine sufficiently meaningful in the evolution of Diderot's thought to have it be the opening selection in a book of translations from the *philosophe's* writings.[1] In a note (p. 329), Kemp informs the reader that, in his development, Diderot outlines part of the argument and demonstration that the soul, spirit, or mind is a product of nature inasmuch as it finds expression with the development of the physical body. " By pushing the argument back beyond the foetus, where Mirzoza starts, to the most primitive germ cells," Kemp tells us, " the development of the faculty of sensation into consciousness, mind, is still more clearly seen to be intimately linked with the increasing complexity of the physical organization (see the *Conversation between d'Alembert and Diderot*)." Here Kemp stops.

What is of particular interest about the above is that the part of the *Bijoux* dealing with the metaphysics of the soul no longer merely prefigures Diderot's *Lettres sur les aveugles* and *sur les sourds et muets* respectively, or those ideas he has in common with the Condillac of the *Traité des sensations* (1754): but it ultimately prepares the way for his masterpiece of 1769, the triptych called the *Rêve de d'Alembert*.

Arthur Wilson, in his extremely conscientious *Diderot: the Testing Years* (1957, 83-87), pauses to make a number of judicious judgments on the *Bijoux*, but lingers over the disquisition on the soul only long enough to refer the matter prudently to another—the fourth scholar to treat the question—Aram Vartanian. Subtly distinguishing, in his book on *Diderot*

---

[1] *Diderot Interpreter of Nature*, translated by Jean Stewart and Jonathan Kemp. Edited by J. Kemp (New York, 1943), 35-38.

*and Descartes*, between the seventeenth-century philosopher and the exponents of Cartesianism, Vartanian intriguingly indicates the influence of the mechanistic biology found in certain sections of Descartes's *Principes* on Diderot. Concerning the chapters on the soul in the *Bijoux*, Vartanian identifies, in accordance with received opinion, the person who locates the soul in the head as Cartesian. Vartanian's position becomes less orthodox when he states that Mirzoza's theory of a wandering soul is an expansion of the Cartesian's distinction between body and soul, not a contradiction of it. Yet the Descartes Vartanian is most interested to reveal as an influence is not the dualistic Descartes of the pineal gland but the Descartes who anticipated, through what Vartanian calls " naturalistic Cartesianism," La Mettrie's *L'Homme machine*. Vartanian emphasizes Mangogul's counterstatements to Mirzoza, which, far from locating the soul in the head, refuse to grant its very existence in the majority of men— a refusal that is consistent with Mangogul's notion that most men are nothing more than automatons.[1]

Still more recently, Robert Ellrich has designated chapter XXIX as an important chapter in the development of Diderot's thought, for it is one of those in the novel presenting " empirical adventures for purposes of moral examination and demonstration." Mr. Ellrich's over-all conclusion differs but little from that of Mr. Vartanian except for the touch of the subjective which the former allows to creep into his terminal statement: " Small wonder, in view of the biased nature of the empirical inquiry, that when the sultan declares women to be animals, the reader finds it hard not to agree."[2]

And finally, Jean Mayer, in a *savant* and detailed introduction to his critical edition of the *Eléments de physiologie* (Paris, 1964), makes many allusions to possible, probable and sure sources for Diderot's reflections on the soul or mind. He makes no mention, however, of the *Bijoux*.

In short, six scholars have, so far, insisted on the importance of Diderot's evolving concept of the soul, and four of them have gone back to focus thought and attention on heretofore neglected pages of the novel. All have made worthwhile and, upon occasion, ingenious contributions to the topic. None, however, has mentioned a source for certain of the early ideas or fancies of Diderot representing concepts that were to carry him far. Had any of the above critics taken into account the existence of such a source, how would they have modified their conclusions, where would their reasoning, their speculations and their erudition have led them? It is a question that might well be asked.

Such a source exists. R. Loyalty Cru in his competent study, *Diderot as a Disciple of English Thought* (New York, 1913), quite overlooked it, as did Charles Dédéyan in his *L'Angleterre dans la pensée de Diderot* (Paris, 1957), who, nevertheless, skilfully documented Diderot's debt to the history of ideas in England. Henri Peyre, writing in 1947, declared: " Une pré-

---

[1] *Diderot and Descartes: A Study of Scientific Naturalism in the Enlightenment* (Princeton, 1953), 242-243.

[2] " The Structure of Diderot's *Les Bijoux indiscrets*, " RR (Dec. 1961), LII, 279-289.

dominance de l'intellectualité est souvent la marque des artistes secondaires de toutes les époques et de toutes les écoles: intelligence et intellectualité, lucidité et maîtrise consciente de soi, limpide clarté qui dissimule peut-être l'absence de profondeur.... Ce sont également là en Angleterre, les marques de Prior, Gay, Butler au XVIIIe siècle." [1]

It is Matthew Prior (1664-1721), poet, essayist, diplomat, friend of the great and near great, with whom we are concerned. A familiar figure in early eighteenth-century Paris and at the court of Versailles, a sometime lover of Mme. de Tencin, and one whom Voltaire called the most amiable of poets, Prior seems to have received short shrift from the *encyclopédistes* in general. Throughout the second half of the eighteenth century in particular, his poetry often appeared in translation in the *Mercure de France* and elsewhere, and even enjoyed the distinction of being imitated by French men of letters.[2] Despite this, as far as can be ascertained, he was mentioned only twice in the *Encyclopédie*, once by Diderot in a reference to burlesque poetry, and once by Jaucourt as one who frequently quoted from *Hudibras*.[3] Yet there is the distinct possibility that, though Prior has for the most part been passed over in silence by figures of the Enlightenment[4] and by studies on the French eighteenth century, he was more familiar to Diderot and his fellow *philosophes* than this neglect would indicate.[5]

The numerous parallels that could be established between the British joiner's son and the son of the French cutler from the point of view of tastes, interests, triumphs and vicissitudes might well be striking but nevertheless contrived by the long arm of chance. Especially striking but perhaps less due to chance is the occasional startling resemblance of ideas in these two writers each of whom so enjoyed giving his imagination the widest possible range.

Nevertheless, despite the heightened interest of Romance scholars in Diderot and, for that matter, in the *Bijoux*, during the past several decades, no one has stepped forward to comment on or make use of the gleanings of the Danish scholar, Leif Nedergaard. In his notes on Diderot, published

---

[1] *Qu'est-ce que le classicisme?* (Paris, 1942), 54-55.

[2] Cf. Charles K. Eves, *Matthew Prior, Poet and Diplomatist* (New York, 1939), 209.

[3] Cf. Lois Gaudin, *Les Lettres anglaises dans "l'Encyclopédie"* (New York, 1942), 32-42.

[4] Voltaire will shortly be called upon again as the exception that would appear to prove the rule; cf. infra. Then too, before the publication of the first edition of Voltaire's *Lettres philosophiques*, Van Effen, in his *Dissertation sur la poésie anglaise*, which was reprinted in *Le Mercure de France* of June 1727 and January 1728, speaks of Prior, " écrivain Anglais que les Français ont pu connaître comme diplomate en France." Furthermore, the Abbé Prévost in the *Mémoires d'un homme de qualité* cites Prior, along with Milton, Spencer, Addison and Thomson, as a major English poet. Chauffepié's *Dictionnaire* of 1753 contained an article on Prior.

[5] No extensive study of Prior and the French has ever been made, though his quite remarkable grasp of Montaigne has been looked into on several occasions. His command of the French language was unusual for his day, and he had many of the works of the older French authors in his library; he often referred to them in his work. Moreover, he knew personally such writers as Boileau, Fénelon, Fontenelle, Saint-Simon and, of course, Mme. de Tencin, among others.

in 1950, Nedergaard offered some three pages of persuasive evidence to the effect that the *philosophe* found in Prior's *Alma* the central conceit and the general argument for the entire chapter of the " Métaphysique de Mirzoza." [1] He was anticipated in his discovery by another scholar whose findings have seemingly passed unnoticed among Diderot specialists. In a brief article almost twenty years before, the Englishman, W. P. Barrett, in an article on Prior and Montaigne, paused long enough to stress Diderot's indebtedness to his compeer from across the Channel. The case presented was a strong one, and Barrett's conclusion was that the dozen pages in which Mirzoza expounded on her " métaphysique expérimentale " were, in the final analysis, " nothing but embroidery of the paradoxes of *Alma*." [2] Before we attempt in turn to inquire into the Diderot-Prior relationship, it would doubtless be well to examine the poem itself.

Matthew Prior's *Alma: or, The Progress of the Mind* (1718), [3] which may take its title from a conjunction of Spenser's House of Alma in *The Faerie Queene* with Donne's *Of the Progresse of the Soule—the Second Anniversarie*, is a mock-philosophical dialogue in Hudibrastic verse about the relation of the soul to the body. Prior's purpose here would appear to be twofold: to take issue with the Cartesian notion that the mind, located in the brain, is connected to the body only through the pineal gland; and to reaffirm the significance of that body, which he feels has been neglected by a world informed by Descartes's dualistic system. According to Prior, the brain is not the soul's natural habitat but rather the final seat of its repose, to be reached only after a long, slow journey extending over many years in the life an individual.[4] The three cantos of the poem are devoted to an account of that journey.

---

[1] " Notes sur certains ouvrages de Diderot," *Orbis litterarum*, VIII (1950), 1-5.

[2] " Matthew Prior's *Alma*," *MLR*, XXVII (1932), 456.

[3] The summary and interpretation of *Alma* which follow represent my own attempt to give the gist of the poem. I have also drawn upon secondary sources for which a selective bibliography would comprise the following: Charles Kenneth Eves, *Matthew Prior: Poet and Diplomatist* (already referred to); L. G. Wickham Legg, *Matthew Prior: A Study of His Public Career and Correspondance* (Cambridge, 1921); four articles by Monroe K. Spears: " The Meaning of Matthew Prior's *Alma*," *ELH* XIII (1946), 266-290; " Matthew Prior's Religion," *PQ* (1948); " Matthew Prior's Attitude toward natural science," *PMLA*, LXIII (1948), 485-507; " Some ethical aspects of Matthew Prior's poetry," *Studies in Philology*, LXV (1948), 606-629; as well as H. B. Wright, " William Jackson on Prior's Use of Montaigne," *MRL*, XXXI (1936), 203-205, and the above-mentioned article by W. P. Barrett. All references to Prior's writings come from *The Literary Works of Matthew Prior* edited by H. Bunker Wright and Monroe K. Spears (Oxford, 1959), which will henceforth be referred to as *Pr*.

[4] Early in the poem, Mat, one of the two interlocutors, sets forth the main idea on which he will later elaborate:
>My simple *System* shall suppose,
>That ALMA enters at the Toes;
>That then She mounts by just Degrees
>Up to the ancles, Legs, and Knees:
>Next, as the Sap of Life does rise,
>She lends her Vigor to the Thighs,
>And, all these under-Regions past,
>She nestles somewhere near the Waste:

In the first canto, "alma" enters the body through the toes, and rises through the legs of childhood [1] to what Prior chooses to call the "middle," which is the vital province of post-adolescence; from that central location, "alma" instructs the heart in matters of love.[2] The second canto offers not only "alma's" ascending progress towards maturation, as "alma" rises from waist to heart, but also an alternative movement, which, dependent upon "Fancy or Desire," places "alma" in, say, the hand of an artist or the throat of a singer.[3] The Cartesian territory of the brain—that supposed domain of later years—replete with "cerebrum" and "cerebellum," though without the pineal gland, is the business of the third canto.

At once accommodating and grandiose, this system, which is a burlesque attempt to reconcile the rather paradoxical neo-Aristotelian view that the

---

>     Gives Pain or Pleasure, Grief or Laughter;
>     As We shall show at large hereafter.
>     Mature, if not improv'd by Time
>     Up to the Heart She loves to climb:
>     From thence, compell'd by Craft and Age,
>     She makes the Head her latest Stage.
>                                      (*Pr.* I, 477)

[1] Hence for some Years they ne'er stand still:
>     Their Legs, You see, direct their Will.
>     From opening Morn 'till setting Sun,
>     A-round the Fields and Woods They run:
>     They frisk, and dance, and leap, and play.
>                                      (*Pr.* I, 478-479)

[2] To Her next Stage as Alma flies, And likes, as I have said, the Thighs....
Another Motion now She makes:
>     O need I name the Seat She takes?
>     The Sport and Race no more He minds:...
>     Sudden the jocund Plain He leaves;
>     And for the Nymph in Secret grieves.
>     In dying Accents He complains
>     Of cruel Fires, and raging Pains....
>     The Nymph is warm'd with young Desire;
>     And feels, and dies to quench His Fire.
>                                      (*Pr.* I, 479)

[3]
>     Mark then;—When Fancy or Desire
>     Collects the Beams of Vital Fire;
>     Into that Limb fair Alma slides,
>     And there, *pro tempore*, resides.
>     She dwells in Nicholini's Tongue,
>     When Pyrrhus chants the Heav'nly Song.
>     When Pedro does the Lute command,
>     She guides the cunning Artist's Hand
>     Thro' Macer's Gullet she runs down,
>     When the vile Glutton dines alone....
>     Again: That Single Limb or Feature
>     (Such is the cogent Force of Nature)
>     Which most did Alma's passion move,
>     In the first Object of her Love,
>     For ever will be found confest,
>     And printed on the Am'rous Breast.
>     O Abelard, ill-fated Youth,
>     Thy Tale will justify this Truth.
>                                      (*Pr.* I, 492)

soul is at once entirely in the whole body, yet entirely in each of its parts, with the Cartesian, essentially separatist attitude, unravels by means of a spirited dialogue between Richard—who is generally taken to be Richard Shelton, whom Prior described as " the partner of my inmost Soul "—and Mat, who is assumed to be an approximation of Prior himself. But at least for the oscillating progress of the dialectic, a contrary, bellicose Richard (the Richard of the poem, of course) prefers " fine *Champaigne*, or muddl'd *Port* " to either " Plato's Fancies " or his soul-partner's system. Yet Richard's function in the structure of the poem is not that of an ironic principle incarnate, a naturalistic but negative foil to Mat's elaborate system-building. For it is significant that Richard, who informs Mat that,

> The plainest man alive may tell Ye,
> Her [Alma's] seat of Empire is the Belly
>
> (*Pr.* I, 509)

should have the last word, or the last thirty lines, to be precise, which are in praise of happiness—or, at least, contentment—uncomplicated by system. Finally, the pragmatic Richard is closer to Prior's position than Mat, and Prior's poem succeeds only as Mat's system fails, as indeed all systems must fail that employ only the modest agent of human reason for metaphysical speculation. Thus Mat's system—the reconciling product of intellectual pyrotechnics that are not only magnificent but absurd—collapses before the awesome prospect of Richard's discontented " Belly."

The poem, then, is a satire on metaphysical systems, more specifically on two opposing theories—still widely discussed—of the location of the mind. These abstruse speculations have as their chief shortcoming a disregard for the fact that, more often than not, men's actions are governed by their bodies. In a final display of scepticism at reason and, at the same time, acknowledgement of the body's demands, the satire ends triumphantly on the following couplet:

> Burn Mat's Des-cart', and Aristotle:
> Here, Jonathan, Your Master's Bottle.
>
> (*Pr.* I, 516)

" Il m'est permis," Molière is supposed to have said with admirable frankness, " de reprendre mon bien où je le trouve." This was a practice of Diderot and Prior as well. The *philosophe* in *Sur ma manière de travailler*, wrote: " Si je trouve quelque chose dans les auteurs qui me convienne, je m'en sers." [1] We have no such avowal on Prior's part, but speaking of the author of *Alma*, Samuel Johnson tells us: " I... have been informed that he poached for prey among obscure authors." [2]

---

[1] See Maurice Tourneux, *Diderot et Catherine II* (Paris, 1899), 450.
[2] *Lives of the Most Eminent British Poets* (London, 1783), III, 35.

The sources for *Alma* have not been firmly established. Since evidence is overwhelming that Prior knew his Montaigne extremely well, there is considerable agreement among scholars that the poem's major conceit came directly from the essay, " De l'Yvrognerie," even though explicit evidence of influence or indebtedness is tenuous indeed.[1] No consideration at all has been given to the possibility that the great physician of Greco-Roman antiquity, Galen, might have been a partial source for the conceit. Nothing is known of the series of lectures which Prior, holder of a medical fellowship at Cambridge, gave on Galen between 1706 and 1710. Charles Eves (p. 38) supposes them to have been " hastily prepared papers, enlivened with wit and read with assurance." Perhaps so, but they must have treated Galen's physiological theories that had more than a little in common with some of Mat's speculations in *Alma*.[2] Prior himself, in his *Essay on Opinion*, hints at a Spanish source which, if it exists, has yet to be brought to light.[3] Finally, there is Dr. John Arbuthnot, the queen's physician and a man of wit, humor, erudition and letters. He was one of the tory wits who met once a week to exchange gossip and read one another's verses, a group from which the famous Scriblerus Club was to be formed. Prior played an important part in these earlier Tory literary gatherings often organized by Swift (cf. Eves, 230-231). A passage in the *Memoirs of Martinus*

---

[1] The passage in Montaigne's essay on drunkenness is as follows: " La chaleur naturelle, disent les bons compaignons, se prent premierement aux pieds: celle là touche l'enfance. De là elle monte à la moyenne region, où elle se plante long temps et y produit, selon moy, les seuls vrais plaisirs de la vie corporelle: les autres voluptez dorment au pris. Sur la fin, à la mode d'une vapeur qui va montant et s'exhalant, elle arrive au gosier, où elle faict sa derniere pose," *Essais* (ed. Pierre Villey, Paris, 1930, II, 31). Monroe K. Spears treats the hypothesis of Prior's debt in the present instance with commendable caution. In " The Meaning " he writes: " It is evident that this passage could have furnished no more than a hint for Prior's " system." Montaigne is speaking of " chaleur naturelle," with reference to sensitivity to physical pleasure, and not of the mind or soul; since he is discussing drunkenness, he makes the throat the final stage. The development of the idea and its contemporary application in *Alma* appear to be entirely Prior's own " (279).

[2] It will be recalled that, for Galen, the nervous system and the vital functions of the human body were explained, at least in part, by the " natural spirit " of the liver, the " vital spirit " of the heart, and the " animal spirit " of the brain. A. C. Crombies states that this physiological approach stressing these spirits and their functions entirely dominated the ideas of the significance of anatomical structures and connections until overthrown by William Harvey. (See his *Medieval and Early Modern Science*, New York, 1959, I, 163).

[3] He declares: " I HAVE read somewhere a Pritty spanish Conceit, that, as we are Born our Mind comes in at our Toes, so goes upward thro our Leggs to our Middle, thence to our Heart and Breast, Lodges at last in Our Head and from thence flies away; The meaning of which is that Childish Sports and Youthful Wrestlings, and Tryals of Strength, Amorous Desires, Couragious and Manly Designs, Council and Policy succeed each other in the Course of our Lives till the whole terminates in Death; The consequence of it is Obvious, Our Passions change with our Ages, and our Opinion with our Passions " (*Pr.* I, 587). Commenting on the above, the German authority on Prior, Engelbert Frey, says: " In dieser Bemerkung ist der leitende Gedanke seiner Almadichtung enthalten. Eine Spanische Quelle dieses Einfalls ist mir nicht bekannt. Vielleicht wollte Prior seine Leser durch diese Andeutung nur auf eine falsche Fährte bringen " (*Der Einfluss der englischen, französischen, italienischen und lateinischen Literatur auf die Dichtungen Matthew Priors*, Strassburg, 1915, 29-30).

*Scriblerus*, that satire directed against false tastes in learning, and perhaps largely conceived by Dr. Arbuthnot, is singularly reminiscent of what we have already seen in both Prior's *Alma* and the somewhat later *Essay on Opinion*. In laboring to discover the location of the soul, Martinus begins his disquisition by stating: " Sometimes he was of opinion that it lodg'd in the Brain, sometimes in the Stomach, and sometimes in the Heart. Afterwards he thought it absurd to confine that sovereign Lady to one apartment, which made him infer that she shifted it according to the several functions of life.[1] Prior's own mention in *Opinion* of a Spanish source for what happens to be the principal invention of his poem has, quite conceivably, not been taken seriously enough; Cervantes's *Don Quixote* remains a possibility.[2] However that may be and *jusqu'à nouvel ordre*, it might well be that all of the above-mentioned possible sources played a rôle in helping Prior develop his own *concetti* in *Alma* at a time when, as Spears has noted, the Cartesian philosophy had given " fresh impetus to speculation on the nature and location of the soul " (" The Meaning," p. 288).

---

[1] The unfinished *Memoirs* appeared in Pope's works in 1741. But a number of noted Scriblerians—Gay, Parnell, Swift, Pope and especially Arbuthnot—were hard at work on the project as early as 1717 (see the booksellers' notice prefixed in 1741 to volume II of Pope's *Prose works*). Work in progress, as was customary with such collaborative literary undertakings, was discussed in correspondence or in the congenial gatherings of the Scriblerus club. The entire passage reads as follows: " Sometimes he was of opinion that it lodg'd in the Brain, sometimes in the Stomach, and sometimes in the Heart. Afterwards he thought it absurd to confine that sovereign Lady to one apartment, which made him infer that she shifted it according to the several functions of life: The Brain was her Study, the Heart her state-room, and the Stomach her Kitchen. But as he saw several offices of life went on at the same time, he was forced to give up this Hypothesis also. He now conjectured it was more for the dignity of the Soul to perform several operations by her little Ministers, the *Animal Spirits*, from whence it was natural to conclude, that she resides in different parts according to different Inclinations, Sexes, Ages, and Professions. Thus in Epicures he seated her in the mouth of the Stomach, Philosophers have her in the Brain, Soldiers in their Hearts, Women in their Tongues, Fidlers in their fingers, and Rope-dancers in their Toes. At length he grew fond of the *Glandula Pinealis*, dissecting many Subjects to find out the different Figure of this Gland, from whence he might discover the cause of the different Tempers in mankind " (ed. C. Kerby-Miller, New Haven, 1950, 137).

[2] Until precise evidence is available, it seems that the only plausible relationship possible between Prior and " a Pritty spanish Conceit " deriving from Cervantes would be the *Memoirs* of *Martinus Scriblerus*. C. Kerby-Miller, in his edition of the *Memoirs*, demonstrates that the general influence of Cervantes is manifestly clear, and even acknowledged by Scriblerus (30, 68-69, 317). Moreover, we know that Arbuthnot was working on chapter XII—where one of the passages on the location of the soul appears—as early as 1714. Prior's *Alma* was presumably written between June 1715 and June 1716, with revisions extending well into the year 1717; there is evidence, furthermore, that Arbuthnot's first draft of chapter XV of the *Memoirs*—the episode of the Double Mistress—was completed by 1717. Its most compelling conceit was that the locus of the soul was to be found in the genitals, a leitmotif that is to run through both Prior's *Alma* and Diderot's *Bijoux indiscrets*. Since Prior was on intimate terms with Arbuthnot, opportunity certainly was not lacking to discuss at leisure the over-all conceit to appear in both the *Memoirs* and *Alma*. It seems reasonable, I think, that Arbuthnot's prose, even though revised by Pope at a later date, preceded the carefully wrought verses of Prior.

A deep-rooted scepticism in *Alma* and elsewhere shows Prior chary of the great metaphysical systems of the seventeenth century. Despite the fact that he views John Locke as simply one more system maker, Prior also enters the mainstream of a fresh, experimental approach towards matters of the mind as he emphasizes the importance of the senses. If anything can be understood about the soul-mind, that understanding will have to come through observation and experience. Only then will there be an appreciation of just how intimate the relation between body and mind really is, such a realization will represent an increased awareness of an organic totality in which the body is not to be undervalued.

And what of *Les Bijoux*? From what circumstances did Diderot's novel spring? Among those that have been repeated time and again are: 1. the occasion to exploit a prevailing taste for the licentious tale in an exotic setting; 2. the wish to satisfy the curiosity and the pocketbook of Mme. de Puisieux through a literary tour de force; 3. a compulsion to give vent to notions on a number of things—literature, the state of the French theatre, science, music, and the nature of dreams. Given also his urgency to complete the novel in a fortnight, Diderot found it expedient to put to use several concepts plucked here and there from the works of other authors. In 1775 he was to say to Catherine the Great: " Il est clair, pour tous ceux qui ont des yeux, que sans les Anglais la raison et la philosophie seraient encore dans l'enfance la plus méprisable."

Prior, in *Alma*, may have had little or no philosophy to offer Diderot. But the poem had in profusion the *données* for Mirzoza's " métaphysique," in short, for an inquiry—half jesting, half serious—into the nature, essential properties and relations of the soul. They had only to be drawn out in prose, in Diderot's impertinent style and with an occasional probing twist of his thought, to fill two chapters of the *Bijoux*.

The same spirited dialogue with the principal conceit and its various corollaries occurs in both works. In the novel as in the poem, past and current hypotheses concerning the soul-mind and its location are reviewed in burlesque. In each, with the growing child, the soul inhabits successive parts of the body—the feet, the legs, the thighs, the midriff. At times, in the mature man or woman, it even reaches the head. Then too, it may remain motionless in, or return repeatedly to, one part of the body, with all the other parts subordinate to it. Thus, in *Alma* we may have " a mere Machine " (*Pr.* I, 509), and in the *Bijoux*, " des automates " (IV, 252). Thus too, in each work the difference in tastes, the diversity of inclinations, and that of characters and dispositions may be accounted for by the place in which the soul has taken up its abode. [1]

---

[1] Both writers have the soul residing in the dancer's legs, the singer's vocal organs, the warrior's armed hand, the glutton's alimentary tract, the libertine's thighs. Furthermore, through innuendo, the *double entente*, or unabashed frankness, the Prior of *Alma* and the Diderot of the *Bijoux* repeatedly and with variations fall back upon the possibilities of the sexual jest inherent in the principal conceit. In *Alma*, we have such lines as: " O need I name the seat she takes? "; " at this Age the active Mind / About the Waste lies most confin'd "; " And Love shall still possess the Middle "; " To those once charming seats below "; " Of the large Round, Her self the Center "; " Fond ALMA to these

"The philosophes," R. R. Palmer tells us, "were popularizers; they read the great books which most people did not read; and reworded the ideas in such a way as to hold the interest of average readers."[1] Prior's *Alma* was not a great book; it was not even a great poem. But Diderot had read it, and he retold it in a fashion that was eminently readable.[2] He had doubtless been drawn by the poet's ingenuity, wit, skill, detachment, and even spontaneity, as revealed in the poem. But he was, it now seems evident, particularly struck by the felicitous treatment of *Alma*'s principal conceit. Diderot's restless, brilliantly associative mind usually knew what to do with a challenging concept, an original idea or ideas when he came across them in his extensive reading. They would serve as a springboard for his soaring scientific imagination, his philosophical speculations and his poetic vision. The problem of the seat of the soul suited perfectly the spirit of the century. In our day, Paul Hazard has suggested the dimensions of the query by depicting Descartes as a thinker who, having overthrown the great among the schoolmen, was now himself overthrown. He had, after all, written only the romance of the soul, not knowing the origin nor the generation of ideas. It was Locke's turn to be the moving spirit of the age.[3]

Voltaire had already written in similar terms in the thirteenth letter of the *Lettres philosophiques* only to go on in an attempt to prove that animals had souls, while, in *L'Homme machine*, La Mettrie preferred to deny souls to animals and human beings alike. He had, moreover, in the *Histoire naturelle de l'âme*—published three years before the *Bijoux*—entitled a chapter, "Différents sièges de l'âme." The *Encyclopédie* reflected, as might be expected, the general concern, and we read in the article "Ame," "Il

---

Parts was gone, / Which LOVE more justly calls his own"; and the like. Already, in chapter XXV of the *Bijoux*, Mangogul says: "Un grand philosophe plaçait l'âme, la nôtre s'entend, dans la glande pinéale. Si j'en accordais une aux femmes, je sais bien, moi, où je la placerais." Mirzoza, in her experimental physics, will push this conceit to its extreme consequences. Still less veiled are the ratiocinations in chapter XV of the abovementioned *Memoirs of Martinus Scriblerus* which arrive at the almost inevitable conclusion that "the Organ of Generation is the true and only *Seat of the Soul*" (158).

[1] *A History of the Modern World* (New York, 1950), 300.

[2] So did Voltaire, but his remarks were written eight years after the appearance of the *Bijoux*. In earlier editions of the *Lettres philosophiques*, he had dismissed the English poet with a charming compliment, but in the edition of 1756 he spoke of some verses by Prior on the famous battle of Hochsted, and of the long philosophical poem, *Solomon*, which restated in 1500 lines the dictum: "All is vanity." But it was *Alma* especially that took Voltaire's fancy and, with his customary lucidity of style, he summarized it for the "average reader" as follows: "C'est de Prior qu'est l'*Histoire de l'Ame*: cette histoire est la plus naturelle qu'on ait faite jusqu'à présent de cet être si bien senti et si mal connu. L'âme est d'abord aux extremites du corps, dans les pieds et dans les mains des enfants; de là elle se place insensiblement au milieu du corps dans l'âge de puberté: ensuite elle monte au cœur, et là elle produit les sentiments de l'amour et de l'héroïsme: elle s'élève jusqu'à la tête dans un âge plus mûr; elle y raisonne comme elle peut, et dans la vieillesse, on ne sait plus ce qu'elle devient: c'est la sève d'un vieil arbre qui s'évapore, et qui ne se répare plus. Peut-être cet ouvrage est-il trop long: toute plaisanterie doit être courte, et même le sérieux devrait être bien court aussi" (*Lettres philosophiques*, éd. Gustave Lanson, Paris, 1930, II, 133).

[3] *La Pensée européenne au XVIIIe siècle* (Paris, 1963), 293.

était difficile de donner la préférence à une partie sur une autre, il n'y en a presqu'aucune où l'on n'ait placé l'âme."

Meanwhile as a countervailing influence, edition after edition of purely theological works devoted almost exclusively to the immateriality and immortality of the soul poured off the presses of the day.[1] But Voltaire, as titular leader of the *parti philosophique*, in his persistent effort to stress man's conflicting views of the soul, was, time and again, brought up short by the impasse definitively expressed in the article " Ame " of his *Dictionnaire philosophique*. Here as elsewhere, he remained convinced that, in the final analysis, one can admit nothing more in oneself than an unknown power of feeling and thinking that goes hand in hand with the organic matter that constitutes living man. This refusal to accept the great metaphysical speculations of the past concerning the properties of the soul bore out well enough Diderot's conclusion of some twenty years before in the *Pensées philosophiques*, when he stated that, " Les subtilités de l'ontologie ont fait tout au plus des sceptiques " (I, 133), and adduced that a better understanding of the workings of nature was needed (I, 133). Moreover, already in the *Essai sur le mérite et la vertu* (1745), he had declared that, " Peu de gens ... se sont occupés à anatomiser l'âme " (I, 67). Small wonder, then, that Diderot, midway between the abovementioned *Essai* on one hand and the forthcoming letters on the blind and the deaf and dumb on the other, should, in 1748, be struck by Prior's metaphor and wish to examine it on his own terms. In doing so he was to pass under review ideas that would lead him to new intellectual positions.

There are three participants in Diderot's dialogue on the seat of the soul. The two poles of dialectic are, of course, represented by the sultan and his mistress. Mangogul maintains an uncompromising, inflexible position that the animating principle of women in general lies in their sexual desires; he concludes that the soul's compulsion to adhere to one location reduces all women and most men to mere automatons.[2] Mirzoza, at the opposite pole, sees the actions of a given human being motivated by a soul whose first principle is mobility, even though it can permanently assume or constantly return to preferred positions. These concepts, as we have seen, are also in Prior. *Alma*, however, as Professor Spears has

---

[1] Typical of the vogue for religious works on the soul were those of the *Abbé* Denis-Xavier; numerous reprintings of such of his books as *Entretiens de l'âme avec Dieu* (1740), *Exercices de l'âme* (1751), and *Elévation de l'âme à Dieu* (1755), enjoyed great popularity.

[2] The historical distinction between the two opposing points of view in the dialogue has been well delineated by Rosalie L. Colie in her quite extraordinary study, *Paradoxia epidemica: The Renaissance Tradition of Paradox* (Princeton, 1966): " Humanist defenses of women are often contrasted to examples of ... medieval misogyny; examples of clerical abuse of women ... abound in the pages of the founders of the Christian Church, until dispraise of women became an accepted convention, with a store of *topoi* drawn upon for didactic purposes by didactic males from cardinals to barnyard cocks.... Humanistic paradoxes assumed that women since Eve had been human beings ... and that as human beings they had souls as well as their notorious bodies ... and that they even had, in the view of some observers, minds " (57-58).

demonstrated, is a significant and characteristic application of Pyrrhonism to contemporary thought (" The Meaning," 268, 290).

Though Diderot is more in sympathy with the views of Mirzoza, which are more imaginative and, in some respects, considerably less reactionary than those of Mangogul, the hints of truths yet to be discovered, we find, emerge from the tensions caused by these two opposing persuasions. In short, a discussion of the soul's slow ascent within its fleshly confines served each writer well. In the one case, it was a heuristic demonstration on the nature and activity of the soul; in the other, a logical demonstration of metaphysical materialism leading toward new ideas on biological and psychological man.

Moreover, the general period in which the *Bijoux* falls is an essential one in the evolution of Diderot's thought. This is true in science and the philosophy of science as recent studies have amply shown.[1] It is equally true for the shift in his religious convictions from deist to atheist. Jacques Roger's article, " Le Déisme du jeune Diderot," opens with " On connaît la rapide évolution religieuse et philosophique de Diderot entre 1745 et 1749," and continues by developing the theme that the *philosophe* was very much a part of his time in his reflections on the relationships " entre les trois personnages du drame métaphysique, Dieu, la nature et l'homme " (*Festschrift*, p. 237).

In Diderot's discussion of the " siège de l'âme," nature and man play leading roles, to be sure, but the supreme being, along with man's immortal soul, has been quite forgotten. Diderot had already assumed in the *Bijoux* the position Yvon Belaval is to assign him along with La Mettrie, Helvétius and d'Holbach. According to Professor Belaval (p. 10), " Tous ' en veulent ' à la distinction des deux substances; il n'y a pas d'âme séparable de la matière et, par conséquent, pas d'Esprit, pas de Dieu," and, in the second place, " Ils refusent d'accepter le principe cartésien selon lequel l'âme est plus aisée à connaître que le corps."

In the *Lettre sur les aveugles*, a year after the *Bijoux*, and in the *Lettre sur les sourds et muets*, three years later, there will be refinements on Mirzoza's " experimental metaphysics." Mirzoza's notion —already underscored in Prior's *Alma*—that a particular individual might be reduced to that part of his body to which his interests and compulsions most often return, has, from time to time, been recognized as the very basis for Diderot's speculations in the two *Letters* and, perhaps, even for Condillac's *statue organisée* in the *Traité des sensations*.[2] There are in the *Lettre sur les aveugles*

---

[1] Cf. Jean Mayer, *Diderot homme de science* (Rennes, 1959), and the introduction to his critical edition of the *Eléments de physiologie* (Paris, 1964). There is also the monumental work of Jacques Roger, *Les Sciences de la vie dans la pensée française du XVIIIe siècle* (Paris, 1963). Even more important to the conclusion of our own inquiry is Yvon Belaval's superb little article, " Sur le matérialisme de Diderot," *Festschrift für Herbert Dieckmann* (München, 1966), 9-21.

[2] Without pursuing the matter further, a number of critics have been content to repeat Assézat's note of 1875 (IV, 250), to which Marie Louise Dufrenoy gave more or less definitive expression in 1946 when she wrote: " Diderot avait donc déjà indiqué dans les *Bijoux indiscrets* l'idée fondamentale qu'il devait vulgariser dans ses deux *Lettres* ... et l'on peut voir ici en germe le principe de la *statue organisée* de Condillac " (117).

such seminal ideas as the possibility of a blind philosopher who is also a deaf-mute insisting that the soul is located in the finger tips (I, 292). In the *Lettre sur les sourds et muets* we find the hypothesis of the *muet de convention* leading Diderot to formulate another idea—that of " decomposing " a man the better to study what he owes to each of his senses. These are echoes from the *Bijoux*, and Diderot, in his second *Lettre*, labels such speculation " une espèce d'anatomie métaphysique " (I, 352), and indeed, we are immediately reminded of Mirzoza's " métaphysique expérimentale."

These echoes will reverberate with special insistence some twenty years later as the suppositions which Diderot first voiced in the *Bijoux* will be heard again in the *Rêve de d'Alembert*. At one moment of the dialogue a delirious d'Alembert is heard to ask whether the dissolution of different parts of the body might not produce men of markedly different characters and, without waiting for an answer, he replies to his own question: " Une chambre chaude, tapissée de petits cornets, et sur chacun de ces cornets une étiquette: guerriers, magistrats, philosophes, poètes, cornet de courtisans, cornet de catins, cornet de rois " (II, 131). Towards the end of the *Rêve* the idea appears again, but in a slightly altered light. Each species of animal, we are told, has its dominant form of instinct: the dog its scent, the fish its hearing, and the eagle its sight. Furthermore, the genius, he concludes, is a particular human being with one part of his physiological make-up far superior to the same part in others: the result is that a d'Alembert is *géomètre*, Vaucanson *machiniste*, Grétry *musicien*, Voltaire *poète* (II, 170).[1]

Despite the complexity of the subject matter in the three dialogues that constitute the *Rêve de d'Alembert* as a whole, the passages discussed above offer no serious problem as to their meaning. There is then little need to establish for purposes of clarification a filiation extending back to the *Bijoux* and Prior's *Alma*. Such does not seem to be the case, however, with the opening paragraph of the *Entretien entre d'Alembert et Diderot*. It is a matter which should, I think, be touched upon before bringing the present inquiry to a close.

In his critical edition of the *Rêve*, M. Paul Vernière [2] tells us that the *Entretien* " pose brutalement le problème; il s'agit de savoir si la science de la vie peut se passer de Dieu. Il faut opter," M. Vernière adds, " entre Dieu, le Dieu mystérieux des religions ... et le naturalisme athée qui dans la nature même trouve le principe de toute organisation et de tout développement." In the final analysis, this confrontation of two opposing points of view is undoubtedly true, for we do see the dialogue developing from the effort to dispose of the difficulties inherent in certain aspects of Christian

---

[1] Pushed to its extreme consequences, this concept continues to play a rôle in the *Suite du Rêve*. But if, on the physiological level, the goat-man of the *Suite* is presently reduced to the sexual urge (II, 190), the same over-all principle, even without the benefit of genius, holds on the intellectual plane as well. In the *Entretien*, Diderot tells d'Alembert, " vous trouverez qu'en tout, notre véritable sentiment n'est pas celui dans lequel nous n'avons jamais vacillé, mais celui auquel nous sommes le plus habituellement revenus " (II, 121).

[2] *Le Rêve de d'Alembert* (Paris, 1951), xxxvii.

doctrine by making life, thought and feeling purely physiological phenomena. But M. Vernière [1] and many other scholars are clearly under the impression that in the opening paragraph of the *Entretien* d'Alembert is debating the existence of God.

Such a conviction doubtless stems in part from the fact that in the Assézat-Tourneux edition of the text there is a capital " E " in the word *Etre* each of the four times it appears in the paragraph. M. Jean Varloot [2] has been able to obtain a microfilm of the copy of the *Rêve* that had been made for Catherine the great. It reveals the word *être* to be written without a capital " E ."

This fact in itself suggests that *être* may not, after all, stand for the supreme being. If, in this connection, we recall that both the *Bijoux* and *Alma* stressed the materiality of the soul, the suspicion arises that not the divinity, but the soul is the subject of d'Alembert's preliminary remarks. Moreover, analysis of the passage lends added weight to the hypothesis that d'Alembert's long, opening sentence is nothing short of the scholastic definition and description of the soul.[3]

The scholastics, it will be remembered, generally defined the soul as the first principle of life in living things. They held the soul of man to be a spiritual substance that is the *form* of the body, or in other words, the soul is that which confers actuality on the body. This union is so close that the scholastic mind would not speak of body and soul, which implies a dichotomy, but of man. Aristotle had said that if the eye were a living creature, sight would be its soul. For Plato and Descartes, on the other hand, the soul is conceived much like a ghost dwelling inside the body and moving about within. But in the Aristotelian tradition, with its hylomorphic theory, the soul is the substantial *form* of the body. It is simple in that it has no parts, it is immaterial, incorruptible, and has all the powers of plant or animal (vegetal and sentient) as well as those of intellect and will, which are properly immaterial. The soul, as conceived by the scholastics, is a substance having powers proper to it, and, like all spiritual substances (angels and God), it can have no other " whereness " than that of existing there where it makes its operations felt. The soul, according to the totality of its specific perfection, exists whole and entire in every part of the body which it informs; but if we consider the totality of its powers, we must say that it exists variously in different parts of the body insofar as they are proper for the performing of its specific functions.

The initial sentence Diderot puts into d'Alembert's mouth as the *Entretien* opens may be broken up into six assertions or statements. Keeping in mind that both *Alma* and the *Bijoux*, through the medium of burlesque, have already taken up the same problems in their discussions of the meta-

---

[1] Diderot, *Œuvres philosophiques* (Paris, 1956), 257.

[2] In his edition of *Le Rêve de d'Alembert* (Paris, 1963), 3.

[3] For the doctrine of St. Thomas Aquinas on the soul, see *De Anima* (*The Soul*, trans. by John Patrick Rowan, St. Louis, 1949), and the *Summa theologica*, questions 75 to 90 (translated and edited by Anton C. Pegis, New York [1945], Vol. I).

physics of the soul, how might the six statements be interpreted in the light of scholastic doctrine? Let us examine them one at a time.

1. *J'avoue qu'un être ... existe quelque part et ... ne correspond à aucun point de l'espace*: Since the soul is the form and the actuality of the body, we must say that it exists wherever the body exists; but *in itself* the soul exists wherever it acts, it is present by its power, and this type of presence cannot be confined to a point of space.

2. *... un être qui est inattendu et qui occupe de l'étendue*: the soul does not have the accidental quality of extension as bodies do; however, when it is informing a living body, we can say that it is present within an extended thing.

3. *... qui est tout entier sous chaque partie de cette étendue*: this doctrine is stated above.

4. *... qui diffère essentiellement de la matière et qui lui est uni*: the soul is immaterial, the body material, yet they are united in the closest of unions.

5. *... qui la suit et qui la meut sans se mouvoir*: the soul *in itself* acts like other spiritual substances in that it exists where it is actually operating, and when it transfers its operation from one point in space to another, it does not cover the intervening space. But the soul *as form of the body* is the principle of life and of movement, and it not only moves the body but moves with the body.

6. *... qui agit sur elle et qui en subit toutes les vicissitudes*: since the soul is the source of life and activity of the body, there is action of soul on body; and since it is the principle of all sentient and intellectual powers, there is action of the body on the soul in the form of sensation and knowledge. Only the will is totally free and independent.

So the notion of the spirit as being within the confines of the human body, and the necessity of denying that it exists here or there in the body, leads to the necessity of stating that the soul exists whole and entire in any and every given part of the body. The imagination balks at this problem of the location of the soul as much as at the problem of interaction between spirit and matter, and both remain for the d'Alembert-Diderot of the *Entretien*'s introductory paragraph " difficiles à admettre."

In a very broad sense, the entire *Rêve* might be said to have as its chief concern the " soul," or the animating principle of life, from which stem, among other phenomena, instinct, unconscious habit and the creative thoughts of the human mind. More specifically, we have a beginning of the *Rêve* sequence, with a serious but brief review of scholastic doctrine on the soul, a middle section where Diderot's metaphysical materialism soon occupies the entire stage of his thought, and an end where, on a bantering note, Bordeu and Mlle. de L'Espinasse speculate on the dilemma the immortal souls of a race of *chèvre-pieds* would oblige the Sorbonne's Faculty of theology to face. The entire dialogue of the *Rêve de d'Alembert* is, as we see, an excellent example of professor Belaval's dictum: " Or, l'examen d'un matérialisme selon ses principes concerne la métaphysique " (p. 9).

The considerable number of references to the soul with their overtones and various shades of meaning that may be found elsewhere in Diderot, need hardly detain us here. Mention should be made, though, of two sets of notes he jotted down comparatively late in life, for in them may be found a clear indication of his definitive position concerning the soul—a position which has already been hinted at, alluded to, and in some cases, openly spelled out, in his previous writings. The first set of notes to appear posthumously comprises the *Eléments de physiologie*, probably composed between 1774 and 1790. There, in the three-page piece, " L'Ame," he uses the same argument as that in the *Entretien entre Diderot et d'Alembert* (II, 114-115) to refute the distinction between the *deux substances*, mind and matter; in the *Eléments* he quickly comes to the point: " Est-ce que l'âme est gaie, triste, colère, tendre, dissimulée, voluptueuse? Elle n'est rien sans le corps. Je défie qu'on explique rien sans le corps " (IX, 377).[1]

The second set of notes is in the form of marginalia only recently brought to light as the *Commentaire inédit de la " Lettre sur l'homme."* [2] In efforts to straighten out the thinking of Hemsterhuis, Diderot repeatedly returns in his marginal comments to the question of the soul. Typical is his reply to the Dutch philosopher's assertion that " Le premier moteur de ce corps, que nous appelons l'âme, est une chose différente de ce corps." Diderot objects with the same patience he has used throughout his marginal notes: " Je n'ai jamais vu la sensibilité, l'âme, la pensée, le raisonnement, sans autre agent ou intermède, que des agents ou intermèdes matériels. Je m'en tiens là. Je n'assure que ce que je vois " (p. 113). This was already Diderot's point of view, though more fancifully expressed, when in chapter XXIX of the *Bijoux* the " soul " was first made manifest in the stirrings of the foetus and the kicking, newborn child, and it had been the opinion of Prior before him.

In the word of advice, *Aux jeunes gens*, which serves as an introduction to the *Pensées sur l'interprétation de la nature* (1754), Diderot asked the reader to have constantly in mind that nature is not God, that man is not a machine and that an hypothesis is not a fact; for those were the principles by which he stood (II, 7). They were, moreover, principles which Mirzoza adhered to when she proposed a new sort of experience, that of putting forward the fundamentals of an experimental metaphysics, fundamentals leading Diderot to speculations that so often were bolder and more advanced than those of his contemporaries. But, as we have seen, Prior's *Alma*—useful because of its witty, thought-catching freshness and because of the provocation of its principal conceit—became a catalyst for Diderot's first sustained attempts to follow his own counsel of a few years before to " anatomiser l'âme " (II, 67).

---

[1] Here, as in *Le Rêve*, Diderot is, of course, in the mainstream of eighteenth-century French materialism, and a number of passages could be cited from d'Holbach, for instance, where the conclusions closely parallel those of Diderot. The following should suffice as an example. D'Holbach writes: " Ainsi l'âme est l'homme considéré relativement à la faculté de sa nature propre, c'est-à-dire, de ses propriétés, de son organisation particulière et des modifications durables ou transitoires que sa machine éprouve de la part des êtres qui agissent sur elle " (*Le Système de la nature*, I, vii).

[2] François Hemsterhuis, *Lettre sur l'homme et ses rapports*, avec le commentaire inédit de Diderot, ed. Georges May (New Haven, 1964).

In all this we are reminded of Paul van Tieghem's statement and its appropriateness in the present instance: " Le mérite d'un génie supérieur consiste dans bien des cas à reprendre une idée banale et usée, ou au contraire perdue dans les œuvres d'un auteur peu connu, ou lancée déjà avec un demi-succès pour lui donner un nouveau lustre et lui imprimer sa marque personnelle, ineffaçable qui l'associera à son nom aux yeux de la postérité." [1]

The English poet's neo-classical scepticism and, as he phrased it, " Pritty spanish Conceit," were swiftly and effortlessly transposed by Diderot into a personal justification of the experimental method on a topic of considerable moment then as now. That this should be so is added proof of the soundness of Arthur Wilson's conclusion in *Diderot: The Testing Years* that " no serious student of Diderot's ideas and their development can afford to overlook *Les Bijoux indiscrets* " (p. 85). Diderot's debt to Prior is unmistakable, and *Alma*, I believe, should henceforth be recognized for the part it played in the *philosophe's* first novel.

---

[1] *La Littérature comparée* (Paris, 1946), 147.

# MOLIÈRE A LA FIN DU SIÈCLE DES LUMIÈRES *

> Il est un petit nombre d'écrivains qui ont un privilège: ils ont peint l'homme, l'humanité même, et comme elle ils deviennent un sujet inépuisable, éternel, d'observations et d'études. Tels sont et seront toujours Molière, La Fontaine, Montaigne.
>
> (Sainte-Beuve, *Nouveaux Lundis*, mars 24, 1862)

En essayant de lier le nom de Molière à la fin du siècle des lumières et surtout à la Révolution française on risque de provoquer immédiatement l'une des répliques les plus célèbres de son théâtre: " Que diable allait-il faire dans cette galère ? "—le " il " se rapportant, bien entendu, à Molière et non au jeune Léandre des *Fourberies de Scapin*.

Il est pourtant incontestable que Molière se trouva étroitement mêlé à la tourmente révolutionnaire et que sa présence continua à se faire vivement sentir pendant toute cette période.

Les divers aspects de la fortune de Molière pendant la Révolution ont été maintes fois étudiées, mais nul essai n'a été tenté, autant que je sache, de présenter une synthèse générale de la question. C'est justement ce que je voudrais faire ici dans les limites étroites dont nous disposons.

Le premier de ces aspects qui a fait l'objet de patientes études au dix-neuvième siècle est celui du sort réservé aux dépouilles mortelles du grand auteur comique. Au premier abord, le sujet peut certes paraître macabre; mais il ne manque pas de jeter une lumière inattendue sur la vénération parfois équivoque qu'on eut alors pour Molière et les à-côtés singuliers de l'idéalisme révolutionnaire.[1] Rappelons-en les grandes lignes.

---

\* Reprinted, with modifications, from *The Age of the Enlightenment. Studies to Theodore Besterman* (1967), 330-349.

[1] Le sort probable des restes de Molière, surtout pendant la Révolution et les années qui l'ont suivie, a souvent piqué la curiosité des savants français, qui ne se sont d'ailleurs jamais trouvés entièrement d'accord sur ce sujet si longtemps enveloppé de mystère. Voici une bibliographie sommaire des ouvrages suscités par la question:

Jean François Cailhava d'Estendoux, *Etudes sur Molière, ou Observations sur la vie, les mœurs, les ouvrages de cet auteur et sur la manière de jouer ses pièces* (Paris, an X, 1802); Alexandre Lenoir, *Musée des monuments français, ou Description historique et chronologique des statues* (Paris, 1821), viii; Ulrich Richard Desaix, *La Relique de Molière*

Depuis de longues années Jean-Baptiste Poquelin, dit Molière, et le grand fabuliste, Jean de La Fontaine, reposaient dans le petit cimetière Saint-Joseph à Paris. Les philosophes n'ignoraient pas l'endroit et Denis Diderot avait écrit ces mots aussi touchants qu'éloquents: " Ce lieu sera toujours sacré pour les poètes et pour les gens de goût " (A.T., VI, 333). " Toujours," voilà bien un grand mot et Diderot n'aurait pu se tromper davantage. Un quart de siècle s'était à peine écoulé que Molière et La Fontaine étaient arrachés à leur éternel repos. Voici comment se passèrent les choses.

C'était en 1792, la Révolution commençait à battre son plein. Cette année fut marquée par un nombre d'incidents qui n'étaient que les signes avant-coureurs de la fureur populaire: la prise des Tuileries par le peuple, la destitution de Louis XVI, les " Massacres de septembre," et l'élection de Robespierre à la Convention.

Le règne de la Terreur n'a pas encore commencé, mais les esprits en fermentation conçoivent bien des idées, bien des projets dont les plus singuliers, les plus fantaisistes, concernant directement Molière enterré depuis plus d'un siècle. Paris est alors divisé en sections dont la plupart portent des noms du passé, des noms militants ou évocateurs des vertus civiques de la Rome antique.

Or une de ces Sections armées avait son siège dans la chapelle Saint-Joseph qui était entourée de cette partie du cimetière où l'on croyait que Molière ainsi que La Fontaine reposaient. Pour faire honneur aux deux grands écrivains classiques et en même temps honorer ce coin de Paris, la Section abandonna son nom d'alors pour s'appeler " Section de Molière et de La Fontaine."

A peine la Section eut-elle reçu son nouveau nom que les citoyens, qui en faisaient partie, décidèrent d'ériger des monuments dignes de ces illustres morts. Or pour donner à ces monuments un éclat et une grandeur exemplaires, il fut décidé de chercher et de trouver les restes mortels—ou " restes sacrés " pour employer la formule contemporaine—de ces deux géants de la littérature française.

L'exhumation de Molière eut lieu le 6 juillet 1792, et celle de La Fontaine le 21 novembre de la même année. Les restes, selon les documents du jour, furent mis dans deux coffres fermés à clef, et aussitôt transférés dans des caisses de sapin " de deux pieds de long sur un pied et demi de large et un demi pied de haut." La chapelle Saint-Joseph ayant été démolie pour faire

---

*du cabinet du baron Vivant Denon* (Paris, 1880); Louis Moland, " Histoire des restes de Molière de 1792 à 1799," *Revue de la Révolution* (1883), II, 405-425.

Voir aussi *L'Intermédiaire des chercheurs et des curieux* (1864), I, 86 (M.T.: " Les Tombes de Molière et de La Fontaine "); 109 (V.D.: " Les Tombes de M. et de L. F. au P. L."); 246 (Fr. L.: " Tombes de M. et de L. F."); (1875), VIII, 452 (Saint-Frusquin: " La Mâchoire de M."); 538 (O. D.: " La Mâchoire de M."); (1959) nouvelle série, IX, 104 (un néophyte: " Tombe commune de M. et de L. F."); 638-639 (Le Raboliot des Lettres: même titre); 1033 (Pierre Vernois: même titre).

Il y a, du reste, dans *Le Temps* du 17 novembre 1885, l'essai de Jules Loiseleur intitulé " Les nouvelles controverses sur Molière à propos de récentes publications, VIII, si les restes de Molière ont eu le sort de ceux de Voltaire."

place à un corps de garde, les sectionnaires mirent les deux caisses dans le grenier du corps de garde.

L'Assemblée avait proclamé la patrie en danger à cause de l'avance des armées alliées; la chute de la royauté étant devenue un fait accompli, l'exécution de Louis XVI n'allait pas tarder. Tant d'événements importants firent bien vite oublier le prestige si récemment acquis par la présence matérielle et spirituelle de deux personnalités littéraires du 17e siècle. Avant la fin de l'année, la Section des poètes n'était qu'un souvenir fugitif; son nouveau nom était la Section Brutus. *Sic transit gloria mundi !* [1]

Aussi, soucieux d'art et de littérature, ces quelques sectionnaires voulaient trouver le moyen de rendre hommage, à leur manière, à ce que, à leurs yeux, représentaient " les restes augustes " de deux Français de grande renommée, aux activités pacifiques et apolitiques.

De ces fidèles il y en a surtout un qu'il serait impossible d'accuser de négligence ou d'indifférence vis-à-vis des augustes débris. C'était l'écrivain et l'auteur dramatique Jean François Cailhava d'Estendoux. Son dévouement sans bornes au souvenir du grand poète comique, son zèle féroce pour tout ce qui le concernait élèvent Cailhava au premier rang de ceux qui l'aimaient non pas sagement, peut-être, mais à la folie. Quand, en 1779, d'Alembert présenta le buste de Molière aux quarante immortels, c'est Cailhava qui composa le *Discours prononcé par Molière le jour de sa réception posthume à l'Académie*. C'est lui aussi qui nous raconte l'émotion qu'il ressentit au moment de la prétendue exhumation des squelettes de Molière et de La Fontaine. Ce fut, semble-t-il, une émotion égale à celle que Hamlet, prince du Danemark dut éprouver devant le tombeau d'Ophélie. Mais laissons la parole à Cailhava lui-même: " J'ai pressé sur mon sein les têtes de ces deux hommes de génie; je les ai baisées religieusement: celle du fabuliste inimitable m'a fait verser des larmes d'attendrissement; je me suis prosterné devant celle du premier des comiques, et j'ai sollicité, j'ai obtenu la permission de la ceindre d'un papier sur lequel est écrit ce vers: 'C'est un homme qui... Ah!... un homme... un homme enfin.'" (*Tartuffe*, I, vi.[2])

Or les dépouilles de Molière avaient été enfermées dans leur caisse quatre mois et demi avant l'exhumation de la Fontaine. Pour que Cailhava pût avoir les crânes des deux poètes dans ses mains, il est évident que la caisse de Molière dut être rouverte au moment de l'exhumation de La Fontaine. On a nettement l'impression, du reste, en lisant des documents que Louis Moland et d'autres savants ont mis au jour, que chacune des deux caisses a été ouverte à plusieurs reprises. Poussés soit par la curiosité, soit par une vénération quelque peu déplacée, certains enthousiastes,

---

[1] Nous lisons, par exemple, dans le *Journal de la Montagne*: " Une députation de Molière-et-Lafontaine communique un arrêté qui change le nom de cette section en celui de section *Brutus*. Pour célébrer l'adoption de ce nom auguste, elle fera prononcer solennellement demain à 5 heures de relevée, l'oraison funèbre des patriotes Marat et Lepelletier." (16 septembre 1793), no. 106, 744.

[2] C'est ainsi que Cailhava conclut—la Révolution enfin terminée—son livre très lu à l'époque: *Etudes sur Molière*, 355.

soyons-en sûrs, n'ont pas toujours montré la plus grande discrétion à l'égard des ossements devenus reliques sacrées. Avec tout ce remue-ménage d'ossements il n'est pas surprenant que certains des os de Molière se soient retrouvés dans la caisse de La Fontaine, et un ou deux des os de La Fontaine dans celle de Molière. Beaucoup plus grave est le fait que dans cette série d'ouvertures et de fermetures des deux caisses quelques-uns des restes se soient doucement évaporés.

Le baron Dominique Vivant Denon, Directeur des musées impériaux et royaux pendant de longues années, fut toute sa vie un grand épicurien et un grand collectionneur. C'est lui, apparemment, qui justifia si bien l'axiome d'Erik Satie: " Si vous voulez vivre longtemps, vivez vieux." Vivant Denon mourut à Paris parmi ses collections en 1825. D'après Anatole France il avait rempli d'une quantité de reliques profanes un reliquaire, vidé pendant la Révolution de ses reliques de saints: cendres d'Héloïse, cheveux d'Ignès de Castro, moustache de Henri IV, dent de Voltaire, sang de Napoléon. Dans le coffret, parmi ce bric-à-brac macabre, il y eut aussi des fragments d'os de Molière et de La Fontaine. C'est ce que nous explique une brochure publiée en 1880, et intitulée *La Relique de Molière du cabinet du baron Vivant Denon*. Collectionneur enthousiaste d'œuvres d'art et de souvenirs, le baron, même aux heures les plus sombres de la Révolution, eut amplement l'occasion de recueillir une variété de reliques dont aucune n'était, semble-t-il, plus facilement accessible que celles de nos deux poètes.

Pendant de longues années au dix-neuvième siècle l'on pouvait voir sous un globe au musée de Cluny un fragment de mâchoire, selon toute probabilité celle de Molière. Si c'était bien son maxillaire inférieur, comme le disait longtemps un certificat apposé sur le socle qui supportait le fragment, comment se fait-il que cette partie de sa mâchoire ait fini par avoir le sort peu enviable d'être transformée en simple curiosité de foire? Les origines de l'histoire remontent à la Révolution. C'est une des plus singulières de cette période, qui n'en manquait pas.

Sous la Convention nationale, l'assemblée révolutionnaire qui succéda à l'Assemblée législative le 21 septembre 1792 pour gouverner la France pendant trois années mémorables, eut une idée géniale. Ce n'était rien moins que de recueillir les os des Français illustres du passé pour les convertir en verre phosphate par une opération chimique. Dans quel dessein? Pour en faire des coupes mortuaires ou—terme plus patriotique—des coupes républicaines; ou bien, et l'expression quelque peu ambiguë est encore plus élégante: des coupes " consacrées à la reconnaissance publique."

En ce qui concerne le pauvre Molière, les comptes rendus que nous possédons se ressemblent tous. Aucun, pourtant, n'est aussi lapidaire que celui publié par un personnage bien informé dans le périodique intitulé l'*Intermédiaire des chercheurs et des curieux* pour l'année 1864. Nous lisons: " ... à l'époque de la Convention, sur un ordre du Comité de salut publique, le chimiste Darcet fut mis en possession d'une partie des ossements de Molière et de quelques autres morts illustres, ... à l'effet d'en tirer du phosphate de chaux qui devait être employé à la fabrication d'une belle coupe en porcelaine de Sèvres où l'on aurait bu patriotiquement à la 'République.' J'ignore si ce vase a été fabriqué...".[1]

Quelques temps après, il paraît que l'ordre en cause fut révoqué. Il en résulta que les corps des "morts illustres" furent rendus aux cimetières et ceux de Molière et de La Fontaine à leurs caisses dans la mansarde mentionnée plus haut. Tout laisse croire, pourtant, que Darcet ne fut pas le seul chimiste choisi par l'Etat pour ce travail de vitrification. Il y a, par exemple, la lettre-requête adressée au ministre de l'Intérieur par Beaumarchais. Dans cette lettre de protestation, le dramaturge déplorait le fait qu'en visitant les collections du Jardin des Plantes, il y avait rencontré au coin d'un laboratoire de chimie, dans la poussière des fourneaux et des matériaux servant à des distillations, le corps exhumé de Turenne portant—ajouta-t-on après—toutes ses médailles.[2]

On a souvent dit que la période révolutionnaire, marquée par un bouleversement politique et social en général et par les excès de la Terreur en particulier, ne fut pas prête à suivre l'exemple de Philinte:

"Je prends tout doucement les hommes comme ils sont."
(*Le Misanthrope*, I. i)

La formule est dans *le Misanthrope*; et *le Misanthrope* est bien la pièce de Molière qui fut, sinon la plus en vogue, du moins celle qui fit le plus de bruit pendant la Révolution. Une des raisons en fut *la Lettre à d'Alembert sur les spectacles* de Jean-Jacques Rousseau, publiée en 1758. L'attaque de Rousseau est d'une importance historique particulière en ce qu'elle montre

---

[1] V. D., "Les Tombes de Molière et de La Fontaine au Père-Lachaise," 109.

[2] Voir *Œuvres complètes de Beaumarchais*, éd. Edouard Fournier (Paris, 1876), 690, "Lettre LII." Il serait à-propos, peut-être, de citer au moins une partie de cette lettre à François de Neufchâteau, homme d'état français et ministre de l'intérieur du Directoire:
"I [sic] brumaire an VII (11 novembre, 1798).
Ministre Citoyen,
Les soins constants que vous mettez pour embellir le jardin national, conservatoire des plantes exotiques, des arbres et des animaux qui arrivent de tous les points du globe, nous prouvent que vos sages vues s'étendent à tout ce qui peut être utile au public, ou sembler digne de sa curiosité. Mais j'avoue qu'au plaisir de voir ces collections se mêle en moi un sentiment pénible, toutes les fois que j'y trouve, au coin d'un laboratoire de chimie, dans la poussière des fourneaux, des matras, et des matériaux servant à des distillations, le corps exhumé de *Turenne*, sans que je puisse m'expliquer les motifs d'un pareil dédain pour les restes d'un chef d'armée que le roi le plus fier de son rang jugea digne de partager la sépulture de sa maison.
"Que peut donc avoir de commun le squelette du *grand Turenne*, avec les animaux vivants que cette enceinte nous conserve?
"Qu'aurait dit Montecuculli, de voir son vainqueur figurer au milieu d'une ménagerie?...
"Je vous prie donc, ministre ami de l'ordre, dont la haute magistrature est de surveiller les objets de décence publique, de prendre en considération cette remarque sur Turenne, qu'un bon citoyen vous soumet.
"Je pourrais bien signer mon nom, ou même en donner l'anagramme, si cette singularité ajoutait quelque chose au mérite d'un aperçu: *qu'importe qui je sois*, si je dis la vérité? C'est de cela seul qu'il s'agit."

les changements qui ont eu lieu dans la société et dans l'opinion publique depuis l'époque de Molière. Elle eut un profond retentissement dans la seconde moitié du siècle, et surtout durant les années révolutionnaires.

Comme les deux *Discours* qui la précédèrent, *la Lettre* fut dans une grande mesure une déclaration de guerre contre le caractère artificiel de la société de l'époque.[1] Ce caractère artificiel est reflété en partie dans l'esprit des salons du jour et en partie dans le théâtre contemporain. *Le Misanthrope* est justement un chef-d'œuvre comique qui a pour cadre les salons de Paris sous l'ancien régime. Le seul personnage de la pièce qui soit sincère aux yeux de Jean-Jacques est, bien entendu, Alceste. Du reste, Alceste a le très grand mérite d'avoir justement les mêmes défauts qu'on reproche à Rousseau: tous deux se piquent de leur franchise et de leur honnêteté; tous deux ont peu de patience pour la dissimilation ou l'hypocrisie; tous deux se trouvent aussi vertueux qu'on peut l'être dans une société non seulement artificielle, mais même dépravée. A cause de ces traits, tous deux tombent dans le ridicule.[2] Tout comme Alceste, Rousseau refuse d'accepter la société contemporaine. Il est donc prêt à s'identifier complètement avec celui qui dit au moment où la pièce touche à sa fin:

> Trahi de toutes parts, accablé d'injustices,
> Je vais sortir d'un gouffre où triomphent les vices,
> Et chercher sur la terre un endroit écarté
> Où d'être homme d'honneur on ait la liberté.
>
> (*Le Misanthrope*, V. iv)

Non seulement Rousseau défend le caractère et les actions d'Alceste, mais il part aussi en guerre contre l'honnête homme par excellence de la pièce, Philinte. Il lui reproche et sa modération et sa fausseté. Bref, il trouve que Philinte, ce sage de la pièce, n'est qu'un homme du haut monde dont les maximes ressemblent à celles des fripons. Pire encore, toujours selon Jean-Jacques, Philinte rappelle ces grands seigneurs qui ne se soucient point du peuple affamé et misérable.

Et voilà Rousseau le porte-parole le plus éloquent de 1789 avant la lettre.[3] En attaquant le théâtre, et, plus précisément, *le Misanthrope* de

---

[1] Voir l'édition critique du *Discours sur les sciences et les arts* par George R. Havens (Modern Language Association of America—Monograph Series, no. XV—New York et Londres, 1946). Dans son introduction et son commentaire se trouve une analyse très utile de l'état d'esprit de Rousseau à partir de 1749.

[2] Sans se nommer, Jean-Jacques se désigne en termes assez transparents pour le lecteur de son temps: " Vous ne sauriez me nier deux choses: l'une qu'Alceste dans cette pièce est un homme droit, sincère, estimable, un véritable homme de bien; l'autre que l'Auteur lui donne un personnage ridicule. C'en est assés, ce me semble, pour rendre Molière inexcusable " (Rousseau, *Lettre à Mr. d'Alembert sur les spectacles*, ed. M. Fuchs, Lille, Genève, 1948, 48).

[3] A cet égard les remarques d'un des plus grands disciples de Rousseau au vingtième siècle semblent parfaitement à-propos. La *Lettre* selon Romain Rolland est un " torrent d'éloquence passionnée qui enflamma l'opinion." Et il ajoute: " Elle est déjà, par endroits, un discours de la Révolution." (*Les Pages immortelles de J.-J. Rousseau choisies et expliquées par Romain Rolland*, Paris, 1938, 24.)

Molière, il obéit à la logique de son système, système qui est à la fois hostile aux raffinements de la société sous l'ancien régime et à son indifférence à la sincérité et à la vertu. Les répercussions en furent, comme on le sait, longues et retentissantes.[1]

Surtout en ce qui concerne les deux personnages principaux de la pièce on était prêt depuis longtemps à accepter une interprétation qui allait être celle donnée par Jean-Jacques. L'acteur Baron, formé par Molière lui-même et mort en 1729, avait refusé de jouer un Alceste ridicule; il tenait à accentuer les qualités supérieures de ce caractère où les exagérations semblaient être légitimes et justes.[2] Du reste, les acteurs qui suivirent peu après Baron furent en général fidèles à son interprétation d'Alceste, homme de cour digne et noble.[3] D'ailleurs La Bruyère avait déjà proposé un Alceste sympathique.[4] Et, dans sa réplique à Rousseau, d'Alembert démontra qu'il n'était pas loin de partager les vues de son adversaire quand il dit du personnage d'Alceste: " Il n'y a personne qui ne l'estime, qui ne soit même porté à l'aimer et à le plaindre." [5] D'autres, suivant l'exemple de Rousseau et de d'Alembert voulaient voir en Alceste, même avant la Révolution, un parangon de vertu. Tantôt se rangeant tout à fait du côté de Rousseau, on s'accordait avec lui pour dire que l'on ne devrait pas présenter le Misanthrope comme un personnage risible. Tantôt—c'est le cas d'Elie Fréron par exemple[6] —on refusait catégoriquement d'admettre avec Jean-Jacques que Molière eût fait de son mieux pour rendre Alceste ridicule.[7]

La vérité est que Rousseau n'était pas si éloigné de Molière qu'il le prétendait. Dans son portrait d'Alceste et ailleurs, Molière avait donné un sens nouveau à la notion de liberté en faisant de l'homme l'auteur de ses propres actions morales et de sa propre vertu. Et c'est précisément la position de Jean-Jacques, homme des lumières, dans ses diverses œuvres et tout particulièrement dans le *Vicaire savoyard* et le *Contrat social*. Molière

---

[1] Voir, parmi tant d'autres, l'étude importante de Margaret M. Moffat, *La Controverse sur la moralité du théâtre après La Lettre à d'Alembert de J.-J. Rousseau* (Paris, 1930).

[2] Cf. Maurice Descotes, *Les Grands rôles du théâtre de Molière* (Paris, 1960), 9.

[3] Sujet traité en détail par Edward Daniel Sullivan, " The Interpretation of Molière's Alceste from 1666 to the Present " (unpublished doctoral dissertation, Harvard University, 1941), 122-123.

[4] " ... le misanthrope peut avoir l'âme austère et farouche; mais extérieurement il est civil et *cérémonieux*: il ne s'échappe pas, il ne s'apprivoise pas avec les hommes; au contraire, il les traite honnêtement et sérieusement. " La Bruyère, *Les Caractères*, " De l'homme " (Paris, Piazza, 1928), II, 189-190.

[5] D'Alembert, *Mélanges de littérature d'histoire et de philosophie*, " Lettre à M. Rousseau " (Amsterdam, Nouvelle édition, 1764), II, 422.

[6] *Année littéraire* 1758), VI, 306.

[7] Cet intérêt renouvelé pour Alceste augmenta encore davantage l'énorme prestige dont jouissait Molière. En 1769, il entra, d'une manière posthume, à l'Académie Française et nombreux furent les écrivains qui concoururent pour son éloge. En 1773, on célébra le centenaire de sa mort, la fameuse édition Le Bret parut et les Comédiens français décidèrent de jouer sans aucune rémunération jusqu'à ce qu'une somme suffisante pour faire élever une statue soit amassée.

aussi bien que Rousseau reconnaissait la souveraineté d'un impératif moral qui n'était pas dicté par le ciel mais que l'homme s'imposait à lui-même.

Autre fait capital: à mesure que le siècle progresse et que le caractère d'Alceste est regardé de plus en plus favorablement, celui de Philinte baisse dans l'estime du public. Ici encore d'Alembert semble accepter le jugement de Rousseau, et il reproche à Philinte d'être " un caractère mal décidé, plein de sagesse dans ses maximes et de fausseté dans sa conduite." [1] Mais c'est en 1790 que les nouvelles interprétations du rôle d'Alceste et de Philinte allaient être exploitées avec grand succès. Depuis quelque temps les affiches de la Comédie-Française avaient fait sensation en annonçant une nouvelle pièce, *le Philinte de Molière ou La Suite du Misanthrope*. Tout le monde se demandait qui avait bien pu avoir l'effronterie de s'ériger en continuateur du grand poète comique. La pièce eut sa première le 22 février, six mois après la prise de la Bastille. C'était une période d'enthousiasme et d'idéalisme qui avait vu l'écroulement de l'ancien régime et qui témoignait du plus grand espoir pour l'avenir. C'est dans cette atmosphère que la pièce de Fabre d'Eglantine s'attira une importance que ses qualités littéraires ne justifiaient pas. Pour le spectateur de 1790 c'était un manifeste de propagande politique émouvant; pour nous, deux siècles plus tard ce n'est plus qu'un document politique et social, une manière de curiosité.

Fabre d'Eglantine, comédien, homme politique et opportuniste, avait su bien accorder sa réfutation du *Misanthrope* avec le climat du début de la Révolution. Molière, quoique toujours vénéré, avait momentanément perdu de sa popularité, et un critique de l'époque pouvait s'écrier " Qui est-ce qui donne aujourd'hui quarante-huit sous pour voir du Molière ? " [2] En effet, la Révolution négligeait les aspects littéraires du théâtre.[3] Fabre, pourtant, avait tout de suite attiré l'attention des spectateurs parisiens en profitant en même temps de la gloire établie de Molière [4] et de la popu-

---

[1] D'Alembert, *op. cit.*, 423.

[2] Voir A. V. Arnault, *Œuvres* (Paris, Bossage, 1826), II, 421.

[3] Cf. Jacques Hérissay, *Le Monde des théâtres pendant la révolution 1789-1800* (Paris, 1922), 69.

[4] L'admiration que Fabre témoignait pour l'auteur du *Tartuffe* et du *Misanthrope* était sans doute sincère et, déjà avant la Révolution, il avait chanté les louanges du " sublime Molière " dans un poème intitulé *A un poète comique, Œuvres mêlées et posthumes de Ph. Naz. Fabre d'Eglantine* (La Veuve Fabre d'Eglantine, Paris, Vendémiaire, an XI), II, 4. En publiant la pièce, il ajouta un Prologue où il proclamait: " A côté de Molière, enfin, je me hasarde " (56); on dirait même, en lisant les vers qui suivent, que le poète révolutionnaire s'abrite à l'ombre du grand homme:

> Mais voyez-vous encor cet essain [sic] ténébreux
> D'aveugles partisans...
> Qui, pour mieux me haïr, feignant d'aimer Molière,
> Fanatiques menteurs de cet homme immortel,
> M'immolent à leur haine au pied de son autel ? "

(*Le Philinte de Molière*, Paris, Prault, 1791, 58). Il se pose aussi en interprète infaillible de Molière dans une assez longue critique défavorable de la première représentation d'une suite au *Misanthrope*, écrite par Charles-Albert Demoustier, intitulée *Alceste à la campagne* (voir l'article de Fabre dans *Les Révolutions de Paris* du 4 au 11 décembre, 1790, LXXIV, 479-482). Cette critique, cependant, est, comme *le Philinte de Molière*, une réfutation de la pièce de Molière.

larité de Rousseau.[1] Fidèle à l'esprit de son âge, il se déclarait publiquement disciple de Jean-Jacques et avouait même avoir pris l'inspiration originale de son Philinte dans *la Lettre sur les spectacles*. Au fond, il ne faisait que suivre l'avis de Diderot qui avait écrit dès 1757: " Telle est encore la vicissitude des ridicules et des vices que je crois qu'on pourrait faire un *Misanthrope* tous les cinquante ans " (A.T., VII, 151). Pour Fabre, Alceste représente un citoyen de 1790, homme sensible et bon, et dévoué aux idées nouvelles.[2] Philinte est peint, par contre, comme un aristocrate borné et égoïste et tout à fait satisfait des conditions politiques et sociales de l'ancien régime. Alceste symbolisait tout ce qui est juste, Philinte, d'autre part, tout ce qu'il y a de pervers dans la société: deux portraits que le spectateur contemporain pouvait reconnaître sans la moindre difficulté.

Bien entendu, sans Molière et sans Rousseau il n'y aurait pas eu de *Philinte de Molière*. Mais il y avait d'autres facteurs qui contribuèrent à la genèse de la pièce. Le portrait que Fabre donne de lui-même ressemble assez à celui de l'Alceste auquel Rousseau s'identifiait une trentaine d'années auparavant.[3] Et puis, par jalousie et animosité personnelle, il voulait attaquer, coûte que coûte, un dramaturge très en vogue à l'époque: Collin d'Harleville. Non seulement Fabre attaquait celui-ci dans le Prologue malicieux de sa propre pièce, mais aussi dans la pièce même; car il tenait à faire croire au spectateur que son personnage principal, Philinte, égoïste et réactionnaire, ressemblait à Collin comme un frère. On peut invoquer comme autre origine de la pièce, le fait que Fabre, membre du club politique de Danton, *les Cordeliers*, voulait faire d'Alceste un déclamateur politique. De tout ceci, il résulte que, pour les spectateurs de l'époque, l'Alceste de Molière prend une signification nouvelle. Dès lors, les acteurs jouant ce rôle aspirent à se faire applaudir en mettant en relief les passages où Alceste s'en prend aux institutions et à la société de l'ancien régime. Quant à Fabre, il n'est peut-être pas sans intérêt de rappeler qu'avant d'être guillotiné il s'est tourné vers un de ses juges en lui adressant les paroles suivantes: " Fouquier, tu peux faire tomber ma tête, mais non pas mon Philinte." [4] Et il avait raison, car sa pièce lui survécut—ne fût-ce que jusqu'à la fin du siècle.

---

[1] C'est toujours dans le Prologue que nous lisons:
> Mon cher, c'est à ce livre, à son intention,
> Que je dois mon ouvrage et sa conception,
> Je le dis hautement. Si le méchant m'assiège,
> Qu'il sache que Rousseau lui-même me protège."
(Paris, Prault, 1791), 58.

[2] Cf. le portrait de l'Alceste de Fabre fait par Wilhelm Fischmann, que le savant allemand conclut en disant. " Alceste ist wohl noch ein Misanthrop, aber er ist menschlicher, sensibler, wohltätiger. Sein Menschenhass und seine Menschenverachtung entspringen dem Mitgefühl für diejenigen, die unter den Boshaften schuldlos zu leiden haben " (Greifswald, Julius Abel, 1930), 108.

[3] Je suis âpre, franc,... ennemi implacable et éternel de la flatterie, haut, fier, quoique timide... " (Cité par A. Aulard, " Figures oubliées de la Révolution," *La Nouvelle Revue*, XXXV, Paris, 1885, 65).

[4] Voir Georges de Froidecourt, " Fabre d'Eglantine, plaideur," *La Révolution Française* (1938 nouvelle série), XIII, 84.

N'oublions pas non plus que le succès d'une pièce à l'époque révolutionnaire, comme dans tous les temps d'ailleurs, dépendait souvent en grande partie du prestige des acteurs. Ceci était tellement vrai alors que des critiques dénoncèrent l'engouement des spectateurs pour certains acteurs et les accusèrent d'accorder une importance plus grande aux diverses interprétations qu'aux chefs-d'œuvre mêmes. Toujours est-il que pendant presque toute cette période le grand acteur Molé jouait, paraît-il, si bien l'Alceste de Molière et celui de Fabre qu'on serait justifié de croire que le monde courait plutôt applaudir son art que celui des deux auteurs.

Mais Molé jouait dans *le Misanthrope* un Alceste tout à fait différent de celui que nous connaissons. Cet acteur renommé travaillait avec Dorat-Cubières, poète médiocre, et révolutionnaire ardent, pour réviser, changer, même " mutiler," dit-on, le répertoire classique, surtout les pièces de Corneille, de Racine, de Voltaire et de Molière. Une de leurs tâches fut d'éliminer toutes les expressions à resonnance aristocratique, depuis " valet de chambre " jusqu'aux mots " cour," " vicomte," et " roi ". Car, pour les citoyens de la Révolution, il n'existait plus de valets de chambre ni de rois.[1]

Le livre de Molé intitulé *Le Misanthrope de Molière avec des variantes du Citoyen Molé*, Paris an II de la Révolution, est assez bien connu même aujourd'hui. Au dix-neuvième siècle cette adaptation de la comédie par l'acteur fut l'objet d'une attaque célèbre de Jules Janin. Dans de tels changements Janin vit des " crimes littéraires de la Terreur," commis par " une main impie." Il se trompait; il y avait plusieurs mains ! On n'a que l'embarras du choix parmi les passages éloquents et passionnés du fameux chapitre XIII de sa *Littérature dramatique*, passages pleins d'indignation vertueuse; quel est celui qui l'emporterait sur tous les autres ? Celui-ci peut-être ferait notre affaire: " Eh ! que voulez-vous que comprenne au Molière du XVII$^e$ siècle, la nation de 93, abrutie par l'alcool et par les discours des clubs, haletante dans les rues pour voir passer les morts qui la saluent, dévergondée, hideuse, sanglante, détachée violemment de son double passé royal et chrétien? Molière en 93, déchiré en lambeaux dans la coulisse et luttant avec peine contre les mélodrames et les tragédies du *Salut public*. O la triste immolation ! "

Comme *le Misanthrope*, *le Tartuffe* subit également des indignités. Les critiques auraient pu s'écrier avec Janin: " O la triste immolation ! " en entendant les acteurs dire:

" Ils sont passés ces jours d'injustice et de fraude, ... etc." au lieu de:
" Nous vivons sous un prince ennemi de la fraude, ... etc."

---

[1] Bien qu'il ait jugé nécessaire de corriger Molière, Cubières ne perdit pourtant jamais l'occasion de l'appeler le plus grand des Français. Dans la *Correspondance dramatique* (Paris, 1810), où il défend la pièce de Mercier, *la Maison de Molière*, et sa propre pièce, *la Mort de Molière*, il écrit: " Molière est notre dieu en littérature " (30). Et dans son *Epître à Molière* (Paris, s.d.) nous trouvons les vers suivants:

La Grèce eut des Myrons; la France des Coustous.
Tous ces Mortels sont grands, nous les admirons tous;
Ils marchent tous de front dans leur noble carrière,
Mais quel Mortel jamais fut l'égal de Molière ? (80)

Les argus du dix-neuvième siècle remarquèrent, du reste, que le dénouement du *Tartuffe* avait été à tel point remanié que " La République, au lieu du prince, exerce sa justice contre l'hypocrite démasqué." [1] Ces critiques se trouvaient cependant dans une position plus avantageuse que ceux qui vivaient à l'ombre du Tribunal Révolutionnaire. Les hommes de Lettres sous Louis-Philippe, par exemple, regardaient souvent d'un œil méfiant cette époque où la modération ne fut pas une vertu. On jugeait donc avec grande sévérité les variantes apportées par le citoyen Molé et d'autres. Changer un groupe de mots, quelques phrases dans l'œuvre dramatique de Molière et de ses confrères fut, pourtant, peu de chose à côté des 16,594 condamnations à mort prononcées dans le pays en dix-sept mois.[2] Du reste, ceux qui remaniaient les pièces de Molière ne faisaient que suivre les ordres du jour. Dans le décret de la Convention Nationale du 2 août 1793 relatif à la représentation des pièces de théâtre on peut lire ce qui suit: " Tout théâtre sur lequel seroient représentées des pièces tendant à dépraver l'esprit public, et à réveiller la honteuse superstition de la royauté, sera fermé, et les directeurs arrêtés et punis selon la rigueur des loix." [3]

Mais Molière lui-même fut dépeint pendant la Révolution comme un grand homme du passé en révolte contre l'ancien régime. Forcé de louer Louis XIV, disait-on, il faisait ses prologues mauvais, et détestables à plaisir.[4] Il employait les platitudes, les lieux communs les plus vulgaires avec une intention marquée, comme pour avertir la postérité du dégoût et de l'horreur qu'il avait pour un travail que lui imposaient les circonstances, son état, et la soif de répandre ses talents et sa philosophie.[5] Mais c'était une manière de justifier Molière qu'on trouve couramment exprimée pendant la Révolution.

Ainsi nous pouvons déjà voir que certaines conclusions du regretté Albert Thibaudet ne sont pas tout à fait acceptables. Il remarquait, il y a

---

[1] Voir A. Liéby, " L'ancien répertoire des théâtres de Paris à travers la réaction thermidorienne," *Révolutions françaises* (1905); cf. Victor Hallays-Dabot, *Histoire de la censure théâtrale en France*, Chap. VI, " La Censure pendant la Révolution " (Paris, 1862), 143-206.

[2] Provenant des recherches et des travaux de Donald Greer, ce nombre est généralement accepté par les historiens.

[3] Et pour corollaire C.-G. Etienne et A. Martainville nous disent dans la Préface à leur *Histoire du théâtre français* (Paris, an X, 1802), " Le trône et l'autel, journellement présentés sur le théâtre comme des objets d'horreur et de mépris, accoutumèrent le peuple à se jouer de ce qu'il avait long-temps vénéré " (I, iii). On dirait que la scène parisienne ne faisait que suivre les ordres du *Journal de la Montagne* où l'on lit pour le 11 septembre, 1793: " Plus de rois sur notre théâtre, s'ils n'y paraissent cruels, sanguinaires, barbares, ou faux hypocrites; en un mot, tels qu'ils sont. Plus de nobles, sinon avec les traits qui, depuis tant de siècles, ont caractérisé cette caste. Plus de prêtres, sinon démasqués."

[4] Aux yeux de Dorat-Cubières le grand crime du roi-soleil fut d'une netteté frappante:
Les beaux-arts autrefois n'étaient-ils pas esclaves
Des tyrans odieux?..........................
Louis, de Despréaux deshonora les pages
Et de Molière même il souilla les ouvrages "
(*Les Progrès des arts dans la République*, Paris, an V, 2.)

[5] *Révolutions de Paris* (an II, déc. 1790), no. 74, 457-458.

une trentaine d'années: " Rousseau et la Révolution l'avaient même traité, avec tous les écrivains de son temps, comme un suppôt de la tyrannie qui ridiculisait les Jacobins en la personne d'Alceste " (*Revue de Paris*, 1930, p. 367). Mais la réfutation de ce point de vue ne doit pas être limitée uniquement au *Misanthrope*. *Le Journal des spectacles* notait que *le Bourgeois gentilhomme* était, par exemple, plus révolutionnaire qu'on ne le pense.[1] Camille Desmoulins disait dans *le Vieux Cordelier:* " Molière dans *le Misanthrope* a peint en traits sublimes le caractère du républicain et du royaliste; Alceste est un jacobin; Philinte un feuillant achevé." [2] D'ailleurs, le *Journal de la Montagne* s'écriait en pleine Terreur: " Molière a démasqué, d'une manière heureuse, les fourberies des prêtres; son Tartuffe est volé à notre révolution." [3]

" Plus de prêtres sur nos scènes, sinon démasqués " devint un cri de ralliement pendant la Révolution.[4] Voilà une explication de la grande popularité de *Tartuffe*, des adaptations du *Tartuffe*, et des suites du *Tartuffe* pendant toute cette période. Un écrivain se plaint à la Préfecture de Police à Paris: " On donne le Tartufe partout ... pourquoi ne donnerait-on pas ma pièce ? " [5] Les attaques contre l'Eglise et le clergé finirent par devenir si acerbes sur la scène parisienne que le public commença à déplorer une telle violence prolongée contre un ennemi déjà terrassé.

Mais la Révolution, surtout au moment de la Terreur, n'eut aucune intention de fuir les extrêmes, quand même il se fût agi de Molière. Le ministre de l'Intérieur, par exemple, reçut une lettre en septembre 1793 caractérisant un aspect outré du jour: " Que les marquis cèdent la place aux patriotes, brûlons, s'il le faut, les chefs-d'œuvre de Molière.... Les arts y perdront quelque chose, mais à coup sûr, les mœurs y gagneront." [6]

---

[1] 9 frimaire l'an IIe (29 nov. 1793); pour confirmation de cette position, voir L. de La Pijardière, " Le Maître d'armes et le maître à danser pendant la Révolution," *Le Moliériste* (avril 1888), X, 2026.

[2] *Œuvres* (Paris, 1874), II, 254.

[3] 4 sept. 1793.

[4] Déjà en 1790 on lit dans *Révolutions de Paris*: " Le Tartufe [sic] a montré et mis à la portée du peuple le [sic] *jésuites* et le *jésuitisme*; pas à pas ces hypocrites impérieux, qui s'insinuoient dans les familles, se sont trouvés soumis à la comparaison que faisoient d'eux les pères, les mères, les fils et les filles, avec l'*hypocrite* de Molière; petit à petit les yeux se sont ouverts, la méfiance s'est étendue, la conviction en a résulté; et quand les jésuites attaqués ont crié au secours, ils n'ont trouvé que des ennemis. Telle est, nous l'osons dire, l'influence puissante des représentations." (No. 74, 456.)

[5] Les deux pièces dérivant du *Tartuffe* qui ont fait le plus de bruit à l'époque sont *Le Tartuffe révolutionnaire ou la suite de l'Imposteur* et *Papelard ou le Tartuffe philosophe et politique*. Il y avait aussi *Hypocrite en révolution*, par P. J. Bourlin [pseud. Dumaniant]. Par contre, parmi d'autres, l'*Autre Tartuffe, ou la mère coupable*, par Beaumarchais, n'eut qu'un succès modeste. On pourrait mentionner aussi: *Les Victimes cloîtrées, A Bas les calottes, ou les Déprêtrisés, L'Esprit des prêtres, Le Prélat d'autrefois, La Journée du Vatican, ou le mariage du pape, Le Prêtre réfractaire ou le nouveau Tartuffe* et *La Papesse Jeanne*.

[6] Cité par Alexandre Tuetey, *Répertoire général des sources manuscrites de l'histoire pendant la Révolution Française* (Paris 1916), IX, 382-383. Dans le même esprit, Aristide Valcour écrivait dans le *Journal de la Montagne*: " Il seroit à souhaiter que nous fussions assez sages pour nous priver, pendant au moins dix ans de la représentation de nos chefs-d'œuvres [sic] dramatiques " (66: 423, 6 août, 1793). De tels sentiments font l'objet mal

Et, en effet, on supprima *les Fourberies de Scapin* et *George Dandin* pour des raisons de moralité. A Angers on trouva même *le Médecin malgré lui* une " pièce absolument immorale." [1] A Caen, un poète se lamentait:
" Hélas ! Qu'êtes-vous devenus
Divin Molière ! O Regnard ! O Destouches ! " [2]

On voit ainsi que les réactions aux pièces de Molière furent nombreuses et variées pendant la décade entre 1789 et 1799, mais que le théâtre de

caché de *la Décade*: " c'est une mesure nécessaire à laquelle tout bon patriote doit souscrire. Mais du moins les Molière, les Corneille, les Racine ne seront jamais exclus d'aucune bibliothèque. L'homme de lettres ira encore s'instruire en silence avec ces grands maîtres; et jamais il ne sera défendu de rire avec *Scapin*, de politiquer avec *Cinna*, de pleurer avec *Andromaque*" (1:140, 30 floréal, an II—19 mai, 1794).

[1] Voir C. Post, " Molière immoral," *Le Moliériste* (1880), II, 94.

[2] L'histoire du théâtre dans les villes de Province pendant la Révolution a fait l'objet de nombreuses études. On retrouve presque toujours les mêmes attitudes: le rire et la comédie ne sont guère à la mode dans une époque d'idéalisme et de violence. Molière lui-même est souvent respecté comme par le passé, mais il arrive qu'un citoyen, animé d'un zèle patriotique et révolutionnaire trop enthousiaste, condamne son œuvre au nom de la pureté.

Sans vouloir donner une bibliographie complète du sujet, nous signalons les travaux suivants: A. A[ulard], " La Police des théâtres en l'an IV," *Révolution française* (1928), LXXXI. 245-246; Jean-Julien Barbé, " Le Théâtre à Metz pendant la Révolution (1790—an II)," *Annales historiques de la Révolution française* (1927), IV, 359-388; Ch. Boell, " Les spectacles républicains à Autun pendant la Révolution," *Mémoires de la Société Eduenne* (1908); Adolphe de Cardevacque, *Le Théâtre à Arras avant et après la Révolution* (Arras, 1884); E. G. de Clérambault, *Le Théâtre à Tours à l'époque de la Révolution* (Tours, 1916); Henri Clouzot, *Le Théâtre à Fontenay-le-Comte pendant la Révolution, le Consulat et l'Empire jusqu'en 1806* (Fontenay-le-Comte 1899); Victor Combarnous, *Notes et souvenirs: l'histoire du grand théâtre de Marseille (31 octobre 1787-13 novembre 1919)* (Marseille, 1927); Paul Courteault, *La Révolution et les théâtres à Bordeaux* (Paris, 1926); Lucien Decombre, *Recherches d'histoire locale, notes et souvenirs. Le Théâtre à Rennes* (Rennes, 1899); Robert Deschamps La Rivière, " Le Théâtre au Mans pendant la Révolution," *Revue historique et archéologique du Maine* (1901), XVIX, 78-100, 191-218, and L, 71-104; Etienne Destranges, *Le Théâtre à Nantes, depuis ses origines jusqu'à nos jours (1430-1893)* (Paris 1902); J. Durandeau, " Le Théâtre à Dijon pendant la Révolution," *Revue bleue* (1888), XLII. 748-750; Louis Duval, *Le Théâtre à Alençon au XVIIIe siècle* (Paris, 1912); Paul d'Estrée, *Le Théâtre sous la Terreur (1793-94)* (Paris, 1913); A. Fray Fournier, *Le Théâtre à Limoges avant, pendant et après la Révolution* (Limoges, 1900); Gaston-Martin, " Le Théâtre et la politique à Toulouse en l'an V," *Révolution Française* (1927), LXXX, 193-211; E. Gautier-Lachapelle, " Les Théâtres pendant la Révolution (d'après une étude inédite de M. Thomas Latour)," *L'Investigateur de l'Institut historique* (1856), 65-76; Gaston Lavalley, *La Censure théâtrale à Caen en l'an VII* (Caen, 1908); Paul de Longuemare, *Le Théâtre à Caen, 1628-1830* (Paris, 1895); P. Moulin, " Le Théâtre à Marseille pendant la Révolution," *Congrès des Sociétés Savantes de Province* (1906); Théodore Muret, *L'Histoire par le théâtre 1789-1851, Première série, La Révolution, le Consulat, l'Empire* (Paris, 1865); J. Noury, *Le Théâtre-Français de Rouen* (Rouen, s.d.); René Paquet, *Le Théâtre à Metz* (Metz, 1908); Jules Pellison, " Le Théâtre à Saintes pendant la Révolution," *Bulletin de la Société archéologique, historique et artistique* (1910-11), IX, 58-60; Edmond Poupe, *Le Théâtre à Toulon (1791-1792)*, Extrait du *Bulletin historique et philosophique* (1905) (Paris, Imprimerie nationale, 1906); Ulysse Rouchon, *Le Théâtre au Puy à la fin du XVIIIe siècle* (Paris, 1909); Henry Rousset, *Le Théâtre à Grenoble, histoire et physionomie, 1500-1890* (Grenoble, 1891); Gilbert Stenger, " Les Théâtres pendant le Consulat: les spectacles de l'an VIII," *Revue d'Art dramatique* (1903), 263-270; Aurélien Vivié, *Les Théâtres de Bordeaux pendant la Terreur (1793-1794): Fragments d'histoire d'après des documents inédits* (Bordeaux, 1868).

Molière lui-même, sans compter les adaptations et les imitations, eut un succès fort impressionnant. Il est difficile d'arriver au nombre exact de représentations à Paris pendant ces années à cause de la multiplicité des théâtres. Fondant mes chiffres sur Joannidès, qui dans ses tables de représentation ne comprend que les pièces jouées à la Comédie-Française, sur la table préparée par M. Listener pour la série *les Grands Ecrivains de la France*,[1] et sur mes recherches personnelles pour lesquelles j'ai dépouillé des périodiques révolutionnaires jour par jour, je suis arrivé aux chiffres suivants, chiffres qui sont assurément en deçà de la réalité.

Pendant cette dizaine d'années dix-huit pièces de Molière furent jouées plus de 500 fois. *Tartuffe* l'emportait sur toutes les autres avec 84 représentations; il était suivi de près par *l'Ecole des maris, le Médecin malgré lui* et *l'Avare*. Quant au *Misanthrope*, généralement considéré son chef-d'œuvre à l'époque, il n'eut que 34 représentations, peut-être parce que cette comédie partageait la scène et les talents de l'acteur Molé avec le *Philinte de Molière*.

Nous venons de parcourir la décade 1789-99, une des époques les plus mouvementées dans l'histoire de la France moderne. Elle provoqua comme on ne le sait que trop bien de profonds bouleversements dont les répercussions continuent à se faire sentir. Nous avons essayé d'examiner la fortune de Molière pendant ces années. Nous avons vu que la présence du grand poète comique se fit constamment sentir d'une façon ou d'autre. D'une manière générale, on peut remarquer un désir prolongé et déterminé de l'honorer et de le révérer. Une des premières manifestations de ce respect fut, ainsi que nous l'avons noté, l'extraordinaire engoûment qui se manifesta pour ses dépouilles mortelles. La majorité de ses pièces furent représentées durant cette période et connurent la plus grande popularité. L'homme Molière devint un héros qui, quoique sujet d'un monarque—et la royauté était alors synonyme de la tyrannie—sut néanmoins faire front à la tyrannie de l'Eglise et de l'Etat. On aima à retrouver dans ses pièces l'esprit même de la Révolution. Selon les exigences du jour, cependant, elles durent subir certains remaniements plus ou moins importants, comme d'ailleurs les pièces de Corneille, de Racine et de Voltaire. Selon des critiques du siècle suivant, elles furent même gravement mutilées. Le fait que suites, adaptations, imitations, " singeries " de ses pièces se multiplièrent alors est un témoignage de plus de sa popularité.[2] Ce n'est que durant la Terreur, quand la violence et l'intolérance atteignirent leur paroxysme, que quelques-unes de ses pièces furent bannies du théâtre au nom de la moralité et de la vertu.

---

[1] *Œuvres de Molière*, nouv. édition, éd. Eugène Despois (Paris, 1873), I, 550. La table de Listener est fondée sur les représentations données sur les cinq principaux théâtres autres que le Théâtre de la Nation pendant les années de la Révolution où les registres de la Comédie n'offrent aucune indication; ces théâtres sont: Théâtre de la République; Théâtre de l'Egalité; Théâtre Feydeau; Théâtre Louvois; Théâtre de l'Odéon—mais il y a au moins une demi-douzaine d'autres théâtres à Paris à cette époque.

[2] Rappelons entre autres: *Alceste à la campagne, Le Misanthrope corrigé, La Suite des précieuses, Le Dépit amoureux (en deux actes)*, sans compter plusieurs de ses comédies mises en musique; et comme nous l'avons déjà vu, un nombre considérable de pièces inspirées du *Tartuffe*. On trouve aussi de fréquentes allusions à Molière lui-même dans des pièces à la mode telles que: *La Maison de Molière, Le Souper de Molière, Les Deux Figaro, Molière à la nouvelle salle*, ainsi de suite.

Molière n'hésitait pas à poser des questions et parfois à proposer des réponses. Moraliste, il était partagé entre les problèmes qui assaillent l'individu et ceux qui, de façon plus générale et permanente, ressortissent à la condition humaine. Les Français des années 1790 ne remarquaient peut-être pas la fréquence des solutions bourgeoises qu'il apportait dans ses pièces aux problèmes de la vie quotidienne; mais Molière proposait aussi aux hommes un mode de vie, et il est fort possible que les révolutionnaires fervents l'aient ressenti plus clairement que nous ne faisons aujourd'hui. Rien d'étonnant à ce que l'ordre en question fût à l'image de celui que Molière admirait dans l'univers naturel, par opposition à l'univers spirituel des chrétiens; on sait en effet qu'il avait subi l'influence de Gassendi, et celle, plus éloignée, de Lucrèce. Cet ordre, adapté au plan humain, aurait fort bien pu devenir celui de l'ensemble de la bourgeoisie montante et, étant un ordre total, résoudre toutes les incongruités de l'existence. Mais Molière savait bien qu'un tel objectif ne pourrait être atteint rapidement. Il voyait de tous les côtés l'intrusion et l'imposture de l'apathie, de la médiocrité, de l'hypocrisie souvent encouragées, encore que de bonne foi, par la bourgeoisie elle-même. Ordre plus apparent que réel, et susceptible de créer le plus grave désordre intérieur parmi les membres de la société. Don Juan et Alceste réagissent là contre, le premier avec une énergie désespérée qui dépasse l'amertume du second. En quoi Molière lui-même pouvait-il croire? Il n'avait pas fréquenté Port-Royal, n'avait pas vécu en la compagnie de Saint François de Sales, Madame Acarie ou Bérulle pour fortifier son espoir en un Dieu tout-puissant et, peut-être, miséricordieux. Il ne pouvait placer son espoir qu'en l'humanité, et c'est de cet espoir que les révolutionnaires saisissaient parfois un éclair dans l'homme et dans ses pièces. Ce point de vue a, lui aussi, son origine dans l'âge des lumières.

D'une manière générale donc, la grandeur et le renom de Molière survécurent à la période révolutionnaire, qui donna même à son œuvre des dimensions nouvelles. Celles-ci allaient être exploitées dans la première moitié du siècle suivant par l'école romantique. Tartuffe deviendra un monstre sinistre, Don Juan, un grand humanitaire, Arnolphe, un homme aussi malheureux que le Werther de Goethe; et quant à Alceste, il pourra dire avec le Rousseau des *Confessions,* " Je suis autre." [1]

L'anecdote bien connue que nous raconte Paul Stapfer dans son *Molière et Shakespeare* nous convaincra facilement que Molière survécut à la Révolution française et fut bien reconnu comme un génie universel: " En l'année 1800, un célèbre acteur anglais, Kemble, vint à Paris. Ses confrères de la Comédie-Française lui offrirent un banquet. A table on causa d'abord des poètes tragiques des deux nations; la supériorité de Shakespeare sur Racine et sur Corneille était vivement soutenue par l'Anglais contre ses hôtes, qui, par politesse ou par conviction, commençaient à céder le terrain, quand tout à coup le comédien Michaut s'écria: " D'accord, d'accord, Monsieur; mais que diriez-vous de Molière? " Kemble répondit tranquillement: " Molière? c'est une autre question. Molière n'est pas un Fran-

---

[1] Cf. O. Fellows, *French Opinion of Molière (1800-1850),* (Providence, 1937).

çais."—" Bah ! un Anglais, peut-être ? "—" Non, Molière est un homme."
… Devant lui s'évanouissent les petites différences de temps et de lieux; aucun peuple, aucun siècle ne peut le revendiquer comme sien; il est à tous les âges et à toutes les nations." [1]

Si cette anecdote n'était pas véridique, elle mériterait de l'être. Pendant une dizaine d'années la Révolution avait donné une nouvelle valeur à Molière comme elle l'avait fait pour Corneille, Racine, Montesquieu, Buffon, et tant d'autres grands écrivains de l'ancien régime. Malgré la violence parfois faite à Molière, à l'homme et à son œuvre, au nom du nouvel ordre, ordre marqué par l'emportement et l'idéalisme, le grand poète comique en est sorti l'égal de Voltaire et de Rousseau—c'est-à-dire non seulement un des plus grands hommes de lettres de la France, mais aussi comme une arme politique des plus redoutables contre les forces réactionnaires du passé.

Tout cela est d'autant plus étonnant que Molière émergeait, avec éclat, d'une époque où l'art théâtral, comme la littérature pure, comptait pour relativement peu de chose. C'était une période où le bourgeois, le marchand et l'artisan jouèrent pour la première fois un rôle capital dans les affaires publiques. Ce sont ces hommes-là, autrefois si peu importants et sur la scène politique et comme spectateurs au théâtre, qui couraient au spectacle et y faisaient prévaloir leur propre goût. A cette époque ce sont les pièces faisant appel aux émotions plutôt qu'aux ressources de l'esprit qui étaient le plus à la mode. Comme l'a fait remarquer un critique qui avait vécu ces années de bouleversement des vieilles valeurs traditionnelles, [2] " la tragédie s'est soutenue dans une médiocrité honorable, et la comédie est dans le plus grand dépérissement " (p. 19). C'était un moment où les dramaturges de talent, tenant à faire plaisir au nouveau public, s'adonnèrent d'abord au drame, puis à un genre qui faisait beaucoup souffrir la bonne comédie— le mélodrame avec ses coups de théâtre sensationnels, ses cris d'horreur, et son amour du sang répandu sur la scène. En dépit de tout cela, Molière, auteur de pièces comiques où dominaient le naturel et la finesse ainsi que le bon sens, fit partie avec Voltaire et Rousseau, de la trinité des trois hommes de lettres les plus vénérés en France au temps où la Révolution touchait à son terme.

---

[1] Paul Stapfer, *Shakespeare et Molière* (Paris, 1887), 23-24.

[2] Alexandre Ricord, *Quelques Réflexions sur l'art théâtral* (Paris, 1811). Il y avait pourtant ceux qui étaient capables de voir le côté amusant de la question. Ainsi, le 5 janvier 1793, on voit à Paris pour la première fois *la Chaste Suzanne*, petite pièce en deux actes agrémentée de couplets dans laquelle l'Ecriture sainte et le Vaudeville se mêlent. Dans le dénouement on se moque du théâtre de l'époque tout en faisant l'éloge de Molière. Voici le refrain de Suzanne:

> " De noirs effets pour du tragique,
> Du calembour pour du comique,
> Du bel esprit pour du plaisant,
> Voilà le théâtre à présent.
> Mais réunir, comme Molière,
> Dans une intrigue régulière,
> Et la morale et l'enjoûment,
> Oh ! c'est de l'ancien testament."

II

# THE NINETEENTH CENTURY

# RACHEL AND AMERICA*

## A RE-APPRAISAL

"Je vais bien, et la jeune Amérique va seule gagner des cheveux blancs aux émotions que lui donneront nos belles tragédies." [1]

So wrote Rachel to her mother in Paris with the steamboat *Pacific* almost in sight of New York. For more than fifteen years the great *tragédienne* had ruled supreme on the Parisian stage. The crowned heads of Europe had showered her with praise and jewels as she turned from one capital to another. London, Vienna, Berlin, Saint Petersburg: a series of amazing dramatic triumphs. And now the toast of a continent, Rachel Félix, unsurpassed as an interpreter of the French classical theatre, was to visit this youthful America. The boat docked at New York August 22, 1855.

Despite inadequate documentation, biographers of Rachel have not hesitated to give considerable space to her American sojourn. But whether it is called "la désastreuse expédition," "the American fiasco," that "lamentable randonnée d'Amérique," or "ce fatal voyage," the exposure is uniformly depressing.[2]

Most critics agree that Rachel's American tour was a failure for three reasons. First, financially it fell far below the expectations of Raphael Félix, brother of the actress and actor-manager of the company. True, the sum of 119,758 dollars for approximately thirty-seven performances in New York, Boston, Philadelphia and Charleston, was more than Rachel had made on any similar tour of Europe.[3] The fact remained that not so long before, Jenny Lind had returned to Europe bearing three times as many American dollars. Second, it was during Rachel's stay in the United States that her consumption-racked body broke down entirely. Indeed,

---

* Reprinted from *Romanic Review* (December, 1939), 402-413.

[1] G. d'Heylli, *Rachel d'après sa correspondance*, Paris, 1882, 208.

[2] See A. de Faucigny-Lucinge, *Rachel et son temps*, Paris, 1910, 208; F. Gribble, *Rachel: Her Stage Life and Her Real Life*, London, 1911, 235; J. Lucas-Dubreton, *Rachel*, Paris, 1936, 181.; H. Fleischmann, *Rachel Intime d'après ses lettres d'amour et des documents nouveaux*, Paris, 1910, 274. Furthermore, the present fourteenth edition of the *Encyclopedia Britannica* refers to Rachel's "tour in the United States ... with comparatively small success," and the *Larousse du XX<sup>e</sup> Siècle*, apropos of her trip to the United States, speaks of "les déboires de cette expédition."

[3] A. de Barréra, *Memoirs of Rachel*, London, 1858, II, 246.

her appearance at Charleston was her last on any stage.[1] The circumstance was an appropriate curtain for lugubrious accounts of Rachel's vicissitudes in America. The third, and from the point of view of the present study, the most important reason for the assumed failure of Rachel's undertaking was an utter lack of appreciation on the part of the American public. One of her French biographers writes: " Ces fils de la navigation et du commerce, d'un esprit mercantile, qui plaçaient à cette époque leur intelligence uniquement à vaincre les difficultés matérielles de l'existence, avaient une foi inébranlable dans leur force et leur valeur personnelles car chacun en ce pays peut développer librement ce qu'il renferme en lui d'aptitudes diverses, mais dépourvus de tout lyrisme, de toute sensibilité, ils ne pouvaient donc être frappés subitement par les beautés du répertoire classique de Racine et de Corneille." [2]

From England we hear: " In America of the mid-nineteenth century, no amount of praise could popularize an entertainment so cold and refined as that provided by Rachel. The facts, much as they may seem to reflect on the level of artistic taste in the Eastern States, are capable of only one interpretation—that, in contradistinction to what had previously happened in Europe, the appearance of Rachel among the American people created only the mildest and shortest-lived excitement." [3]

These representative opinions are not based on a careful perusal of American periodicals in 1855, but merely on two documents utilized *ad nauseam* by successive biographers. The first of these is Léon Beauvallet's *Rachel et le nouveau monde, promenades aux Etats-Unis et aux Antilles*, Paris, 1856.[4] Beauvallet, an actor in Rachel's company, hoped by his rattle-headed vivacity and his farcical descriptions,[5] to win a wide reading public for his experience of American life while traveling in this country.

The second document is Jules Janin's *feuilleton* " Rachel et la tragédie aux Etats-Unis," published in the *Journal des Débats* [6] shortly after Rachel's arrival in New York. This article which beseeched the actress, " Faites

---

[1] James Agate expresses the sentiments of most of Rachel's biographers when he points out that her American venture brought not only disappointment, but ill health as well (*Rachel*, New York, 1928, 162). Louis Barthou is much nearer the truth when he states that previous to her American tour, Rachel's health had already been " ruinée par les fatigues du théâtre et par les jeux de l'amour " (*Rachel*, Paris, 1926, 148).

[2] A. de Faucigny-Lucinge, *op. cit.*, 213.

[3] B. Falk, *Rachel the Immortal*, London, [1935], 273.

[4] Translated into English the same year, the book was dismissed by American letters as a ridiculously absurd exaggeration of the experiences of Raphael Félix's dramatic troupe in the western hemisphere. See *Southern Literary Messenger*, July, 1856, 80; *Harper's New Monthly Magazine*, XIII, 407; *North American Review*, LXXIV, 561-562; *Putnam's Magazine*, VIII, 100. Fleischmann is mistaken in affirming that the book is " aujourd'hui introuvable " (*op. cit.*, 274). Copies are readily accessible on both sides of the Atlantic.

[5] The seriousness of Beauvallet's intentions may be gathered by the following description of the Lafayette Guard trying to serenade Rachel during a rain storm: " In the gutters, now swelled into rivers, flageolets and double basses were seen floating at the mercy of the waters ! " (*Rachel and the New World*, Dix, Edwards, New York, 1856, 191).

[6] October 15, 1855.

comprendre à ces marchands, fils de la navigation et du commerce, les grandes pensées exprimées en si beaux vers," infuriated a sensitive American public only too eager to look well in the eyes of Europe. It is not surprising then that our newspapers arose as one to counterattack the indiscreet Parisian dramatic critic.[1]

Now Janin's remarks concerning the low cultural level of the American theatre-goers might have passed unnoticed among Rachel's European biographers had not Beauvallet reprinted the article in its entirety in his own book. As a result of these two documents in one, we find in studies pertaining to the actress repeated duplication of the declarations of both these early critics. For instance Beauvallet's statement that the American spectator preferred Rachel's interpretations of the French nineteenth-century theatre [2] to those of French classical tragedy.[3] This assertion has been repeated in at least five biographies [4] and yet, as we shall see, there is abundant evidence to prove that the contrary is the case.

The question immediately arises as to what extent the French dramatists in general, later to be illustrated by the great actress, were known to the American reader during the first half of the nineteenth century.

American literary critics themselves acknowledged that this country's tastes regarding French letters were influenced by English prejudices. Reprints of observations and articles on French writers first published in England are not uncommon in periodicals before the turn of the century. Consequently, reflecting British criticism, America found Corneille stiff, formal and demoded and Racine artificial, effeminate and deficient in the higher essentials of drama. However, though cultural America did not always receive the outstanding writers of the age of Louis XIV with the greatest warmth, it accepted them as monuments of a great cultural tradition.[5]

Again following the footsteps of the English, American critics refused to accept whole-heartedly the French romantics. All in all, men of letters agreed with James Rees that " The plays of Dumas and Victor Hugo are

---

[1] Students of Rachel have failed to point out that Janin subsequently acknowledged, although with a certain anonymity, the injustice of his notorious *feuilleton*. In his *Rachel et la Tragédie*, Paris, 1859, 500, we read: " Un ami de mademoiselle Rachel, la voyant éperdue et perdue en ces pays si nouveaux, écrivit de Paris un injuste feuilleton où il déclarait que les Américains étaient indignes d'entendre *Andromaque, Athalie, Esther*.... Les Etats-Unis répondirent, ce qui était vrai, qu'ils étaient restés les sincères et sympathiques admirateurs de ces chefs-d'œuvre et de leur interprète."

[2] Particularly Hugo's *Angelo*, and *Adrienne Lecouvreur* of Scribe and Legouvé.

[3] *Op. cit.*, 146.

[4] G. d'Heylli, *op. cit.*, 212-213; A. de Barréra, *op. cit.*, II, 246; A. de Faucigny-Lucinge, *op. cit.*, 218; N. H. Kennard, *Rachel*, Boston, 1886, 276-277; T. Martin, " Rachel," *Monographs*, London, 1906, 262.

[5] Cf. *Mirror of Taste and Dramatic Literature*, III (Philadelphia, 1811); *Southern Literary Messenger*, VIII (December 1842) and IX (February 1843); H. W. Longfellow, *The Poets and Poetry of Europe*, revised edition, Philadelphia, 1871; S. T. Goodrich, *Literature Ancient and Modern*, Boston, 1845, 222; *North American Rewiev*, 231-232 (January 1854).

of the worst class, chiefly founded upon some portions of history which it would have been well had they never been recorded." [1]

Insinuations of Rachel's biographers to the contrary, we do see that the more critical of the American public had definite ideas concerning French playwrights during the first part of the century. Furthermore, before the advent of the actress, the theatre-goer had ample opportunity to see French drama behind the footlights. Of the fourteen plays performed by Rachel in this country [2] at least five had been produced repeatedly, usually in translations or adaptations, before 1855. Of the classical theatre *Andromaque* had been played in the original as early as 1827,[3] and Ambrose Philips' *The Distressed Mother* was familiar to American audiences even before this date.[4] *The Roman Father*, founded on *Horace*, represented Corneille. Of the later playwrights, Hugo's *Angelo* was performed under two adaptations,[5] as was Dumas' *Mlle. de Belle-Isle*.[6] In Latour's *Virginie* was recognized the same subject as treated by Sheridan Knowles in his well known *Virginius*.[7] Scribe's *Adrienne Lecouvreur* had been played numerous times both in New York and in the provinces previous to Rachel's appearance.[8]

For those not acquainted with the French theatre through actual performances other opportunities were offered before Rachel's arrival. Appropriate public lectures and readings were given both in New York and Boston.[9] Furthermore, finishing schools were exercising their students in reading the principal plays in which Rachel was to appear, as a part of the regular school routine.[10] Ever since 1843 there had been noted a passion for French literature in this country [11] and by 1855 the names of great French playwrights were not to ring unfamiliarly in American ears.

---

[1] "The French Theatre," *Dramatic Mirror*, February 26, 1842.

[2] Rachel appeared in the following plays during her American tour: *Adrienne Lecouvreur, Andromaque, Angelo, Bajazet, Horace, Jeanne d'Arc, Lady Tartuffe, Mlle. de Belle-Isle, Marie Stuart, Le Moineau de Lesbie, Phèdre, Polyeucte, Virginie*. She also gave readings from *Athalie, Esther, Le Cid* and *Le Misanthrope*, recited the *Marseillaise* and read in public the poem " Rachel à l'Amérique " by Régis de Trobriand, editor of the *Courrier des Etats-Unis*.

[3] H. M. Jones, *America and French Culture, 1750-1848*, Chapel Hill, 1927, 34.

[4] A. H. Quinn, *A History of the American Drama*, New York, 1923, I, 24.

[5] Richard Penn Smith's and John Brougham's.

[6] Cf. R. H. Ware, *American Adaptations of French Plays on the New York and Philadelphia Stages from 1834 to the Civil War*, Philadelphia, 1930, 11.

[7] New York *Herald*, November 14, 1855; New York *Tribune*, November 15, 1855.

[8] New York *Times*, September 7, 1855. Two plays used as curtain raisers, *Le Chapeau d'un Horloger* and *Le Dépit amoureux*, were played by the company without Rachel. They were already well known to the American public as *Betty Martin* and *The Lovers' Quarrels* (cf. Boston *Advertiser*, October 23, 1855; Boston *Journal*, October 24, 1855).

[9] Particularly the lectures of Robert Kemp (see G. C. D. Odell, *Annals of the New York Stage*, VI, 179), those of J. F. Astié, published as *Louis XIV and the Writers of His Age* (Jewett, Boston, 1855) and the popular readings of M. Malignon (cf. Boston *Advertiser*, October 15, 1855).

[10] Boston *Advertiser*, October 15, 1855.

[11] Cf. *The Knickerbocker*, XXII (November 1843), 503.

But what of the tragic actress herself? Soon after Rachel's successful début at the Comédie Française, her reputation reached the shores of the New World. Her triumphs in Paris and elsewhere were faithfully recorded in American newspapers and periodicals. The slightest incident attached to her name became news for the dailies [1] and more detailed accounts appeared in leading reviews on the Atlantic coast.[2]

By 1838 trips to France were extremely common and American travellers abroad such as Longfellow, Edwin Forrest, Olive Logan, T. Allston Brown, George W. Curtis, Samuel Goodrich, Augustus Gardner, James Jarves, and Horace Greeley, saw Rachel in Paris and many of them wrote of their experience in works published before 1855.

In the early fifties Rachel's name as a great actress was a by-word in this country. And yet Raphael Félix was a cautious man. By a series of publications he sought to educate further the American public. The first of these was a pamphlet entitled *The Biography of Mdlle. Rachel with Contemporary Criticisms by the most Eminent Writers, and Analytical Notices of the Characters in Her Repertoire Written and Compiled from European Authorities and Edited by John Darcie.*[3] Here we find the scandalous stories concerning Rachel (already common knowledge in America) emphatically denied.[4] We are told of her reception throughout Europe and are informed as to what scenes in the various plays citizens of the United States should applaud. The American editor in a preface frankly lays the case before the public and concludes: " Europe has unanimously pronounced Mlle. Rachel to be the greatest tragédienne of the age—nay, perhaps the greatest classic artiste that ever lived; and it only remains to be seen if the New World will, in its young and vigorous judgment, confirm the verdict of the Old."

---

[1] For instance, examining the *New World* over a period of three months we note: November 9, 1839, mention of a throat ailment; January 11, 1840, her return to the Paris stage; February 8, 1840, description of her performance in *Cinna*; also February 8, 1840, Rachel anecdote.

[2] Among these may be mentioned the following: " Mademoiselle Rachael [sic], The French Tragic," *Dramatic Mirror*, I (August 14, 1841); " From our Paris Correspondent," *Southern Literary Messenger*, XV (March 1849), 180-184; " Mademoiselle Rachel," *Littell's Living Age*, XXVI (July, 1850), 356; " Louis Philippe and Mademoiselle Rachel," *Eclectic Magazine*, XXXIII (December, 1854), 525-532; " Rachel," *Putnam's Magazine*, VI (September, 1855), 290-298; " Rachel," *Harper's New Monthly Magazine*, XI (October, 1855), 681-687.

[3] John Darcie and Wardle Corbyn, New York, 1855; it is possible that Gustave Naquet, publicity manager for Félix's American enterprise, was the real author of this brochure.

[4] Obviously a puritanical reaction was expected even by Rachel's manager in what concerned her rather tempestuous life. As a matter of fact, New York newspapers were to comment upon the small number of women in the audience at her American début. However, it was not long before women were almost as numerous as men in the audiences which applauded her. An interesting letter by a Boston gentleman published in the Boston *Daily Journal* (October 8, 1855) would lead us to believe that, in particular, the wealthy and fashionable people of this center of puritanism were more than willing to accept Rachel. We read: " I know upwards of one hundred gentlemen who intend to spend at least one hundred dollars each for their families to see Rachel at the Boston theatre in her best rôles."

Félix's other publications consisted of the chief plays to be given with the original French in one column and a poor English translation in the other. These pamphlets were so widely utilized in the theatres of Boston and New York that Rachel was disquieted each time her audience turned the page in unison.

And so in the words of Darcie's booklet the time had come for Rachel " to imprint the mark of her genius upon the history of the stage of the New World."

The consensus of opinion in Europe with echoes in the United States had been that Rachel's tour in America was doomed, not only to financial failure but to complete artistic failure as well. But let us glance rapidly at the reactions recorded in the periodical literature of the day.[1]

The editor of *Harper's Monthly* writes: " Rachel has come, and seen, and conquered. Here in New York we have all been talking about her. We have all rubbed up our French and been to see her. We have grown suddenly familiar with French tragedy. ' What a great poet is Corneille ! ' we have discovered; we, who had all thought the French drama to be only the synonym of stately stupidity. ' How soft and sweet is Racine ! ' we have all murmured; we, who had supposed Racine to be only a rhymer of grand old Greek stories.... Jenny Lind's first night was an event. Grisi's hardly. Alboni's and Sontag's not so.... But Rachel's first night was truly triumphant." [2] The *Courrier des Etats-Unis* speaks of her American début in the following terms: " Parmi les soirées mémorables que nous avons vues à New York ... nous en cherchons vainement d'une grandeur aussi réelle, d'un enthousiasme aussi sincère." [3] The New York *Times, Tribune, Daily News, Sun* and *Advertiser* were equally moved. But it was not the approbation of a day. A paragraph appearing more than a month later in the *Tribune* was typical of the acclaim which continued to greet Rachel: " Last night was indeed a night memorable both for Rachel and those who saw her. The one was more inspired, the other more enthusiastic than on any previous occasion. There can be no doubt that a crowd surging and swelling from parquet to ceiling, by sending a thrilling influence on the heart of the actress and reflecting the electric touch back upon the audience creates in a great degree that wondrous grandeur in conception, and perfection in execution, which made the Camille of last night more sublime in her bursts of indignation and more thrilling in her pangs of agony than the Camille of any former evening." [4]

The *United States Review* comments: " We have seen the great French tragedian, and are obliged to register our opinion, that she is the greatest artist in her line who has ever trodden on the boards in New York. She has brought us a new style, and made us acquainted with a purely new school of acting.[5] The editor of *Putnam's Magazine* points out that in acting

---

[1] Rachel opened in New York September 3 and closed at Charleston December 17.
[2] XI (November 1855), 842-843.
[3] September 4, 1855.
[4] October 9, 1855.
[5] " Rachel at the Metropolitan," V (October 1855), 349.

before an American audience Rachel has been successful in that she " has mastered the mind and reached the heart of a strange people, who care nothing for classical proprieties." [1]

Boston was no less warm in its reception of the actress. The *Journal* confesses that all that had been said by the New York press was completely justified.[2] The *Atlas* is in raptures [3] and the *Courier* is certain that her New York début was less elegant and grandiose than the one in Boston [4] while the *Advertiser* describes in detail the sensation caused by her initial appearance in " The New Athens." [5]

Even the last performance of Rachel's entire career—that of Charleston —though described by biographer Gribble as having been " played to a thin and almost indifferent house," [6] seems to have been a triumph. The Charleston *Weekly News* notes that days in advance good tickets were difficult to procure,[7] and both this journal [8] and the Charleston *Courier* [9] testified that a crowded theatre gave the actress a tremendous ovation for this her only performance in the south.

Finally, we have Rachel's own impression concerning her American experience as given by one of her acquaintances. We are told: " She [Rachel] spoke with evident delight and gratitude of her kind reception here, and was agreeably surprised to meet, both in the press and the auditorium, that peculiar kind of appreciation (*appréciation nuancée*) which is at once encouraging to the feelings and stimulating to the efforts of an artist." [10]

The point must be immediately made, however, that the feeling was widespread that Rachel rather than Corneille, Racine or Hugo imbued the tragedies presented with a reality of power, a significance and a sense of actuality not their own.[11] In this respect, to be sure, America concurred with France, for during the previous decade the Comédie Française had been poorly attended whenever Rachel was not among the cast.

---

[1] V (October 1855), 446; cf. *The Knickerbocker*, XLVI (November 1855), 550 and A. H. Guernsey's article in *Harper's Monthly* entitled " Rachel," XI (October 1855), 681-687.

[2] October 23, 1855.

[3] October 23, 1855.

[4] October 23, 1855.

[5] October 23, 1855; it is true, however, that a certain coldness became manifest in the Boston press for a few days resulting from a controversy with the unscrupulous Raphael Félix.

[6] *Op. cit.*, 245.

[7] December 14, 1855.

[8] December 20, 1855.

[9] December 18, 1855.

[10] C. Marie, " My Acquaintanceship with Rachel," *Harper's Monthly*, XVI (May 1858), 808.

[11] This notion is found in the following newspapers and reviews: New York *Tribune*, October 4, 9, 15, 26, November 15; New York *Herald*, October 9; Boston *Advertiser*, October 23; *Saturday Evening Gazette*, October 27, *Harper's Monthly*, XI, 126, 687, 843; *Putnam's Magazine*, VI, 406, 448; VII, 335.

Since, in the mind of the American public, Rachel's interpretative genius was so closely bound up with the tragedies she was portraying, it is sometimes difficult to determine precisely what opinions were held concerning Corneille and Racine. Frequently it was a question as to whether the *tragédienne* was more convincing in *Phèdre*, or *Horace*, in the rôle of Monime or that of Pauline. Nevertheless, evidence seems to point to the fact that *Phèdre*, although less familiar to the theatre-going public, made the greatest impression on the American mind.[1] The New York *Tribune* makes a compromise: " If Camille is the most beautiful and touching of Rachel's characters Phèdre is the most powerful and exciting. Complications and contrasts of passion reach their highest point in this most tragic of all plays." [2] The *Times* finds that *Phèdre* has the advantage over most French productions, for its style is chaste while the language is pathetic and intense. Consequently Racine is more popular than Corneille and with justice.[3]

In both New York and Boston the recalcitrants were won over by Racine's tragedy. We read a representative observation: " What pure and sorrowful Camille had failed to do was done by the superb Phèdre, victim of Fate, vainly contending against passions inspired by an implacable deity and the crimes by which they sought gratification and safety." [4] Just how deep an impression did this play make on the capital of Massachusetts? We know that after Rachel's departure an adaptation in English was made for the Boston stage and first played there in January 1858 although it did not reach New York until after the Civil War.[5]

Now if it is true that Rachel's genius was acknowledged on every hand it is equally true that her American public refused to give its unqualified approval to the French classic drama. The evidence in hand indicates that there are two principal reasons for this: French classical verse form and Shakespeare.

The American traveler in Paris had already found alexandrine verse, with its ever recurring rhyme, disagreeable to the foreign ear.[6] Consequently we are not surprised to find the spectator of 1855 warned that French tragedy is written in rhymed couplets [7] which are referred to as " unyielding alexandrines." [8] The *Times* finds this type of verse form " a kind of barrel

---

[1] The editor of *Putnam's Magazine* would not have agreed. With *Horace* in mind he writes: " Nothing that she [Rachel] performs so moves, exalts, and kindles the spectator's mind and heart as do the harrowing scenes which paint the agitations, the despair, and the frenzy of the Roman maiden " (VI [November 1855], 558).

[2] October 26, 1855.

[3] September 5, 1855.

[4] New York *Tribune*, October 26, 1855; cf. New York *Evening Post*, September 5, 1855; *Boston Atlas*, October 24, 1855; *Saturday Evening Gazette*, October 27, 1855.

[5] Ware, op. cit., 43.

[6] A. K. Gardner, *Old Wine in New Bottles*, New York, 1848.

[7] *Boston Atlas*, October 22, 1855.

[8] *Harper's Monthly*, XI (October 1855), 687.

organ music that grows very wearisome."[1] and the *Tribune* observes that *Virginie* would be a pleasant play " were it not for the monotonous Alexandrian measure, dropping ceaselessly the same sound at the close of every line, and thus exciting the same sweet but sleep-disposing influence as the fall of waters or the hum of bees."[2] Because of this insistence on verse form, asserts *Putnam's Magazine*, " the story grows languid, the interest of the plot disappears. The characters are really so many charming declaimers of charming lines."[3]

To be sure, it was admitted that all strong emotion tends to express itself in rhythmic form from whence it was indeed concluded that the blank verse of Shakespeare was an appropriate vehicle for tragedy. However the use of formal couplets in French classical tragedy was criticised as being carried to an unnatural excess.[4]

Such a reaction is to be expected. American dramatic appreciation was steeped in the tradition of Shakespeare. One actress, writing of the fifties, says: " Editions of his [Shakespeare's] works succeed each other with astonishing rapidity, and in no country has the great dramatist called forth to his illustration of late years, higher genius, profounder knowledge, or better taste than our own."[5] And another writes: "At least twenty-four of our forty-two week season was given over to Shakespearian productions, and every actor and actress had the Bard on their tongue's tip."[6] The *Courrier des Etats-Unis* foresaw that America's penchant for Shakespeare might harm Rachel's chances of success in this country, when it published shortly before her New York début the following warning: " Pour éviter le danger des désillusions, et l'impression fâcheuse d'un désappointement, il ne faut s'attendre à aucune de ces violences d'actions, de ces successions d'événements qui abondent dans la tragédie anglaise; il faut oublier ces moissons de situations qui mûrissent d'acte en acte, de scène en scène, dans les immortels chefs-d'œuvre de l'immortel Shakespeare."[7]

Despite this admonition, disappointment was felt and the French classics were frequently compared with Shakespeare to the advantage of the latter. Still critical opinion was not unusually severe as a typical comment in the *North American Review* shows: " In the drama, although it must be conceded that France has produced no unique [sic] like our own inspired and immortal Shakespeare, yet the names of Corneille, Racine, and Molière, will redeem her stage from any charge of intellectual poverty."[8]

Did Raphael Félix include modern drama in his sister's repertoire partially in the hope of catering to America's taste for Shakespearian

---

[1] September 5, 1855.

[2] November 15, 1855; cf. *Saturday Evening Gazette*, October 27, 1855.

[3] VI (October 1855), 404.

[4] See *Harper's Monthly*, XI (October 1855), 686-687.

[5] O. Logan, *Before the Footlights and Behind the Scenes*, Philadelphia, 1870, 401.

[6] C. Morris, *Life on the Stage*, New York, 1901, 33.

[7] September 3, 1855.

[8] LXXXI (October 1855), 333.

action? If so, the stratagem failed. The French nineteenth-century theatre was no more highly esteemed at the time of Rachel's sojourn than previously. During both periods America's dislike for the French romantics appears chiefly ascribable to the pseudo-immorality of their dramas. *Putnam's Magazine* states: " The dramas of Hugo and Dumas reflected nothing—it was no intellectual mirror of man or nature.... The materialism, the vague and feverish ambition, the discontent, the imperious passions, and the imbecile will of a transitional and discordant age passed from the characters of the men themselves into their works. To call them scholars of Shakespeare is simply an absurdity, and almost a blasphemy. They have but one thing in common with Shakespeare—the number of their dramatis personae." [1]

*Angelo* represented Hugo in Rachel's presentations and the *Herald* dismissed it as " three hours of trash," [2] while the *Evening Post* tersely remarked that the game was not worth the candle.[3] In Boston the play was less well received than Corneille and Racine because " The taste for Victor Hugoisms is not very violent in Boston and *Angelo* is one of the worst of that class of literary monstruosities [sic]." [4]

Scribe's *Adrienne Lecouvreur* was considered " a mere melodrama, a vaudeville of costume, with a frightful catastrophe appended." [5] Along with *Angelo, Jeanne d'Arc, Mlle. de Belle-Isle* and *Marie Stuart* it was considered vastly inferior to Corneille and Racine by the press of New York and Boston and was less cordially received by the spectator.[6]

America's ultimatum was expressed by an anonymous critic as early as October 1855: " The modern drama of France boasts, as yet, no name worthy to be compared with those of the great classicists.... And lofty as must be the place accorded to Corneille and to Racine, in the world's regard, France has not yet produced a dramatic writer worthy to stand with Aeschylus and Euripides, with Calderon and with Goethe, around the throne of Shakespeare." [7]

We may conclude, Rachel's biographers notwithstanding, that the great actress did *not* play before an American audience both totally ignorant of and apathetic toward her offerings. Could her own remembrance of her reception in the United States have been a bitter one? Twice in letters written after her departure she expressed the desire to return to America.[8]

---

[1] VI (October 1855), 410.

[2] September 20, 1855.

[3] September 20, 1855.

[4] Boston *Atlas*, October 25, 1855; cf. Boston *Courier*, October 24, 1855.

[5] *Putnam's Magazine*, VI (October 1855), 297.

[6] Cf. New York *Times*, September 7, 1855; New York *Evening Post*, September 7, 1855; New York *Herald*, September 10. November 9, 1855; *Courrier des Etats-Unis*, September 15, 1855; Boston *Courier*, October 25, 1855; Boston *Atlas*, October 25, 1855; Boston *Advertiser*, October 29, 1855.

[7] *Putnam's Magazine*, VI, 410.

[8] *Harper's Monthly*, XVI (May 1858), 811; Heylli, *op. cit.* 234.

America most certainly thought her tour in the New World was a success. From a variety of quarters it was pointed out that her visit could not but have both a permanent literary as well as artistic influence on American culture [1] and shortly after her departure from New York the *Tribune* has this to say: " Perhaps the cultivated taste of America was never put to a severer test than in this instance, in which a great artist trusts for victory to her art alone, and that art exhibited in a tongue to which a majority of her audience are strangers. She came and her victory may almost be described in the terse, triumphant words of Caesar." [2] That Rachel had left her mark may be deduced from the fact that a French theatre opened in New York in the late fifties in which artists from the Théâtre-Français, the Odéon and the Théâtre des Variétés acted.[3]

England and France had both said that should Rachel attempt to carry her art and her genius across the ocean she would meet with disappointment and failure. America replied: " She brought the New World the most consummate excellence which the culture of the Old World has produced, and she found us ready to receive, to enjoy, and to appreciate." [4]

---

[1] *Putnam's Magazine*, VII (March 1856), 335; *Harper's Monthly*, XII (May 1856), 852; *The Knickerbocker*, XLVI (November 1855), 550; *North American Review*, LXXXIV (April 1857), 527.

[2] November 18, 1855.

[3] See Odell, *op. cit.*, VII, 163-165, 338-340.

[4] *Putnam's Magazine*, VII (March 1856), 335.

## *MADAME BOVARY*, CENT ANS APRÈS *

Le " succès de scandale " ne date certes pas d'hier. Au siècle dernier, comme de nos jours, un écrivain inconnu pouvait devenir célèbre en quelques heures, pour peu qu'il ait eu la chance de voir la publication de son premier ouvrage déclencher les foudres des Pouvoirs. Outrages aux mœurs, outrages à la religion : rien de tel pour assurer le succès, le triomphe, la gloire. Il ne restait plus, pour que ce triomphe accidentel durât, se transformât en culte littéraire, en immortalité, qu'à avoir du génie.

Scandale, génie, tout cela fut l'apanage de Gustave Flaubert, et cela éclata aux yeux de tous il y a un peu plus de cent ans, en 1857. Quelle patience de la part de l'auteur, quelle impatience de la part des autorités ! Flaubert s'était crucifié, cinq ans durant, sur les versions successives d'un roman qui ne cherchait à conter qu'une histoire provinciale. Ce " Christ de la littérature," comme on devait l'appeler plus tard, passait des jours et des jours sur une page, torturé par le sens intérieur de la perfection, par les affres d'un style qui se voulait l'équivalent sonore de la réalité visuelle et de la vérité mentale. Se battant les flancs, s'appliquant la discipline, Flaubert suait sang et eau pour mettre au monde la plus minutieuse des héroïnes. Hélas, nous étions en plein Second Empire: pour la police, *Madame Bovary* n'était qu'un adultère sordide, photographié avec un réalisme inutile et surtout choquant. La chance ou le destin voulut que ce long martyre, que cette persécution à la fois outrageante et vertueuse, se terminassent en apothéose. Flaubert fut acquitté, Flaubert fut glorieux. Et, dès avril 1857, *Madame Bovary* reparut, entière cette fois, sans la moindre trace des ciseaux de la censure.

Lorsque nous affirmons aujourd'hui, en toute confiance, que *Madame Bovary*, à l'égal de *Don Quichotte* ou d'*Anna Karénine*, constitue un moment privilégié dans la longue évolution du roman européen, nous oublions que telle n'était pas l'opinion commune au XIXe siècle. Incontestablement, le succès auprès des lecteurs fut immédiat et grand, tandis que Flaubert jouait l'indifférence olympienne. C'est que le lecteur n'y voyait guère qu'un chef-d'œuvre de méchanceté, une analyse chirurgicale autour de laquelle flottait l'odeur suspecte des salles d'opération: quelle sensation, quel attrait morbide ! Mais la critique fut d'un autre avis, qui tenait à la vertu

---

* Exposé présenté à Columbia University durant la session d'été de 1967.

et aux distractions saines. Voyez-vous, le *style* de Flaubert la laissait insatisfaite. Sans doute la souhaitait-elle plus " travaillé." D'autres part, *Madame Bovary* paraissait d'un matérialisme abject; le roman était immoral, il insultait aux mœurs, à tous les bons sentiments. Le grand Sainte-Beuve, patelin et prudent, déconseillait la lecture de *Madame Bovary* aux femmes. Le livre était trop cru, il pouvait blesser la délicasesse du sexe faible. Peut-être pouvait-il leur donner des idées?

Ce n'est que lentement qu'un nimbe de légende, qu'une auréole de sainteté se formèrent autour de *Madame Bovary* et de son auteur. Certes, on trouve dans le roman des scènes d'un naturalisme clinique, et qui n'ont pas cessé de choquer, surtout à l'étranger. Mais même Outre-Manche, même Outre-Atlantique, on s'habitua peu à peu à l'idée rassurante qu'après tout Emma finit par payer cher ses goûts romanesques. Le premier choc passé, on discerna dans le livre des intentions ironiques: un mari beaucoup plus stupide que la moyenne des maris, un clerc de notaire extrêmement vulgaire, un pharmacien qui battait tous les records. Cela plut. Aussi étrange que cela puisse paraître, on oublia, pour terminer, les côtés érotiques et libres du roman. Du coup, *Madame Bovary* devint, de femme adultère et perdue, une victime de la grossièreté des hommes et de la société épaisse; du coup on conseilla, aux jeunes gens et aux jeunes filles, la lecture et la relecture de passages passionnés et *purs*, tel celui-ci:

" Je t'aime à ne pouvoir me passer de toi, sais-tu bien?... J'ai quelquefois des envies de te revoir où toutes les colères de l'amour me déchirent. Je suis ta servante et ta concubine! Tu es mon roi, mon idole! tu es bon! tu es beau! tu es intelligent! tu es fort."

Il s'était tant de fois entendu dire ces choses, qu'elles n'avaient pour lui rien d'original. Emma ressemblait à toutes les maîtresses; et le charme de la nouveauté, peu à peu tombant comme un vêtement, laissait voir à nu l'éternelle monotonie de la passion, qui a toujours les mêmes formes et le même langage. Il ne distinguait pas, cet homme si plein de pratique, la dissemblance des sentiments sous la parité des expressions. Parce que des lèvres libertines ou vénales lui avaient murmuré des phrases pareilles, il ne croyait que faiblement à la candeur de celles-là; on en devait rabattre, pensait-il, les discours exagérés cachant les affections médiocres; comme si la plénitude de l'âme ne débordait pas quelquefois par les métaphores les plus vides, puisque personne, jamais, ne peut donner l'exacte mesure de ses besoins, ni de ses conceptions, ni de ses douleurs, et que la parole humaine est comme un chaudron fêlé où nous battons des mélodies à faire danser les ours, quand on voudrait attendrir les étoiles.

Ce passage, qui se trouve au chapitre XII de la Deuxième partie, est l'un des textes assurément les plus connus du roman. C'est même l'un des passages les plus célèbres de la littérature française du XIX$^e$ siècle. Ce qui intrigue ici, c'est l'identité des personnages. En un sens, Madame Bovary est toutes les femmes, comme son amant nous représente tous—toutes choses égales d'ailleurs. Mais, plus précisément, comme l'avait souligné

Baudelaire, parlant il est vrai du livre tout entier, le *je* y est le *moi* de l'auteur, du Gustave Flaubert. Si l'on arrive à oublier l'omniprésence flaubertienne, le texte que nous venons de citer est pourtant bien un texte lyrique, où se trouvent glorifiés la poésie de l'adultère et le sublime de l'amour non conjugal. Et, dès lors, le scandale cesse, puisque nous retrouverons cette poésie et ce sublime en remontant le cours des siècles, jusque dans l'amour courtois et l'*Art d'aimer* d'André le Chapelain, dont la vertu ne saurait être mise en doute. En un sens, le roman de Flaubert n'est qu'un lieu poétique commun, né au fond du Moyen Age, et où seules sont nouvelles les *coordonnées flaubertiennes*, permettant une vision et une solution plus rapides de l'amoureux problème....

Désormais Emma n'est plus un monstre, mais un modèle. Emma n'est troublante que parce que nous la voyons troublée par l'émotion la plus pure, la passion la plus profonde, voire la plus métaphysique. Mieux encore: tandis qu'on reprochait naguère à Flaubert la férocité de ses *strip-teases* psychologiques, nous tendrions aujourd'hui à voir en lui une victime des limitations philosophiques et linguistiques inhérentes à la nature même de la communication interpersonnelle. Nous ne concevons plus Flaubert comme un naturaliste sauvage, disséquant des personnages pantelants pour donner les leçons de réalité aux civilisés dépravés et choqués. Nous l'appréhendons plutôt comme un rude primitif, aux prises avec des problèmes d'intercommunication qui laissent pantelants les meilleurs linguistes et les " nouveaux romanciers " les plus subtils. Les compliments d'Emma ne nous frappent plus par leur sauvage sincérité, mais plutôt par leur gaucherie primitive. Emma n'exagère l'expression verbale qu'en désespoir de cause, parce qu'elle sait, obscurément, que tout langage est inadéquat, et qu'elle veut exprimer l'inexprimable. Emma est bien le *moi*, non pas celui de Flaubert toutefois, mais celui de tout le monde, le *je* de chacun. Et Rodolphe est, de ce *je*, l'*autre*, celui que nous sommes condamnés à opposer à notre moi, l'*autre* opaque, et qui ne permettra jamais l'adéquation entre notre pensée et notre expression. De là l'incompréhension mutuelle et la double tragédie du texte, qui nous apparaît aussitôt comme symbolique de la condition humaine: Emma *croit* que Rodolphe n'a jamais aimé qu'elle, Rodolphe *croit* qu'Emma a l'attitude banale des coquettes et des filles. Le coup de génie a été d'habiller cette primitive et ce sauvage, où apparaît à nu le roc et le tuf de l'existence humaine, où chante le dialogue pur du moi et de l'autre, en crinolines et en fracs de la société la plus policée. En se penchant sur notre texte, nous y entendons, au-delà des phrases romantiques et des rires satisfaits, le cri sauvage du moi cherchant, et ne parvenant pas, à percer la carapace de l'autre, ce cri que Flaubert entendait si souvent sur les lèvres de Louise Colet, dans une auberge sur la route de Paris.

Et les hyperboles d'Emma pointent aussi vers une autre expression, vers un autre inexprimable, ceux de l'art. Comme Emma n'arrivera jamais à faire comprendre à Rodolphe les profondeurs de son moi et de son amour, ainsi Flaubert, aux prises avec les problèmes du style, et malgré les cris sauvages de son " gueuloir," ne parviendra jamais à atteindre ses propres profondeurs et celles de la création littéraire. Qu'il s'agisse de langue ou de style, d'expression passionnelle ou d'expression littéraire, les platitudes déchirantes d'Emma et le sourire fat de Rodolphe sont *exemplaires*, à la fois métaphysiques et personnels, primitifs et raffinés, civilisés et sauvages, impurs et *purs*.

Les quelques réflexions qui précèdent témoignent de la faiblesse des interprétations contemporaines de *Madame Bovary*. Le livre semblait plat; il était métaphysique. Le roman paraissait immoral: mais en bon juge en la matière, l'Anglo-Saxon Henry James, déclarait qu'il méritait d'être lu à l'Ecole du dimanche, afin qu'y soit commentée la vigueur avec laquelle Flaubert condamnait, sinon le péché, du moins ses conséquences.

Ainsi *Madame Bovary*, sans doute à l'encontre des intentions explicites de l'auteur, devenait l'équivalent Second Empire de *Manon Lescaut*, de *Clarissa* et des *Liaisons dangereuses*: un livre qui ne troublait le lecteur que pour mieux le garder de l'enfer des passions—et de celui de la mauvaise littérature.

Les spécialistes de la littérature du XIX$^e$ siècle liront toujours les romans de Flaubert parce que Flaubert est un mythe, le mythe de l'intégrité artistique et de la conscience esthétique, et parce que Flaubert est peut-être le seul écrivain qui ait pu dire de bonne foi que le succès était pour lui une conséquence et non un but. Mais sans doute le plus authentique de l'écrivain se retrouve-t-il, d'une part dans *Madame Bovary*, et de l'autre, dans les treize volumes d'une *Correspondance* où paraissent toutes les nuances de de la vivacité. Pour nous, *Madame Bovary* est avant tout l'effort désespéré d'un être qui s'efforce de ressaisir l'amour humain dans son intégrité spirituelle et sensible; et la tragédie d'Emma est d'avoir échoué dans la quête la plus abrupte.

Pourtant, certains écrivains du XX$^e$ siècle n'ont pas hésité à parler sévèrement de Flaubert et de son moment historique. Ni pour Sartre, ni pour Malraux, ni pour Gide, ni pour Proust, *Madame Bovary* ne constitue une réalité signifiante. Sartre reste enfermé dans une philosophie existentialiste qu'il alourdit de prises de position à la fois politiques et paradoxalement idéalistes, et dont il proclame depuis peu la non-valeur, à l'ombre de la grande philosophie marxiste. Malraux, déjà entré dans la légende, s'empêtre dans une psychologie de l'art et dans le gouvernement d'une République qu'il n'arrive pas à révolutionner. Gide, malgré ses rodomontades et ses effets de style, commence à dater; il sera bientôt aussi compliqué et aussi touchant qu'une entrée du Métro de Paris. Proust seul a assez d'envergure pour pouvoir se mesurer à Flaubert. Mais cet artiste et ce philosophe du passé était peu préparé à comprendre les présents déchirants et ironiques de *Madame Bovary*. Dans la grande mêlée autour de Flaubert, c'est le colosse normand qui reste inaccessible, et entier, tandis que tout autour de lui ses adversaires tombent ou abandonnent la lutte.

La critique contemporaine a peut-être des vues moins vastes, mais plus justes. Flaubert a été récemment l'objet de recherches, d'analyses et d'exégèses où l'Ancienne Critique a mis le meilleur de ses méthodes et de son esprit. Ce qu'elle nous a appris de positif sur l'écrivain est précieux, indispensable même; et nous connaissons Flaubert mieux depuis qu'on nous a tant dit sur sa famille, ses amis et la façon dont s'élaboraient ses chefs-d'œuvre.

Reste à voir l'apport de la Nouvelle Critique. Jean-Pierre Richard, l'un des champions de la critique thématique, nous a déjà donné, de Flaubert, une image originale et neuve.[1] Et l'on sait tout ce que René Girard a réussi à tirer de lumineux et d'universel d'une analyse en profondeur des structures flaubertiennes.[2] Mais il serait intéressant de savoir ce que d'autres " néo-critiques " pourraient nous apprendre sur les paysages intérieurs du maître normand. Quelles sont les structures marxistes qu'un Goldmann pourrait découvrir, sous-jacentes à Emma ou à Monsieur Homais ? Charles Mauron est mort trop tôt pour nous décrire les lents cheminements du complexe d'Electre dans l'âme d'Emma, de celui de la castration chez son époux. Mais ne pourrait-on demander à Jean-Paul Weber quels thèmes hantèrent l'imagination créatrice de Flaubert, quels spectacles grotesques ou navrants avaient frappé, de façon indélébile, son inconscient, à travers quelles " modulations " innombrables ces thèmes se révèlent, toujours les mêmes et toujours autres, dans l'œuvre et le destin de l'auteur ?

Nous souhaitons, en toute sincérité, que le génie et l'œuvre de Gustave Flaubert, au lieu d'être inlassablement dépoussiérés et repeints, soient enfin *éclairés*. Et qu'importe si certains de ces éclairages nous révèlent autant sur l'esprit du critique que sur l'âme de l'écrivain ou le caractère des personnages ? L'important, n'est-ce pas de sortir de l'impasse où nous condamnent certains disciples de Lanson ? l'important, n'est-ce pas d'aller, avec Platon, à la rencontre de l'écrivain, " *avec toute son âme* " ? L'éclat de l'Idée nous récompensera alors de ce que les plus récents lecteurs de Flaubert apportent de subjectif, voire d'arbitraire, dans leurs analyses.

---

[1] Cf. J.-P. Richard, *Littérature et sensation*, 1954.
[2] R. Girard, *Mensonge romantique et vérité romanesque*, 1961.

# MAUPASSANT'S *APPARITION* *

## A SOURCE AND A CREATIVE PROCESS

Montaigne was expressing a fundamental principle of literary criticism when he wrote that in order to judge an author, " il faut sçavoir ce qui est sien et ce qui ne l'est point, et en ce qui n'est pas sien combien on luy doibt en consideration du chois, disposition, ornement et langage qu'il y a fourny." [1]

Critics have not failed to stress the fact that Guy de Maupassant, singularly preoccupied with the morbid, the fantastic and the insane, wrote a great number of tales revolving around these themes.[2] " As a perhaps inevitable consequence," states Professor Atkin in a scholarly article, " they have almost unfailingly been coupled with the tragic disintegration of their author's genius." [3] There has, then, been a widespread attempt to link these tales of the fantastic with the author's personal experiences. But in such instances opinions are dangerous for it is difficult to determine to what extent a composition has a bearing upon the life of a writer, or vice versa, without the most accurate material observation or the most definite facts. Altogether too often entirely plausible explanations are both false and misleading.

Maupassant felt strongly that if a writer's work belonged to the public, his private life and his more intimate creative processes belonged to himself alone. " Pas un aveu, pas une confidence qui éclairât sa vie ou son œuvre," writes Pol Neveu in the Conard edition of *Boule de Suif*. " Nous savons peu de chose concernant la méthode de travail de Guy de Maupassant. Il n'a point fait de confidences à ce sujet," adds Gérard de Lacaze-Duthiers.[4]

Maupassant has indeed been of little help to scholars interested in establishing sources for, and literary procedures of, his short stories and

---

* Reprinted from *Romanic Review* (Feb. 1942), 58-71.

[1] *Essais*, Alcan edition, 1930-1931, III, 314.

[2] Among the stories in this category are: *Apparition, L'Armoire, L'Auberge, A Vendre, Berthe, Conte de Noël, La Folle, Fou, Le Horla, Un Lâche, Lui?, Mademoiselle Cocotte, Magnétisme, La Main, Misti, La Nuit, La Peur, Qui Sait?, Solitude, Suicides, Sur l'Eau, Le Tic*. " Terreur," a poem appearing in *Des Vers* (1880) indicates Maupassant's interest in such matters at the beginning of his literary career.

[3] " The Supernaturalism of Maupassant," *PMLA*, XLII, 186.

[4] " Notes sur Guy de Maupassant," *La Pensée Française*, September, 1926, 11.

novels and perhaps this was intentional, for, as René Doumic points out, " Un portrait achevé ne doit laisser transparaître ni les préparations ni les dessous. Cela même est la méthode de Maupassant qui ne nous montre jamais que des résultats." [1]

It is a generally accepted fact, however, that Maupassant, always hard-pressed for subjects,[2] gathered anecdotes from doctors, innkeepers, farmers, postmen—in fact from all available sources. It has further been established that such stories as *Boule de Suif, La Maison Tellier, Ce Cochon de Morin, Boitelle* and *L'Aventure de Walter Schnaffs*, are founded on incidents in real life, furnished by obliging friends.

And yet, students of Maupassant have been singularly unsuccessful in bringing to light written sources for his various tales. " Maupassant never plagiarized," asserts one of his English critics.[3] Nor does he stand among the accused in Georges Maurevert's *Le Livre des Plagiats*. However, a contemporary of Maupassant, Jean Jullien, did charge him with plagiarism in two instances. In 1889 Jullien pointed out that *Le Port* was simply a new version of his own *Le Capitaine Chamorin* written three years earlier.[4] A few months later he accused Maupassant of stealing the plot of *L'Endormeuse* from Charles Morice's *Suicide-House*.[5] Jullien's indictment of Maupassant elicited no comment from the critics of the day nor has anyone since supported his claims. Likewise, scholars have completely passed over Brander Matthews' suggestion that *Le Horla* is based on Fitz-James O'Brien's startling tale, *What Was It?*[6] Although *Le Horla* is not the *conte* with which we are chiefly concerned, consideration of the American critic's hypothesis deserves a place in the analysis of Maupassant's creative processes. As Matthews did not himself attempt a comparison of texts and as no other critic has insisted upon the resemblance, we here present some of the more striking parallel passages:

---

[1] " L'Œuvre de Guy de Maupassant," *Revue des Deux Mondes*, November 1, 1893, 206.

[2] We read in a letter to his mother (October 30, 1874), " Essaie de me trouver des sujets de nouvelles," (*Correspondance*, Conard ed., CXXXI). Cf. Adolphe Brisson's remarks concerning Madame de Maupassant's rôle in providing plots for her son (*Portraits Intimes*, 4e série, Paris, Colin, 65).

[3] R. H. Sherard, *The Life, Work and Evil Fate of Guy de Maupassant*, London, T. Werner, Laurie, 1926, 331.

[4] *Echo de Paris*, March 15; however, according to Charles Lapierre, the plot of *Le Port* had been suggested to Maupassant by his friend, Robert Pinchon (*Souvenirs Intimes de M. Ch. Lapierre* republished in *Souvenirs sur Maupassant* by A. Lumbroso, Rome, Bocca frères, 1905, 611).

[5] *Art et Critique*, September 22. Auriant in " Une belle histoire de plagiat " (*Mercure de France*, December 1, 1939, 463-468) discusses the question but feels that it is Stevenson's *Suicide-Club* which may have inspired both French authors. But upon comparing *Suicide-Club* and *L'Endormeuse* one is compelled to feel that Maupassant's debt to the Scotsman is negligible.

[6] Critics have either followed Edmond de Goncourt (*Journal*, IX, 147) in stating that the subject of *Le Horla* was given Maupassant by Porto-Riche or have asserted with René Dumesnil (*Guy de Maupassant*, 226) that it was suggested by Léon Hennique. Matthews first offered his own theory in 1903 (" A Note on Guy de Maupassant," *The Bookman*, XVIII, 172).

| *What Was It?* | *Le Horla* [1] |
|---|---|
| Doors were opened without any visible agency. | Des portes fermées le soir étaient ouvertes le matin. |
| While I was lying still as a corpse, hoping that by a perfect physical inaction I should hasten mental repose, an awful incident occurred. A Something dropped, as it seemed, from the ceiling, plumb on my chest, and the next instant I felt two bony hands encircling my throat, endeavoring to choke me.... I was ... bitten with sharp teeth in the shoulder, neck, and chest.... | A peine couché, je fermais les yeux et je m'anéantissais. Oui, je tombais dans un néant absolu, dans une mort de l'être entier dont j'étais tiré brusquement, horriblement par l'épouvantable sensation d'un poids écrasant sur ma poitrine, et d'une bouche qui mangeait ma vie, sur ma bouche. |
| ... and all in the bright glare of a large jet of gas I absolutely beheld nothing! | L'impossibilité de le voir m'exaspérait et j'allumais toutes les lumières de mon appartement, comme si j'eusse pu, dans cette clarté, le découvrir. |
| Let us reason a little Harry. Here is a solid body which we touch, but which we cannot see. The fact is so unusual that it strikes us with terror. Is there no parallel though, for such a phenomenon? Take a piece of pure glass. It is tangible and transparent. A certain chemical coarseness is all that prevents its being so entirely transparent as to be totally invisible. It is not theoretically impossible, mind you, to make a glass that shall not reflect a single ray of light—a glass so pure and homogeneous in its atoms that the rays from the sun shall pass through it as they do through the air, refracted but not reflected. We do not see the air, and yet we feel it. | Ah! vous souriez! Pourquoi? Parce que cet Etre demeure invisible. Mais notre œil, messieurs, est un organe tellement élémentaire qu'il peut distinguer à peine ce qui est indispensable à notre existence.... Placez devant lui une glace sans tain parfaite, il ne la distinguera pas et nous jettera dessus comme l'oiseau pris dans une maison qui se casse la tête aux vitres. Donc, il ne voit pas les corps solides et transparents qui existent pourtant; il ne voit pas l'air dont nous nous nourrissons.... Quoi d'étonnant à ce qu'il ne voie pas un corps nouveau, à qui manque sans doute la seule propriété d'arrêter les rayons lumineux. |

---

[1] The first version of *Le Horla* which appeared in *Gil-Blas* (October 26, 1886) is utilized, the subject having been more fully developed in the definitive version of 1887. Both *What Was It?* and *Le Horla* are stories told in the first person of experiences with an invisible monster. O'Brien and Maupassant each call the creature the " Invisible " with a capital " I."

Examination of the above and similar likenesses between the two tales suggests that *What Was It?* (first published in 1859) may have served at least as a *point de départ* for *Le Horla*. As we shall see shortly, Maupassant was quite capable of going back into the years to find inspiration in some printed text for a story of his own. But if more convincing evidence does come to light concerning Maupassant's debt to O'Brien, much critical comment on *Le Horla* will have to be seriously revised.

Such a revision is indicated in the case of *Apparition*, one of Maupassant's better ghost stories.[1] One critic asserts that, " *Apparition* could have hardly been conceived by a perfectly healthy mind." [2] Another suggests that the hallucination which appears in the tale may have been inspired by the writer's use of stimulants such as ether, cocaine, morphine and hashish.[3] And although a German critic finds no indication of a pathological frame of mind in the composition of *Apparition*,[4] an eminent physician is of quite the opposite opinion.[5] Still another believes the tale so illogical and so unreal that he raises the question: " Does he [Maupassant] therefore become by definition Romantic? " [6]

Now it seems apparent that the foregoing opinions are based on the assumption that the plot of *Apparition* is Maupassant's own.[7] Such is not the case, however, for there is evidence to show that Maupassant has used a definite literary source. To find this source we must go back well over a quarter of a century before the story's appearance in *Le Gaulois* in 1883. At the time of Maupassant's birth, Jules Lecomte,[8] referred to by

---

[1] Saintsbury calls it " of the best." (*History of the French Novel*, London, Macmillan, 1917-1919, II, 509).

[2] B. M. Woodbridge, " Maupassant's Realism," *The Texas Review*, October 1922, 13. Cf. Ernest Boyd's remark: " Of that unhealthy mind there was a glimpse in ... *Apparition*." (*Guy de Maupassant, A Biographical Study*, New York, Knopf, 1926, 128-129).

[3] E. Maynial, *La Vie et l'œuvre de Guy de Maupassant*, Paris, Mercure de France, 1907, 227-228.

[4] P. Mann, *Guy de Maupassant, Sein Leben und seine Werke*, Egon Fleischel, Berlin, 1908, 261.

[5] Docteur N. Bajenow, " Guy de Maupassant et Dostoiewsky, Etude de psychopathologie comparée," *Archives d'Anthropologie Criminelle*, XIX, 39.

[6] O. H. Moore, " The Romanticism of Guy de Maupassant," *PMLA*, XXXIII, 102.

[7] Only one critic has attempted to seek a literary prototype for the tale. Hubert Matthey in his generally authoritative *Essai sur le merveilleux dans la littérature française depuis* 1800, suggests that Maupassant has appropriated the manner of Mérimée in ending *Apparition* with the tangible blond hair which recalls the little spot of blood on the king's slipper at the end of *La Vision de Charles XI* (Payot, Paris, 1915, 206; see also 296).

[8] Jules-François Lecomte was born at Boulogne-sur-Mer, June 20, 1814, and died in Paris, April 22, 1864. Author of a large number of books as well as of the notorious *Lettres de Van Engelgom*, he founded, directed or wrote for such publications as *Le Navigateur*, *La Revue Maritime*, *La France Maritime*, *L'Indépendance Belge* and *Le Monde Illustré*. In 1858 the Goncourts refer to him in their *Journal* as: " Un homme rempli d'histoires qu'il tire comme des tiroirs, et qu'il raconte sans chaleur et avec le même accent, ainsi qu'il lirait un procès-verbal. Sans goût littéraire, mais fureteur sagace, intelligemment curieux, le seul homme, à l'heure présente, qui dans la presse soit un chroniqueur un peu universel, un peu informé de ce qui court, de ce qui se dit, de ce qui se fait ... (I, 189)."

his contemporaries as " le prince des chroniqueurs," was writing weekly *feuilletons* entitled *Courrier de Paris* for *L'Indépendance Belge*. On Sunday, January 17, 1852, the following account appeared over Lecomte's name: [1]

### COURRIER DE PARIS

(*Correspondance particulière de* " L'INDÉPENDANCE BELGE.")

Le monde moral a parfois des courants bien singuliers ! Savez-vous, Monsieur, ce qui fait aujourd'hui l'objet des conversations d'une foule de coins du feu ? Le coup d'Etat et ses conséquences—me dira-t-on. Pas du tout !—Ce sont les revenants ! Et par ce mot, je n'entends point parler de ces vieux de la vieille, que depuis quelques semaines nous rencontrons dans les alentours de l'Elysée et du Ministère de la guerre, traînant un vieux sabre ébréché sur tous les os de l'Europe, et promenant des galons noircis sur les habits moisis ... non ! Les revenants dont on parle et dont je parle sont d'une immortalité plus charnelle que celle que donnent la gloire et l'Académie ; oui, ce sont des êtres plus effrayants et moins pensionnés.

Et c'est bien le cas de constater une fois de plus ici quelle action puissante, irrésistible, la littérature et l'art exercent sur les idées d'une nation impressionnable ! Cette fois, c'est le boulevard qui nous vaut cela. Sans *le Vampire*, sans *l'Imagier de Harlem*, et un peu aussi *les Rêves de Matheus*, du diable si on songerait au diable ! et voilà que tout Paris, comme on dit, ayant été palpiter dans les salles sombres, y *revenant* lui-même, devant ces histoires d'un autre monde qui, n'ayant pas le sens commun, figent tous les sens, on s'est mis de toutes parts à évoquer des foules de récits pleins de frissons le soir, en cercle non politique ... rangé devant le feu où la flamme s'affaisse ... se voyant à peine sous les projections épuisées de la lampe estompée d'abats-jour ! Ne riez-pas ! on vous mettrait à la porte ... si on osait l'ouvrir !

C'est ainsi que, l'autre soir, dans le salon d'une grande dame polonaise, où se trouvaient réunies en silence une douzaine de personnes défiantes, on attendait avec impatience et terreur à la fois, *l'apparition* ... de M. de R*** arrivant, je dirai presque de l'autre monde ! La pluie fouettait les doubles vitres sur lesquelles se croisaient d'amples rideaux de brocatelle d'un rouge sanglant. Une main complice de minuit, heure traditionnelle du crime, avait baissé la carcel ; le foyer expirant n'exhalait plus que de temps en temps comme un soupir, qui allait tirer des angles dorés des meubles de Boule, ou des cadres brunis, une étincelle semblable à un regard lancé de l'ombre. Personne n'osait dire un mot, tout ce monde attendait superstitieusement M. de R***. [On parlait de séquestration à propos

---

[1] A story entitled " A Mysterious History," appearing on March 1, 1852 in the *International Magazine*, V, 306-307, which had been translated from *L'Indépendance Belge*, led to the discovery of Lecomte's tale. As *L'Indépendance Belge* for the year 1852 is not obtainable this side of the Atlantic, we quote Lecomte at length. *Apparition* may be found in the volume *Clair de Lune*. A few extracts from Maupassant's tale have been inserted with brackets into Lecomte's text for purposes of general comparison.

d'un procès récent. C'était à la fin d'une soirée intime, rue de Grenelle, dans un ancien hôtel, et chacun avait son histoire, une histoire qu'il affirmait vraie. Alors le vieux marquis de la Tour-Samuel, âgé de quatre-vingt-deux ans, se leva et vint s'appuyer à la cheminée.]

Etait-ce un mort? Non. Voici son histoire. Au commencement de décembre dernier, un de ses amis vient le trouver.—Comte!—lui dit-il,—vous savez quelle invincible répugnance j'ai à retourner dans mon château de Normandie, où j'ai eu le malheur de perdre ma femme, l'été dernier! [Voici les faits tout simples. C'était en 1827, au mois de juillet.... C'était un ami de jeunesse.... Devenu follement amoureux d'une jeune fille, il l'avait épousée.... elle était morte subitement....] Pourtant, j'ai laissé là dans un secrétaire, des papiers importants qui me sont aujourd'hui indispensables pour des affaires de famille... Rendez-moi un service, prenez cette clé, et allez les chercher... La mission est délicate, je ne puis la confier qu'à vous [... je te demanderai de me rendre un grand service, c'est d'aller chercher chez moi dans le secrétaire de ma chambre... quelques papiers dont j'ai un urgent besoin. Je ne puis charger de ce soin un subalterne ou un homme d'affaires, car il me faut une impénétrable discrétion et un silence absolu. Quant à moi, pour rien au monde je ne rentrerai dans cette maison.... Je te donnerai la clef.] M. de R*** céda aux instances de son ami et partit le lendemain même. Le chemin de fer de Rouen le déposait à une station d'où, en deux heures, il pouvait arriver au château. Lorsque la voiture s'arrêta à la grille, un jardinier se présenta, qui parlementa à travers les barreaux, sans l'ouvrir. Le comte s'étonna de ces défiances qui résistaient même à la lettre d'admission dont l'avait muni—je dois dire armé—son ami. [En approchant du château, je cherchais dans ma poche la lettre que j'avais pour le jardinier.... un vieil homme sortit d'une porte de côté et parut stupéfait de me voir. Je sautai à terre et lui remis ma lettre. Il la lut, la relut, la retourna, me considéra en dessous, mit le papier dans sa poche et prononça:—Eh bien! qu'est-ce que vous désirez?] Enfin, après une courte absence qui fut sans doute employée à aller se consulter avec quelqu'un le jardinier revint et ouvrit. Lorsqu'il fut dans la cour d'honneur, M. de R*** examina la façade du château dont les cent fenêtres étaient toutes fermées, à l'exception d'une seule. Là un des volets, peut-être soulevé par le vent, avait quitté ses gonds, et était tombé à terre où il était resté. Cette fenêtre était, comme il le vit ensuite, précisément celle de la chambre où il devait aller remplir la commission qu'il avait acceptée....

Le comte, impressionné par la singularité de l'accueil, observait tout avec soin. Il vit une petite fumée qui s'échappait tournoyante d'un des conduits de cheminée disposés dans l'architecture du toit.—Le château est-il habité?—demanda-t-il.—Non!—dit sèchement le jardinier. [Le manoir semblait abandonné depuis vingt ans.] Et en même temps il tira la porte d'un petit escalier de service par lequel il précéda le comte, ouvrant, à chaque étage qu'on gravissait, des espèces de petites lucarnes encastrées dans l'architecture rococo de la façade.

Arrivé au troisième, le jardinier s'arrêta, et montrant une porte, dit: C'est là!—et sans rien ajouter, il se mit à redescendre. M. de R***, sans plus s'étonner de ces façons maussades, ouvrit la porte, et se trouva dans un cabinet obscur. La lumière qui venait de l'escalier lui permit de voir une seconde porte qu'il franchit, et il pénétra dans la chambre éclairée par le volet détaché. L'aspect de cette chambre était froid, nu, abandonné. [L'appartement était tellement sombre que je n'y distinguais rien d'abord. Je m'arrêtai, saisi par cette odeur moisie et fade des pièces inhabitées... des chambres mortes.] Il y avait la cage d'un oiseau envolé ou mort, posée à terre. Le secrétaire désigné par son ami était en face de la fenêtre; sans s'arrêter à une investigation inutile, il alla droit au meuble et l'ouvrit... [... j'allais au secrétaire... j'ouvris le tiroir indiqué.]

En cédant à la clé, le secrétaire grinça fortement. Un autre bruit répondit à ce bruit: celui d'une porte qui s'ouvre. M. de R*** se retourne, et dans l'encadrement d'une autre chambre pleine d'ombre, il voit une forme blanche, qui étend les bras vers lui: [... un grand et pénible soupir, poussé contre mon épaule, me fit faire un bond de fou. ... Une grande femme vêtue de blanc me regardait. ...]

—Comte! dit une voix faible, mais expressive.—Vous venez m'enlever les lettres de Théodore?... Pourquoi?

(Théodore n'est pas le nom du propriétaire du château qui avait donné mission à son ami.)

—Madame!—s'écria M. de R***—qui êtes-vous?

—Ne me reconnaissez-vous pas, toute changée que je doive être?...

—La marquise!—s'écrie M. de R*** surpris jusqu'à l'épouvante.

—Oui... c'est moi. Nous étions amis autrefois; vous venez ici me causer un mal affreux. Qui vous envoie? Mon mari? Que veut-il encore? par pitié, laissez-moi ces lettres!...

Et en se parlant ainsi, l'apparition faisait signe au comte d'approcher. Il approcha, repoussant de son esprit toute impression surnaturelle, et persuadé qu'il était en face de la marquise vivante au milieu d'un étrange mystère; il la suivit dans la seconde chambre. Elle était vêtue d'une robe— j'allais dire d'un suaire—de couleur grise. Ses cheveux, qui firent pendant dix ans le désespoir envieux d'une foule de femmes du grand monde, flottaient en désordre sur ses épaules. Le jour qui n'arrivait dans cette chambre que par reflet de la première, ne permit d'abord au comte que de constater la maigreur extrême et la pâleur tombale de la marquise. A peine entrée là, elle lui dit, changeant brusquement de discours:

—Je souffre d'incroyables douleurs de tête... ce sont mes cheveux qui les causent, il y a huit mois que je n'ai été peignée... comte, rendez-moi ce service... peignez-moi!

Et s'étant assise, elle présenta un peigne à M. de R***, qui obéit subjugué. La dame ne parla plus; lui ne l'osa. D'ailleurs, il l'avoue lui même, il était fort troublé. [Oh! Monsieur, vous pouvez me rendre un grand service!... Je souffre affreusement. Je souffre, oh je souffre! Et elle s'assit doucement dans mon fauteuil. Elle me regardait:—Voulez-vous? Je fis "Oui" de la tête, ayant encore la voix paralysée. Alors elle me tendit un peigne en écaille et elle murmura:—Peignez-moi, oh! peignez-moi....] Sans doute il faisait mal son office de camérier, car la patiente exhalait de petits murmures plaintifs. Tout à coup, elle se leva, disant:—Merci!— et disparut dans les profondeurs obscures de la chambre. Le comte attendit quelques instants, regardant du mieux qu'il pouvait ... ne voyant rien, n'entendant rien ! [Soudain elle me dit: " Merci ! " m'arracha le peigne des mains et s'enfuit par la porte que j'avais remarquée entr'ouverte. Resté seul, j'eus, pendant quelques secondes, ce trouble effaré des réveils après les cauchemars.] Il prit alors le parti de rentrer dans la première pièce; ses yeux se portant sur le secrétaire, il le vit tout en désordre. Il put, toutefois, y prendre les papiers de famille qui faisaient l'objet de sa mission. [Je saisis brusquement les trois paquets de lettres sur le secrétaire ouvert.... le meuble refermé, il attendit ... appela ... rien ! Il s'en fut, il avoue que ce fut très volontiers ....

En bas, personne. Le cocher qui l'avait amené était contre la grille prêt à repartir. M. de R*** crut ne devoir pas prolonger là son séjour. En route, et essayant de recueillir ses esprits sur l'étrange incident de sa visite au château de***, il s'aperçut que ses vêtements étaient couverts de cheveux de la marquise.... [Mes yeux, par hasard, descendirent sur ma poitrine. Mon dolman était plein de longs cheveux de femme qui s'étaient enroulés aux boutons.]

Au lieu de rentrer sur-le-champ à Paris, il alla à Rouen, trouver un riche fabricant, dont la résidence de campagne est contiguë au château où il venait d'avoir cette aventure. Adroitement interrogé, le voisin ne répondit rien qui y jetât quelque lumière. Deux jours après, M. de R*** revenait à Paris: c'était le 3 décembre. Il chercha le marquis sans pouvoir le rencontrer. Le 4, ce dernier ne rentra pas à son hôtel. [Je me rendis chez lui le lendemain.... Il était sorti la veille au soir et pas rentré. Je revins dans la journée, on ne l'avait pas revu. J'attendis une semaine. Il ne reparut pas.... Je ne sais rien de plus.] On croit, depuis, qu'il a été une des victimes du boulevard Montmartre, là où était son club. C'est cette histoire que M. de R*** avait promis de raconter l'autre soir, chez la vieille dame polonaise, où on l'attendait jusqu'à minuit. Il vint, comme on allait se séparer ... et montra les cheveux de la marquise. J'en ai un là, sur la table où j'écris ceci ....

Il est certain que si, depuis un mois, le théâtre ne nous avait pas montré tant de vampires et d'apparitions à Harlem et ailleurs, le récit du comte de R*** ne terrifierait pas toute la société parisienne, et que moi-même, si je n'avais pas *saisi aux cheveux* cette occasion de fixer ici un reflet des singulières préoccupations du moment ....

Passons à des choses plus irréfragablement positives, des morts incontestés.

In plot then, Lecomte's *feuilleton* and *Apparition* are the same. In a fashionable drawing-room, a nobleman relates a personal experience. A friend, grief-stricken by the loss of his wife, had approached him with the singular request that he go in the strictest secrecy to the family château and there procure papers in a locked desk. The nobleman, furnished with a key and a letter of introduction, arrived at the dilapidated manor-house but it was with difficulty that he persuaded the gardener to let him enter. Having once located the desk in a large, sombre room, he began to gather up the papers. But the task was interrupted by the appearance of a phantom or a woman. Complaining of a pain in her head, she begged him to comb her hair. He did so, after which she thanked him and fled. Greatly alarmed he picked up the papers and hastily departed. Not until later did he notice long strands of hair clinging to his coat. When he tried to find the friend who had sent him on the mission, the man had disappeared.

If Maupassant has invented nothing here we are nevertheless given the opportunity of seeing his creative processes at work. Appropriating a story of average interest, he has, through the suppression, expansion, transformation and exaggeration of details, constructed with great artistry a strange and moving tale.

Suppressed are most of the particulars Lecomte utilizes in explaining away the supernatural in his anecdote. First, our chronicler strives to give a setting in harmony with his subject: " La pluie fouettait les doubles vitres.... Une main complice de minuit, heure traditionnelle du crime, avait baissé la carcel," etc. But a jocular note has put us at our ease: " Ne riez pas ! on vous mettrait à la porte ... si on osait l'ouvrir ! " Confronted by the " apparition," M. de R*** recognizes his friend's wife and she in turn is convinced that her husband has sent him to take from her the letters of Théodore. We have, then, grounds for assuming that the woman, not dead after all, has been confined to the château because of infidelity. Her insistence that M. de R*** comb her hair to alleviate the pain in her head, leads us to believe that the incarceration has driven her to insanity and when the desk is found ransacked it seems more than likely that she rather than a ghost wished to keep Théodore's letters from him. With the château once behind, M. de R*** notices his coat covered with the woman's hair and as proof of his adventure shows several strands of it to his drawing-room audience. Lecomte confesses that one strand was presented to him and in order to convince the reader more fully that this is not a story of the supernatural, he adds: " Passons à des choses plus irréfragablement positives, des morts incontestés."

In his treatment, Maupassant immediately seized upon what was to be the main-spring of his tale—overwhelming fear having as its victim one who has experienced the seemingly inexplicable.[1] Like Lecomte, Maupassant endeavored to create at the outset a mood of apprehension. But the external and hackneyed details used by the former—the beating rain, the blood-red curtains, the dim light of the lamp and the flickering hearth—have been suppressed and their place has been taken by insistence upon the " horrible épouvante " which years before first gripped and still dominates the narrator, giving the story its *raison d'être*. Maupassant also eliminated certain details furnished by Lecomte which might too readily lead to a plausible explanation of the apparition, such as smoke rising from the chimney of the deserted mansion, the open window, the resemblance of the woman to the supposedly dead wife and especially the episode of Théodore's letters. Nor in the *dénouement* did he follow Lecomte's example by offering a logical explanation for the sudden disappearance

---

[1] As we have seen, a very common theme in the works of Maupassant.

of the proprietor of the château. These are unnecessary details which not only would have slowed up the narrative, but, more important still, would have destroyed the illusion of substance and shadow that Maupassant was attempting to create. But we cannot agree with Professor Moore who is of the opinion that the author is here dealing with the supernatural and that *Apparition* " is a vast world of unreality which Maupassant discloses to his readers." [1] As Professor Atkin has pointed out,[2] a solution is suggested for the careful reader. The narrator, old Marquis de la Tour-Samuel, himself feels that there must be some logical explanation for his amazing experience. Moreover, the tale's opening sentence, " On parlait de séquestration à propos d'un procès récent," leads us to infer that this too may be an instance of sequestration. Nor are details lacking to suggest that a living being rather than a ghost inhabits the château. The room upon close examination reveals " un lit sans draps, mais gardant ses matelas et ses oreillers, dont l'un portait l'empreinte profonde d'un coude ou d'une tête comme si on venait de se poser dessus." Furthermore the " apparition " does not vanish into thin air but flees through a door left slightly ajar which immediately becomes " fermée et inébranlable." We may conclude that if Maupassant rejected some of the more obvious explanatory details furnished by Lecomte, he was merely resorting to the mode of procedure he was to lay down four years later in the prefatory essay to *Pierre et Jean*: " Les partisans de l'objectivité . . . évitent avec soin toute explication compliquée, toute dissertation sur les motifs, et se bornent à faire passer sous nos yeux les personnages et les événements." [3]

While suppressing the irrelevant and trite in Lecomte's story, Maupassant was nevertheless able to give an impression of plenitude to his own version. This was made possible by skillful expansion of action and descriptive detail which was merely indicated in the source. Thus, from Lecomte's brief and colorless exposé of his friend's arrival and his astonishing request, Maupassant builds two absorbing scenes. In the first we have an account of the chance meeting, a vivid description of the friend broken by suffering, the revelation of his tragic past and his appeal, all told with great simplicity and yet with a wealth of detail. A second meeting is arranged for the following day. Here, we have a psychological portrait of the friend —his agitation, his confusion and his feeling of distrust. Under Maupassant's pen, the two-dimensional character of Lecomte has become a human being of undeniable interest to the reader.

Likewise, the terse sentence of the original text touching upon the trip to the château has been enlarged so that we see the marquis, filled with the joy of living, trotting across meadows listening to the larks and walking his horse through a peaceful forest, snatching at leaves in passing. It would be unjust to accuse Maupassant of verbiage here for not only is the author adroitly building up suspense but he is, at the same time, com-

---

[1] *Op. cit.*, 102.

[2] *Op. cit.*, 217.

[3] *Pierre et Jean*, " Le Roman," Conard ed., xvii.

posing a scene in order to mark more clearly the contrast with those to follow.

Particularly striking is Maupassant's improvement upon and expansion of the original in his depiction of milieu. It was essential to the effectiveness of the story to give an impression of abandonment to the château. This Lecomte did by mentioning the closed shutters. Maupassant, however, sought a few precise details which would evoke a graphic and complete picture of the scene—the rotten, half-open gate, the weed-choked paths and the overgrown flower beds. In a similar manner, Lecomte's cold, bare, abandoned chamber is depicted in *Apparition* as sombre, with armchairs pell-mell, the window shutters caked in rust and the moldy stale odor " des chambres mortes " permeating all. Following Flaubert's dictum,[1] Maupassant has sought the sudden, distinct effect produced by a few chosen particulars standing out in sharp relief. Moreover, these details go far towards creating an atmosphere in conformity with the preternatural drama to follow.

We may say, then, that Maupassant's method of expansion on this story was to seize upon some material point offered by Lecomte and to develop it, taking pains that the creation be in perfect harmony with the story as a whole.

Maupassant departed from the original text also through the process of transformation—and in particular, the transformation of characters. It cannot be properly said that there has been any alteration in the character of the château's owner. As we have already seen, the skeleton outline afforded by Lecomte has been given flesh and blood in Maupassant's version. The same, however, is not true in the case of the gardener. Lecomte has drawn him as a sullen, defiant creature, who, at first grudgingly and then with seeming indifference, led the visitor to the room in question. The gardener of *Apparition*, on the other hand, is dumbfounded by the arrival of the marquis. He hesitates, he stammers, he seems desirous of restraining the determined arrival from committing a foolhardy action: " Alors, vous allez dans ... dans sa chambre ? " For all that, he yields to the ingression.

The character of the supposed apparition has undergone a change as well. In the primitive text the woman would appear to be unquestionably on this side of the grave. She is excitable, even voluble. She reproaches her husband and she pleads with their common friend; then too, there is a suggestion of coquetry in her challenge: " Ne me reconnaissez-vous pas, toute changée que je doive être ? " As the count follows her from one room to the other our reaction is that this is not the stuff of which phantoms are made. When we compare such a woman with the nebulous, ethereal creature who announces herself by a sigh to the startled marquis, the contrast is striking. She stares fixedly and in silence. When she does speak it is but a murmur. Her soft phrases are punctuated with sighs and moments of pause; no gesticulations, no lost motions, no animated conversation, and she disappears as she came—as though from another world.

---

[1] Cf. *idem*, xxiv.

Furthermore in the rewriting Lecomte's protagonist has been transfigured from the calm, self-assured count, momentarily alarmed by his recent unusual experience, to the marquis of Maupassant. The latter, still shaken, his imagination still inflamed by an event undergone fifty-six years before, clearly reveals his character to the reader in the tale he tells. Proud and sensitive, he had been offended by the sealing of the letter entrusted to his care. His mood of elation on the trip had abruptly changed to one of petulance when he found himself temporarily thwarted by the gardener. And it is not surprising that his febrile imagination had been aroused by his adventure.

Fear is the *leitmotif* of *Apparition* and Maupassant has transformed the characters we have just discussed in order to depict in all its puissance the gradual ascendency of horror in one man. The concern of the gardener, the apparently unaccountable presence and actions of the unearthly visitant, the overwrought state of the marquis's nerves, all lend to the portrayal of this emotion a sense of unity which is entirely lacking in the original.

We may here speak of the process of exaggeration in Maupassant's creative method. The entire development has been organized so as to magnify the current of uneasiness, at times scarcely perceptible in Lecomte's tale, to the mounting tide of horror which grips the marquis and by its very force pervades the reader. Three scenes in particular dominate the story by their sharp depiction of the obsession of fear. At the very beginning the marquis, in a troubled and subdued tone which seems a pledge of the sincerity of his emotion, describes the deleterious effects of his experience upon his mind. The second scene takes place at the moment of the "apparition." Here, Maupassant minutely analyzes overwhelming terror in all its desperation: "L'âme se fond; on ne sent plus son cœur, le corps entier devient mou comme une éponge; on dirait que tout l'intérieur de nous s'écoule." The third sets forth the physical reaction, the uncontrollable panic which grips a person once he has recovered from the paralysis of the moment.

A glance at the original is sufficient to show that the painstaking and implacable descriptions of different phases of fear, of irresistible horror, and its result are much more developed in Maupassant's version. To obtain such vividness of effect, Maupassant must obviously have been very familiar with the emotion.[1] Consequently, it is not unlikely that he drew from his own past wherein the sensations, accumulated from all his previous experience, lay dormant. This supposition seems to be borne out by the exclamation of the marquis: "Oh! personne ne peut comprendre à moins de les avoir ressenties, ces épouvantables et stupides terreurs." Maupassant's own experiences obviously and inevitably furnished the motive force of his imagination which in turn gave such conviction to the portrayal.

To date there have been two articles purporting to show how Maupassant utilized his own "contes" in composing his novels.[2] However,

---

[1] Such is the opinion of Maynial, *op. cit.*, 244, and of Bajenow, *op. cit.*, 8.

[2] E. Maynial, "La Composition dans les romans de Maupassant," *Revue Bleue*, October 31, 1903, 562-565, November 7, 1903, 604-608; L. Barthou, "Maupassant Inédit; Autour d'' une Vie,'" *Revue des Deux Mondes*, October 15, 1920, 746-775.

there has been no investigation showing how Maupassant made use of a published tale to write one of his own. Lecomte's *feuilleton* has, in the present instance, afforded us the opportunity for such a study. We have seen how Maupassant has taken possession of the original subject, sifted the relevant from the irrelevant, transformed certain details while amplifying and developing others. Immediately perceiving the essential—the depiction of the obsession of fear—he has magnified and analyzed this emotion against a background both fantastic and plausible. His distinction lies in having given to his tale so great an illusion of reality that the reader's mind turns to re-examine the premises, hesitating between a rational explanation and an explanation based on the supernatural. His genius is revealed by his ability to transfigure into something rich and strange the substance and the ideas of another, for if the theme of *Apparition* is Lecomte's, the artistic consummation is Maupassant's alone.

# III

# THE TWENTIETH CENTURY

# MASTER OF REAL FICTION*

André Gide, an avid reader and early admirer of Simenon, once called him " perhaps the greatest and most truly novelistic novelist in French literature today." Although the statement may be interpreted in a number of ways, we know that for Gide, a novel's primary function is to give life to what is possible rather than to reproduce reality (*Journal des Faux-Monnayeurs*). And indeed critics have noted that Simenon has so developed his natural gifts as a storyteller that his world of fiction often conjures up a sense of reality which, while seeming a true image of the world around us, becomes more convincing to the reader than everyday reality itself. It has also been noted that while his narrative art reveals the author's conscious skill, it also seems to have been prompted, as one critic put it, " by some inner compulsion, as though to tell stories were a necessary activity of his being. " And as favorable comment during the past decade has multiplied on both sides of the Atlantic, " Simenon authenticity and conviction " has almost become a byword. To have at least a partial understanding of how Simenon achieved the position he now holds in the eyes of many discerning critics, some idea of his development as a writer is necessary.

Of Breton and Dutch origins, Georges Simenon was born in Liége, Belgium, on February 13, 1903. His father, Désiré, eked out a living for a family of four in an insurance agency. When the son was five, his mother began to take in students of both sexes from the University of Liége in order to round out the family income. Most of these young people were foreigners, and Rumania, Poland, and Russia were particularly well represented. As a result, by the time he was twelve Simenon, already with ambitions as a writer, knew Gogol and Dostoevski better than he did Balzac or Flaubert.

When he was sixteen his formal education at the Jesuit College of Saint-Servais ended abruptly with the death of his father. Almost immediately he became a reporter on the Liége *Gazette* and within a month had started writing a column which appeared for the next three years. At

---

* This piece first appeared in slightly modified form in the *Saturday Review* (February 21, 1953).

seventeen, with the publication of his first book, *Au Pont des Arches*, he had become a novelist.

Simenon was twenty when he moved to Paris and embarked in earnest upon the first part of his remarkable writing career. Convinced that a novelist, like a painter, actor, or musician, must first become an artisan with a thorough command of his craft, he wrote within the next few years some two hundred " popular novels " (*romans populaires*) under seventeen pseudonyms. Though this mass of material was financially profitable, he considered it merely a preparation for a career as a serious man of letters. Before long he was inserting one chapter of real literary merit into each of these rapidly conceived novels. By his own confession, the chapters thus interpolated had little to do with the plot and were perplexing to his readers, but they helped him serve the ten years of apprenticeship he had pledged himself.

In 1930, at the age of twenty-seven, he took another step toward literary self-realization when he wrote his first detective novels and created the character of that calmly perceptive French sleuth, Inspector Maigret, who was to become as famous on the continent as Sherlock Holmes already was in Britain and America. In the field of detective fiction, Simenon continued to work out his own salvation as an author. Increasingly he applied his skill to the economical use of words, the brief but vivid description, and the cohesion between characters and background. His stories were already taking on a marked psychological aspect as they were focused more and more on character rather than action. Seen in this light, the transition from detective fiction, to which Simenon devoted three years of intensive writing, to the *roman d'atmosphère*, the psychological novel, novel of ideas, or simply " plain novel," as his subsequently predominant literary form has variously been called, was not so abrupt as has sometimes been stated.

In fulfillment of his promise that at the age of thirty he would abandon the mystery novel to enter the literary field proper, he published the *Gens d'en face* in 1933. In this, the first of a new series of novels, the action revolved around the Russian seaport town of Batum, and the depiction of customs and characters assumed an importance that it had not had in his previous work. Of particular interest to us is the Preface (the first Simenon ever wrote) which stressed the new step he had taken. In part, the author says: " J'ai écrit un roman. Batum est vrai. Les gens sont vrais. L'histoire est vraie.

Ou plutôt, chaque détail est vrai, mais l'ensemble est faux....

Ce n'est pas encore ce que je veux dire. C'est un roman, voilà ! Est-ce que ces mots-là ne devraient pas suffire ? "

With such novels as *Les Pitard* (also published in 1933) and *Le Coup de Lune* (1935), Simenon was gradually emerging as the writer of singularly gripping psychological studies. Not until 1937, however, was it generally recognized that he had irrevocably committed himself to the *roman tout court*. It was then that *Le Testament Donadieu* appeared (translated into English as *The Shadow Falls*). The author's mastery of psychological detail deeply impressed the critics: his probing, relentless, lucid analysis of the disintegration of a French upper middle-class family suggested that here was a writer on the threshold of a significant contribution to modern literature. Though it was hailed almost immediately as his first great novel, Simenon prefers to see it simply as his first long one. In the author's terminology, it is a "*roman-chronique*" or family chronicle encompassing the lives and dramas of a relatively large number of characters, whereas he feels his natural bent lies in concentrating on one or two principal characters depicted in moments of sharp crisis. This fictional form he has designated as the "*roman-crise*," and it was brilliantly realized in 1938 in *L'Homme qui regardait passer les trains*. *Pedigree*, written in 1942-43 and published in 1948, strongly reminiscent of the *roman-fleuve* technique, was received with acclaim, but it remains a work apart in Simenon's creative effort. The concept of the *roman-crise* was still apparent in his first novel written in America, *Trois Chambres à Manhattan* (1946). It was even more successfully carried out in *Lettre à mon juge*, composed in Florida in 1947 and later translated as *Act of Passion*. Other novels, such as *La Neige était sale* (*The Snow Was Black*) and *Les Volets verts* (*The Heart of a Man*), continued to reveal the magnetic intensity with which he etched the psychological contours of a character in a critical phase of his life's drama.

Such is a brief account of some of Simenon's major works to date. A number of the factors that have gone into the making of his present worldwide renown as a novelist should nevertheless be passed in quick review.

Simenon has long made a practice of traveling extensively and living in many parts of the globe. A born observer, he has undeniably profited from this desire to know the whole world and its peoples. All manner of settings have thus been provided for his novels. But more important, his varied existence has afforded many opportunities to study the detailed manifestations of human nature under the most diverse conditions. Recent critics seem entirely justified in acknowledging that his stories are often psychological studies that could only result from wide experience and deep understanding.

On the other hand, Simenon has always held that if an author follows his characters through, and if they are human, they will create the plot themselves. In fact, he tells us, it is the novelist's task to re-create a world every bit as real as our everyday world; and it is even more important that he re-create men more human than those we rub elbows with, so that they may freely manifest all the possibilities inherent in their personality.

This view was given fuller expression when, in 1943, he contributed to a symposium on the Novel in the French periodical, *Confluences*. There he foresaw the genre evolving toward "*le roman pur*," the novel shorn of all that can be depicted through such media as the cinema, radio, and magazines. Thus conceived, the novel would be reduced to its primal elements, for, he said: "There remains living matter, man remains, naked or clothed, the man of everywhere or the man of some particular place, man and his eternal drama." Those who have followed Simenon's development as a writer through the years will agree that with each successive book he has drawn close to, if indeed not attained, effectual mastery of the novel as he believes it should now be.

Only one other point need here be touched upon. Critics have of late dwelt on the fact that his stories have a fascination which is difficult to define. It is again Gide to whom we may turn for at least a partial answer. The following entry appears in his *Journal* for January 13, 1948:

" Simenon's subjects often have a profound psychological and ethical interest, but insufficiently indicated, as if he were not aware of their importance himself, or as if he expected the reader to catch a hint. This is what attracts and holds me in him. He writes for the " vast public," to be sure, but delicate and refined readers find something for them too as soon as they deign to take him seriously. He makes one reflect; and this is close to being the height of art; how superior he is in this to those heavy novelists who do not spare us a single commentary ! Simenon sets forth a particular fact, perhaps of general interest; but he is careful not to generalize; that is up to the reader." [1]

This appreciation was written three years before Gide's death. Much critical comment appearing since reveals that readers of discernment are reaching the same conclusions in their evaluation of Simenon's contribution to the modern novel. But Simenon, with characteristic prudence, says that his " apprenticeship " seems to stretch on indefinitely.

Perhaps in recent years no other writer's name has been proposed with such regularity and futility for the Nobel Prize in Literature as Simenon's. Another perennial and equally unsuccessful nominee has, of course, been the late Robert Frost, whose claims for consideration were almost entirely poetic and highly valid. Many questions might be raised as to why he, like the great Giuseppe Ungaretti of Italy, was unable to meet the not always exacting requirements of the Swedish Institute for a laureateship. Even were a volume or so of verse included among Simenon's varied literary accomplishments, he could hardly hope to achieve the eminence of an Ungaretti or a Frost. Looking at Simenon's prolific output—pot boilers, *romans policiers*, essays and psychological novels—one wonders if this very productivity has not irrevocably removed the name of the Belgian writer from the list of likely candidates. Although amazement is invariably voiced on the publication of each successive novel that a single author could produce so much and so well, doubtless it will not be determined for years to come whether among this wealth of volumes there may, after all, be an authentic masterpiece. Be that as it may, it seems safe to say that the Nobel Prize for Literature will forever elude Georges Simenon's grasp as it has that of so many others.

---

[1] André Gide, *Journals*, trans. Justin O'Brien, Vol. IV. Permission to quote granted by Alfred A. Knopf, Inc.

# UN CRITIQUE LITTÉRAIRE DE LA NOUVELLE VAGUE : JEAN-PAUL WEBER *

Le renouvellement est la loi fondamentale de la littérature. Que serait le roman français si nous en étions restés à Maupassant ou à Anatole France ? Que n'aurions-nous perdu si les poètes, au lieu de se métamorphoser au gré de découvertes, s'étaient bornés à répéter docilement les leçons délectables, des romantiques ?

Ce renouvellement perpétuel est-il négation permanente ? Pas nécessairement ; à l'intérieur d'une Ecole, un Nerval ne nie pas Hugo ou Musset, mais plutôt découvre, parmi leurs chants, des cantilènes possibles, en mineur, moins improvisées et plus grêles. Et Pascal ne nie pas Descartes, puisqu'il parle un dialecte cartésien. Pourtant, il faut souvent un œil bien exercé pour discerner, sous les apparences d'une révolution tapageuse, des indices sûrs d'un cheminement continu. « Enfin Malherbe vint.... » Il y a dans ces mots le principe d'une *table rase*. De Marot à Ronsard, de Parny à Lamartine, d'Henry Régnier à Apollinaire, la distance est considérable, voire vertigineuse. Montaigne est un initiateur, Descartes un révolutionnaire, Baudelaire un voyageur sans retour, Mallarmé, Proust, Robbe-Grillet sont de savants chimistes de qui les explosifs, par leurs effets destructeurs, barrent les chemins du passé. Un grand écrivain peut vivre dans la vallée. La plupart des grands mouvements collectifs, ou Ecoles, escaladent les flancs de la colline, mettant leurs pas dans ceux d'un guide hautain et sûr. A peine sont-ils de l'autre côté que de nouveaux versants les tentent. Le passé est souvent comparable, en histoire littéraire, à la tête de Méduse, qui fige ceux qui la fixent de trop près.

Est-ce pour cela que la critique littéraire, elle aussi, à notre sens, doit subir la loi du renouveau ? La vérité est qu'une histoire littéraire trop attentive à son passé risque de nous donner finalement, de son objet, une idée statique. L'impressionnisme d'un Lemaître nous mettra toujours en présence d'un paysage intérieur unique, celui des impressions de Lemaître. Le dogmatisme d'un Brunetière—ou d'un Alain—nous fera connaître les pensées et les arrières-pensées d'un Brunetière ou d'un Alain. Le lansonnisme universitaire, qui nous a valu pourtant une abondante moisson d'inestimables travaux et de précieuses découvertes, aplatit les perspectives, raccourcit les distances, télescope les différences ; il nous présente de la vie

---

* Reprinted from *Saggi e ricerche di letteratura Francese*, V (1965), 213-236.

littéraire, qui est prodigieuse diversité, une image d'autant moins vraie qu'il la veut davantage exacte, parce que, développant toutes les réalités dans le plan du témoignage objectif et de la conscience subjective, le critique lansonien manque le principe de la diversité des êtres, qui est l'âme de l'œuvre. De là vient que la critique littéraire traditionnelle sera toujours plus sensible aux ressemblances qu'aux oppositions, elle recherchera toujours plutôt les sources d'un écrivain que son essence hautaine, irremplaçable, elle s'efforcera toujours de tout ramener au conflit d'un petit nombre de forces impersonnelles — classicisme, baroque, paysage, état d'âme— tandis que la réalité littéraire, la chose littéraire, est faite de révolutions et de nuances, de négations et de meurtres, et qu'il est vain de chercher à superposer, au chaos vivant des œuvres qui s'entre-pillent et s'entretuent, une valse cérémonieuse d'écoles, de styles ou de concepts.

Le renouveau n'est donc pas, dans le domaine de la critique littéraire, un danger à éviter, un péril à conjurer, mais une nécessité et une grâce. Le critique doit dépasser les méthodes les plus éprouvées, les consignes les plus sûres, parce que l'obéissance sans hésitation ni murmure, la résistance sans esprit de recul conduisent, en cette matière, sous les apparences trompeuses d'un terrain puissamment défendu, à une défaite essentielle. En s'agrippant aux accidents des "leçons du passé," l'historien risque de transformer un terrain voué, par nature, aux évolutions d'une armée indisciplinée et ardente, en une forteresse immobile, offrant le flanc à d'innombrables mouvements tournants. Et toute tentative pour endiguer, par le moyen d'une ligne Maginot réputée imprenable, l'imprévisible courant de l'invention littéraire, aura nécessairement pour résultat de masquer la réalité, et de se rendre aveugle aux faits. Le châtiment immanent, inscrit dans une critique figée, est l'inadéquation, l'impossibilité de lutter avec une littérature de plus en plus indocile, l'altération et l'appauvrissement du spectacle que nous offre spontanément la permanente révolution littéraire.

Sans doute l'idée, d'allure nietzschéenne, que le critique doit être dépassé, n'est-elle pas nouvelle. Au-dedans comme au-dehors de la critique littéraire, on prend de mieux en mieux conscience des limites du lansonnisme. Freud est peut-être l'un des premiers à avoir senti qu'il convient de creuser au-delà des apparences explicites, et que l'œuvre existe comme un message chiffré. En un buissonnement hardi, à partir du tronc psychanalytique, la critique littéraire contemporaine, en France, nous présente toute une variété de doctrines et d'ouvrages qui veulent transcender le donné: depuis Bachelard, tantôt psychanalyste tantôt phénoménologue, et Sartre, aux positions nuancées et parfois contradictoires, jusqu'aux subtiles analyses d'un Jean-Pierre Richard, d'un Starobinski, d'un Georges Poulet. Parmi les auteurs participant de cette tendance nouvelle, visant au renouvellement de toutes les perspectives, une œuvre se détache, toute récente, et relativement peu connue encore: celle de Jean-Paul Weber.

Ce critique et historien de la littérature française nous vient d'ailleurs: de la philosophie. De ses origines philosophiques, il a gardé le goût des idées générales, la nostalgie des définitions, et un certain sens, très philosophique, du relativisme universel. Je m'empresse d'ajouter que la philosophie n'interfère pas, chez lui, avec l'érudition proprement littéraire, mais qu'elle surmonte plutôt celle-ci, l'existentialisme couronne les études littéraires de Sartre, ou la psychanalyse celles de Bachelard.

Jean-Paul Weber s'est fait connaître par un petit volume élégant sur *La Psychologie de l'art*.[1] Il y situe, dans le cadre des doctrines antérieures, ses propres vues, ramassées « nucléairement » en quelque sorte, sur la contemplation, l'inspiration et la création esthétique, et plus particulièrement littéraire. La doctrine globale de cet ouvrage est ensuite reprise, développée et appliquée au cas particulier de l'invention littéraire dans la thèse de doctorat ès lettres intitulée *Genèse de l'œuvre poétique*,[2] qui contient l'analyse thématique de huit poètes français, Vigny, Hugo, Baudelaire, Verlaine, Mallarmé, Apollinaire, Valéry et Claudel. Tout récemment, un autre volume de théorie et d'analyse a paru, *Domaines thématiques*,[3] réunissant des études sur Poe, Gogol, Nerval, Lautréamont, Kafka et Julien Gracq. Enfin, un nouvel ouvrage, reposant sur les mêmes bases, fera connaître bientôt des perspectives thématiques sur l'œuvre de Stendhal.[4] L'ensemble de ces livres désigne nettement—jusqu'à nouvel ordre—un littéraire.[5] Aussi bien, Weber, qui a enseigné d'abord la philosophie à Paris, enseigne-t-il actuellement l'histoire de la littérature dans une Université new-yorkaise.

Jetant un coup d'œil global sur l'œuvre publiée de Jean-Paul Weber, nous discernons aisément deux lignes de force. D'une part, Weber propose au lecteur une approche nouvelle de l'écrivain et de ses écrits: on peut appeler cette méthode, et le champ de ses applications immédiates, *analyse thématique*. D'autre part, Weber présente, destinée surtout aux philosophes, une doctrine esthétique générale, dont l'analyse thématique n'est qu'un cas particulier; appelons cette doctrine *esthétique des profondeurs*, ou *esthétique des sources*. Nous nous bornerons à examiner ici, avec quelque détail, l'analyse thématique,[6] ne consacrant, faute de place, que de brèves remarques au versant proprement esthétique des recherches weberiennes.

L'analyse thématique repose sur la notion de thème: " Nous entendons par *thème*, dit Weber, un événement ou une situation (au sens le plus large du mot) infantiles, susceptibles de se manifester — en général inconsciemment — dans une œuvre ou un ensemble d'œuvres d'art... soit symboliquement, soit " en clair "—étant entendu que par *symbole* nous comprenons

---

[1] Presses Universitaires de France, 1958, 3ᵉ édition sous presse.

[2] Gallimard, " Bibliothèque des Idées," 1961.

[3] Gallimard, " Bibliothèque des Idées," 1964.

[4] *Stendhal ou les cristallisations de la Morsure*, sous presse.

[5] Signalons également des articles dans la " *Revue d'Esthétique*," la " *Revue de Métaphysique et de Morale*," " *Modern Language Notes*," la " *Nouvelle Revue Française*," etc., ainsi que la thèse complémentaire sur les *Regulae* de Descartes (1964). Jean-Paul Weber est également l'auteur de deux récits publiés chez Gallimard, *Meurtre à l'observatoire* et *L'Orient extrême*.

[6] " Les travaux de J.-P. Weber s'orientent, depuis sa *Psychologie de l'art* (1958), vers une *analyse thématique*... " (G. Rosolato, " Genèse de l'œuvre poétique, " *Les Temps modernes*... (Novembre 1961); 592). Voir dans Ch. Mauron, *Des Métaphores obsédantes au mythe personnel*, Corti, 1963, une esquisse de l'histoire de la *critique thématique* en France (13-15, 26-31).

181

tout substitut *analogique* du symbolisé." [1] Le thème, c'est donc " la trace qu'un souvenir d'enfance a laissée dans la mémoire d'un écrivain." [2] Ainsi se dévoile d'emblée la dimension que les analyses weberiennes ajoutent à l'œuvre: la dimension de l'enfance. L'œuvre d'art, et le phénomène art dans sa totalité, ne sauraient être compris qu'en étant placés dans la lumière, incertaine et violente, qui vient des *sources*.

Toutefois la notion de thème appelle un complément contrastant, qui est l'idée de *modulation*.[3] " Nous appellerons *modulation* ou *orchestration* d'un thème... sa résurgence symbolique dans une œuvre ou un destin qu'il oriente." [4] Plus simplement, on pourrait entendre " par *modulation*, tout *analogon* du thème, en d'autres termes, le thème symbolisé." [5] Idéalement, on pourrait comprendre l'ensemble des œuvres d'un écrivain comme un *domaine de correspondance*, au sens baudelairien:

> Comme de longs échos qui de loin se confondent
> Dans *une ténébreuse et profonde unité*,
> Vaste comme la nuit et comme la clarté,
> Les parfums, les couleurs et les sons se répondent...
>
> L'homme y passe à travers *des forêts de symboles*...,[6]

ces parfums, ces couleurs étant, chez un écrivain, ceux d'

> Une bizarre fleur qui parfume sa vie
> Transparente, *la fleur qu'il a sentie, enfant,*
> Au filigrane bleu de l'âme se greffant.[7]

Mais, dans la pratique, les choses, comme il se doit, se compliquent.

Tout d'abord, Weber pense que l'œuvre surgit, constamment, d'une source ou d'un thème *unique*:[8] " l'œuvre total d'un écrivain... exprime, à travers une multitude en droit indéfinie de symboles, c'est-à-dire d'analogies, une hantise ou un *thème* unique." [9] Seules feraient exception des œuvres

---

[1] *Genèse de l'œuvre poétique*, 13.

[2] *Domaines thématiques*, 9.

[3] Otto Hahn (*Les Temps modernes* (mai 1963), 2087, n. 2) indique que les expressions *thème* et *modulation* apparaissent déjà chez Sartre (*Baudelaire*, 222, et *Genet*, 500). Mais chez Sartre—qui d'ailleurs n'emploie plus le mot " thème " dans *Critique de la raison dialectique*, où il se sert du mot " coloration " (71)—*thème* signifie " la forme générale de l'anecdote " ou encore " le mouvement général d'un comportement." Chez Weber le mot *thème* a un sens plus précis et plus unifié. D'autre part, " modulation " signifie chez lui *variation*, au sens musical du terme. Weber considère l'œuvre totale d'un écrivain comme une " partition " musicale, où il s'agit de découvrir le ou les thèmes *développés* ou *modulés* par le compositeur (mais inconsciemment).

[4] *Genèse de l'œuvre poétique*, 15.

[5] *Domaines thématiques*, 9.

[6] Baudelaire, *Correspondances*.

[7] Vers cités (à propos de Weber) dans H. Mondor, *Autres Précisions sur Mallarmé*, 147.

[8] C'est ce que Weber appelle *monothématisme* de l'œuvre (*Domaines*, 27).

[9] *Genèse*, 19.

d'auteurs doués de tempérament névrotique: " Il semblerait que la valence thématique soit fonction du degré d'intégration de la personnalité: un poète équilibré comme Valéry serait dominé par un thème unique; un écrivain comme Nerval ou comme Gogol, moins fortement intégré, pourrait créer dans un système bithématique ou même plurivalent." [1] Quoi qu'il en soit de ce dernier point, soulignons que le monothématisme weberien n'est pas une construction rationnelle, indépendante de l'expérience. Tout montre que l'idée d'un thème unique orientant toutes les perspectives d'une œuvre donnée, est issue au contraire des lectures illuminées par la notion de *symbole* ou d'*analogon*. Ce n'est pas parce que Weber voulait, antérieurement à toute lecture, trouver un seul thème chez Poe, qu'il l'y a découvert; c'est parce que le thème de l'Horloge, d'abord clairement aperçu à travers une modulation ou symbolisme incontestable,[2] appliqué *ensuite* au déchiffrement des autres œuvres poesques, a conduit à constater des modulations similaires et inconscientes ailleurs.[3]

Notons dès à présent que le monothématisme reconnu par Weber a été l'objet d'assez sévères critiques.[4] Sans doute s'agit-il d'une méprise: loin d'imposer à toute œuvre une monotone unité thématique, Weber reconnaît qu'à côté d'auteurs " modulant indéfiniment le même thème, dont ils se contentent de varier les aspects ou profils," il en est d'autres qui " offrent une thématique proliférante, buissonnante, telle modulation du thème devenant thème à son tour, susceptible à son tour d'être modulé à l'infini." [5] Le monothématisme, affirme Weber, est " susceptible d'une pluralité de faciès qui en atténuent la sévérité... Il est fort possible... qu'un certain nombre de textes que précisément nos investigations ne parviennent pas à ramener au commun dénominateur thématique puissent s'expliquer par des souvenirs d'enfance absolument indépendants " (surtout dans le cas d'une névrose caractérisée).[6] Et Weber penche finalement " vers une conception de monarchie thématique tempérée—le thème fondamental éclairant l'essentiel de l'œuvre, et des souvenirs moins importants expliquant ses aspects mineurs—et non pas vers une conception de monarchisme absolu." [7]

La distinction entre *thème* et *motif* est capitale. " Par *motif* nous entendons tout élément linguistique revenant avec insistance dans l'œuvre d'un écrivain... Le *thème* s'en distingue en ce qu'il n'est que secondairement un phénomène de vocabulaire; quoiqu'il puisse être présent *en clair* dans l'œuvre du poète, il n'y figure généralement que sous une forme symbolique." [8] Ainsi les études purement stylistiques sont, pour Weber, condamnées à demeurer à la surface de l'œuvre: elles n'en explorent que les *motifs*. Si

---

[1] *Domaines*, 26.
[2] *Genèse*, 23; *Domaines*, 38 sqq.
[3] *Genèse*, 19-29.
[4] *Domaines*, 26-29.
[5] *Genèse*, 504-505.
[6] *Domaines*, 27.
[7] *Ibid.*
[8] *Genèse*, 17.

l'on veut aller plus loin, il faudra creuser plus profond, et retrouver, au-delà des constantes linguistiques, les sources invisibles qui alimentent le paysage de l'œuvre, lui donnent son allure personnelle et ses nuances irremplaçables.

Les présupposés d'une telle doctrine, qui met l'accent sur l'unité inaperçue et la genèse invisible, sont assez nombreux. Le principe le plus important en est la *réalité de l'inconscient* que, après James, Bergson et Freud, Weber admet inconditionnellement, contre le Sartre de *L'Etre et le Néant*.[1] Comme chez Freud, l'inconscient est, chez Weber, une force capable d'orienter, à l'insu du sujet, ses volontés, états d'âme et créations esthétiques. Plus précisément—avec Wordsworth et Baudelaire—Weber pense qu'un souvenir d'enfance est apte à diriger, de façon constante, les puissances créatrices d'un écrivain.[2] La création poétique lui apparaît ainsi comme la résultante de deux vecteurs, dont l'un est le thème sousjacent à la conscience actuelle de l'artiste, et l'autre, sa virtuosité formelle.[3] Il admet encore qu'un auteur peut connaître son thème, sans soupçonner le rôle primordial que le thème peut jouer dans la création d'une œuvre.[4] Toutes ces implications des notions fondamentales de thème et de modulation convergent finalement vers l'idée que nous ne sommes pas conscients de ce qui nous pousse à écrire, que l'auteur ne sait pas pourquoi il écrit, ni pourquoi il écrit ce qu'il écrit. Cette idée, Weber ne cherche jamais à la démontrer. Sans doute pense-t-il qu'elle est trop évidente pour avoir besoin de démonstration. Puisque cette idée se retrouve à la base des esthétiques freudienne et issues de la psychanalyse freudienne, la question se pose de savoir quels sont, au juste, les rapports entre Freud et Weber.

Ce problème à déjà fait couler pas mal d'encre. Weber lui-même a consacré à la réfutation de l'esthétique psychanalytique plusieurs pages de sa *Psychologie de l'art*[5] et des *Domaines thématiques*.[6] " Nous croyons sincèrement, dit-il, qu'on ne peut nous accuser d'être un freudien, parce que, de la psychanalyse freudienne, nous n'admettons point le dogme qui lui paraît consubstantiel: la réduction des névroses et " sublimations " au seul complexe d'Œdipe, avec son corollaire, le complexe de la castration." [7] Un psychanalyste comme le D<sup>r</sup> Rosolato a pu écrire: " Pour Weber, il ne saurait être question de psychanalyse sinon pour quelques emprunts "; et il parle d'" une méconnaissance farouche." [8] De même, un critique d'obédience freudienne, Charles Mauron, prononce à propos de Weber les mots:

---

[1] *La Psychologie de l'art*, 1, note 1. Les positions sartriennes semblent moins abruptes dans *Critique de la raison dialectique*, parue depuis.

[2] *La Psychologie de l'art*, 31-33.

[3] *Domaines*, 29-31 (*L'analyse thématique n'explique que le mystère*).

[4] Ainsi chez Julien Gracq. *Domaines*, 295.

[5] *Psychologie*, 77-85.

[6] *Domaines*, 19-21.

[7] *Ibid.*, 19.

[8] " *Les Temps modernes*," (novembre 1961), 600 et n. 1.

" une fausse psychanalyse." [1] La cause est donc entendue: l'analyse thématique de Weber n'est pas la psychanalyse. Weber refuse les complexes tout faits du freudisme (le " platonisme des complexes "), et s'il admet les notions psychologiques—plutôt que psychanalytiques—d'*enfance* et de *symbole*, il cherche à dépister, dans l'œuvre, un thème *exclusif* et *personnel*. Aussi bien, il est facile de mesurer l'écart toutes les fois que les analyses weberiennes portent sur un auteur psychanalysé selon les méthodes traditionnelles.[2]

Peut-être pourrait-on rattacher les vues de Weber à celles qui ont été exprimées par un psychologue français tombé, trop jeune, sous les balles d'un peloton d'exécution allemand: Politzer, qui reprochait justement à la psychanalyse de s'enliser dans de faciles généralisations, et qui visait à " dramatiser " et à " personnaliser " la psychanalyse.

En matière de critique littéraire, facilement subjective, les méthodes ont sans doute plus d'importance que les principes, ceux-ci constituant plutôt la conséquence et la vérification de celles-là. Or, si, par ses principes, Weber paraît se rattacher à des auteurs qui ont pu l'influencer, les méthodes de l'analyse thématique sont entièrement originales. Weber les a décrites minutieusement tant dans sa thèse que dans les *Domaines thématiques*. L'exposé de ce dernier ouvrage paraît plus systématique et plus clair [3]; mais on doit se reporter également à celui de la thèse.[4]

Weber parle d'analyse thématique *progressive et régressive* [5]; on pourrait aussi bien employer les termes de *déduction* et d'*induction* thématiques. Il y a *déduction thématique* lorsque le critique se trouve en possession d'un souvenir d'enfance dûment authentifié et qui, à l'examen, se révèle omniprésent, sous une forme symbolique, dans l'œuvre tout entière d'un écrivain. Il y a *induction thématique* quand divers indices, dont Weber dresse la liste, permettent de présumer l'existence d'un " thème " que, dans le cas le plus favorable, un souvenir d'enfance découvert après coup permet d'authentiquer. Reste à commenter et à préciser ces formules méthodologiques.

Que signifie d'abord l'omniprésence, sous une forme symbolique, d'un souvenir d'enfance? Prenons l'exemple de Valéry.[6] Le *souvenir thématique* figure en toutes lettres dans les œuvres de Paul Valéry [7]: âgé de trois ans, le futur écrivain tombe dans le bassin du jardin public de Sète où il manque de se noyer. Le contenu du souvenir comporte la vision du bassin, où vivaient des cygnes; un petit enfant chargé d'un manteau et de collerettes empesées, et qui jette des graviers dans l'eau; une bonne qui oublie de le surveiller, et met " en grand péril " son " petit destin "; la noyade du

---

[1] *Des Métaphores obsédantes...*, 340. Cf. également 213, et " Le Provençal " du 21 mars 1961, qui invoque le " bon sens," mis bizarrement au service du freudisme.

[2] C'est le cas de Poe, de Mallarmé, de Baudelaire, etc.

[3] *Domaines*, 13-18.

[4] *Genèse*, 19-29.

[5] *Ibid.*, 24-25.

[6] *Ibid.*, 388-451.

[7] *Ibid.*, 388-389.

" cygne improvisé," d'abord " flottant par le soutien des robes empesées qui formaient des poches d'air," et qui finit par perdre connaissance; enfin le sauvetage inattendu.

Voilà donc un *souvenir d'enfance*. Comment prouver qu'il s'agit bien d'un *souvenir thématique*, au sens weberien du mot ? Weber y parvient en montrant que les divers éléments ou l'ensemble de ce souvenir figurent, sous une forme aisément reconnaissable, dans la quasi-totalité des poèmes que l'enfant se noyant parmi les cygnes écrira, devenu adulte.

Ainsi, la *noyade* apparaît dans les textes suivants :

Hideusement s'en va sous les flots blafards     (Rêve);
Et le soleil mourant... ondoyait     (La Marche impériale);
   Du cygne funèbre qui dort
   Charmant tombeau sur la fontaine     (Intermède);
C'est un effondrement dans un puits de tristesse
                                    (Pessimisme d'une heure);
S'enfoncent pesamment dans l'onde calme et plate     (La Mer);
   mourant oiseau qui plonge     (Ibid.)
Car une chair, illuminant l'humide azur
Vient d'y plonger...     (Luxurieuse au bain);
Tes regards se noyaient dans la source d'argent     (Myriam);
Le pur soleil descendait dans le sel d'écume     (" Vers libres ").

Arrêtons ici cette énumération, qui risquerait de devenir fastidieuse. L'important, c'est qu'à côté de cette " dominante " de l'œuvre valéryenne, qu'une analyse statistique eût pu découvrir, à la rigueur, nous trouvons d'autres allusions, d'autres hantises, qui s'enracinent incontestablement dans le même souvenir. Ainsi l'image de quelque chose de blanc qui glisse sur l'eau, ne rappelle-t-elle pas très précisément les brefs instants d'avant la noyade, durant lesquels le petit Valéry vêtu de blanc imitant à son insu les cygnes ?

   O soirée à peine frivole
   D'une mince lune sur l'eau     (Intermède);
   La plume d'ombre un peu lointaine
   Du cygne funèbre qui dort...
   Se mire à l'eau sainte et lucide     (Ibid.);
Neige sur l'onde ! un souffle insensible le pousse
Comme un vaisseau fantôme enfui parmi l'azur     (Le Cygne);
   Ta nudité s'enflamme et tu nages splendide     (Luxurieuse au bain);
Car l'Archange à l'autel de Lune lentement
Pour la suave et la blanche cérémonie
Apparaît (telle une lumière sur les eaux)     (La Messe angélique);
   Leur fourrure à l'éclat des glaciers baignés d'aube     (Les Chats blancs);
Fuir ! sur un fleuve calme et si calme et si lent
Dans l'ivoire incrusté d'argent d'un canot frêle
Qui sur l'eau glisse comme un rêve - vague et blanc !     (Sur l'eau);

>Des blancs torses s'y baignent (" Vers libres ");
>    la chair
>Amèrement vomie au soleil par la mer (Naissance de Vénus);
>Sur les cygnes dolents qui frôlent les roseaux
>— Galères blanches et carènes lumineuses—
>Elle effeuille des lys et des roses neigeuses
>Et les pétales font des cercles sur les eaux (Féerie);
>Un fruit de chair se baigne en quelque jeune vasque (Baignée);
>O mes baisers jetés à la calme fontaine,
>Roses vaines que vers mon image lointaine
>Epand sur l'eau ma main suave avec effroi ! (Narcisse parle.)

On pourrait montrer de même, en puisant dans le recueil d'exemples fourni par Weber dans son chapitre sur Valéry, que d'autres versants du *souvenir thématique* se retrouvent également, tels quels, ou sous une forme légèrement différente, *analogique*, dans l'œuvre de l'écrivain: le bord du bassin fatal; les cygnes; les graviers jetés par l'enfant; le sauvetage, etc. Assurément, si l'on s'hypnotise sur les exemples concernant tel ou tel versant particulier, le doute est possible: ne s'agit-il pas d'un pur hasard ? N'est-il pas arbitraire, après avoir isolé quelques vers ou fragments, de les rapporter à un souvenir d'enfance ? Ne pourrait-on pas invoquer plutôt la liberté de l'artiste, l'inspiration, les contingences d'une existence d'artiste ? —Mais ce qui emporte la conviction, ce sont les considérations suivantes:

1) tous les aspects du souvenir d'enfance se retrouvent dans l'œuvre: ce qui ne peut être dû au hasard seul;

2) il est possible de grouper un très grand nombre de textes sous l'un ou l'autre aspect du souvenir d'enfance;

3) il est impossible de parvenir aux mêmes résultats, c'est-à-dire d'établir des rapports nombreux et précis entre la Noyade parmi les cygnes et les poèmes d'un adulte, en partant de l'œuvre d'un autre écrivain, par exemple Victor Hugo, Verlaine, ou même Mallarmé;

4) enfin, certains textes de Valéry, que nous ne pouvons examiner en détail, faute de place, présentent sous un voile d'analogies transparentes la quasi-totalité des épisodes du souvenir en question: ainsi la " symphonie marine " (vaisseau; l'horizon se peuple de galères; orage menaçant; tout est mobile et périlleux; salut—le tout transposant évidemment l'épopée de la noyade et du salut de Valéry-enfant) [1]; ainsi *Narcisse parle*, où ne manque que le salut final [2]; ainsi la version ancienne d'*Anne* [3]; ainsi le

---
[1] *Ibid.*, 395-396.
[2] *Ibid.*, 406-408.
[3] *Ibid.*, 410.

*Cimetière marin*, qui chante la marche d'Oiseaux sur l'eau, le spectre de la Mort, enfin le jaillissement de l'onde, salut:

Courons à l'onde en rejaillir vivant! [1]

Tant d'épreuves et de contre-épreuves ne sauraient être attribuées au hasard, aux contingences, ou aux hantises du lecteur. Il s'agit bien d'un ensemble de hantises complexe, structuré, objectivement décelable, propre au seul Valéry, et dont le rattachement à la structure analogue du *souvenir d'enfance* ne saurait faire par conséquent de doute: ce qui suffit pour promouvoir le souvenir d'enfance au rang d'un *souvenir thématique*.

On voit ainsi, dans le cadre d'une *analyse thématique déductive*, comment opérer la jonction entre un souvenir d'enfance et l'œuvre: en recherchant, entre le souvenir et l'œuvre, des analogies précises, nombreuses, structurées, et telles qu'on n'en puisse pas trouver de semblables entre ce même souvenir d'enfance et des œuvres d'autres écrivains. Si l'on demande maintenant comment trouver le souvenir d'enfance qui soit bien le souvenir thématique, le thème de l'œuvre globale, sans doute Weber répondrait-il—à en juger par les analyses publiées—que cette découverte est le fruit à la fois de la patience du lecteur et de l'intérêt suscité par l'enfance de l'auteur. Lorsque les souvenirs d'enfance manquent, la méthode déductive est évidemment impraticable. Lorsque nous sommes en présence d'un petit nombre de souvenirs, il y a des chances que l'un d'entre eux soit le souvenir thématique: il faut alors partir de chacun d'eux comme d'une " hypothèse de travail," et vérifier s'il se retrouve analogiquement dans les œuvres. Bien entendu, plus on connaît de souvenirs d'enfance, et plus les chances augmentent de discerner parmi eux le, ou les, souvenirs thématiques proprement dits.

L'analyse thématique inductive s'impose là où les souvenirs font défaut ou sont en nombre insuffisant. Elle se présente, selon Weber, sous plusieurs formes:

*(a)* méthode du *texte révélateur*. Elle consiste à " partir du déchiffrement thématique d'un texte suffisamment bref et explicite pour que le thème s'y inscrive presque en clair, et d'emblée." [2] Weber cite le cas de l'analyse de Poe, qui " a débuté par *Le Diable dans le Beffroi*, conte bref où le village *Quelle-heure-est-il* se déchiffre immédiatement comme cadran, et la rencontre du Diable et du Sonneur en haut de beffroi, à midi, comme rencontre des deux aiguilles en haut de ce cadran même." [3] Une fois le *thème de l'Horloge* établi par ces déchiffrements immédiats, il devient possible, selon les procédés analogiques définis plus haut, de tenter d'interpréter comme *contes horlogers* une foule de textes poesques. Weber parvient même à les répartir en " cycles ": il y a ainsi un " cycle de douze heures," dont font partie *le Masque de la Mort rouge* (sonnerie de minuit, l'ombre de l'horloge d'ébène qui se projette, à la fin du conte, sur le Masque),

---

[1] *Ibid.*, 438-441.
[2] *Domaines*, 14.
[3] *Ibid.*

*Le Corbeau* (minuit lugubre, onze Nevermore—comme, dans *Le Diable dans le Beffroi*, treize coups d'horloge), *La Chute de la Maison Usher, Ligeia, Une descente dans le Maëlstrom*; un " cycle de sonneries successives ": *Hans Pfaall* (le ballon alunit à *midi*, sommet de sa course, puis revient vers la terre, point le plus bas, en lâchant *six sacs*—sonnerie de six heures), *Un cœur révélateur* (chaque nuit, vers *minuit*, le cœur assimilé à une montre, l'angle droit suggérant la position des aiguilles à *trois* heures, la hantise du nombre *trois*), *Le Puits et le pendule* (double exécution du prisonnier par un mécanisme horloger, puis par une chute abyssale); le " cycle des poids " (*Hop-Frog*, soixante caryatides, minuit, remontée de Hop-Frog à l'aide d'une chaîne); *Le Scarabée d'or* (montée et descente d'un scarabée pesant, massif, couleur d'or, attaché à une ficelle), etc.; sans oublier l'extraordinaire *Faux du Temps* (*The Scythe of Time, A Predicament*), où la grande aiguille d'une horloge guillotine lentement l'héroïne du conte, aux environs de *cinq heures vingt-sept* ....

Une fois la quasi-totalité des textes déchiffrée à l'aide du code horloger, il devient possible—c'est le deuxième temps de la méthode du " texte révélateur "—de rechercher le *souvenir thématique* qui a pu orienter dans le sens de l'horloge l'imagination créatrice de Poe: Weber croit tenir au moins une réminiscence directe de ce souvenir thématique dans *William Wilson*, qui transpose l'enfance écossaise de Poe, et mentionne la présence à l'école d'" une horloge d'une dimension prodigieuse." [1]

*(b) Méthodes des hantises linguistiques.* Dans certains cas, écrit Weber, " c'est l'insistance de l'écrivain sur une idée ou sur un objet, c'est la persistance de certains noms, de certains verbes... de certaines images même, qui trahissent, involontairement, une obsession inconsciente, et peuvent suggérer un souvenir d'enfance, qu'il appartiendrait au chercheur de découvrir." [2] Ainsi les textes de Nerval cernent indiscutablement la hantise du *feu* (abondance de termes relatifs au feu, au volcan, au rouge, au sang, au jaune, à l'or, au soleil, à la lumière et à ses dérivés: lueur, luire, clarté, éclaircir, briller, étincelle, éclair, foudre, rayon, etc.).[3] Il ne suffit pas, certes, de la constater: il faut tenter de la préciser, de la centrer sur un événement qui aurait chance d'être privilégié, et qui renverrait à un souvenir d'enfance. Semblablement, les poèmes de Mallarmé renferment de très nombreux vers relatifs à l'oiseau, à l'aile, à la plume; au vol; au mouvement ailé; à la chute; et l'ensemble de ces textes converge visiblement vers l'image, qui pourrait être thématique, de la chute d'un oiseau.[4]

*(c) Méthode du point de fuite.* Dans un cas au moins, Weber semble avoir recours à un procédé plus intuitif: dans le cas de Baudelaire. " Chez Baudelaire, confessons que nous avons été d'abord induit en erreur par la

---

[1] *Ibid.*, 42. Mais cf. aussi 27, n. I, sur la possibilité d'un thème secondaire.

[2] *Domaines*, 14.

[3] *Ibid.*, 148 sqq.

[4] *Genèse*, 224 sqq.

fréquence des allusions au sein, qui nous a paru orienter vers le thème de l'Allaitement. Pourtant, si quelques poèmes semblaient recevoir un sens thématique valable... d'autres textes demeuraient, malgré nos efforts, tout à fait en dehors de la thématique entrevue.... Nous avons eu soudain l'intuition, beaucoup plus tard, en lisant un ouvrage de Gide, qu'un fantasme analogue à celui que Gide avouait... pouvait expliquer plusieurs poèmes de Baudelaire [1]; intuition que nous avons pu à la fois vérifier par des recoupements biographiques, et généraliser au-delà de l'attente, puisque la quasi-totalité des poèmes de Baudelaire a fini par s'intégrer au domaine modulateur du Revenant." [2]

Weber note enfin que, " le plus souvent, la recherche thématique procède par une combinaison plus ou moins libre des trois procédés indiqués: souvenir d'enfance authentique, texte révélateur, hantise stylistique." [3]

Ainsi nous nous trouvons en présence d'un ensemble de procédés parfaitement définis, constituant une méthode susceptible d'être appliquée, de toute évidence, à n'importe quelle œuvre globale d'écrivain, de poète, voire de philosophe.[4] La question qui se pose aussitôt est, évidemment, celle de la validité de cette méthode.

Son originalité ne fait pas de doute. Elle ne doit rien aux procédés classiques de la psychanalyse, fondés sur un dictionnaire de symbolismes universels, et l'existence de quelques complexes cliniques classiques. La stylistique s'aventure rarement dans les domaines inconscients, ou ceux de l'enfance. Bachelard, Georges Poulet, J.-P. Richard, Butor récusent, souvent avec violence, l'idée même d'une méthode générale, se fiant de préférence à leurs intuitions personnelles. On pourrait penser à Ch. Mauron.[5] Mais les techniques de cet auteur sont à base de superpositions de poèmes, qui n'impliquent, au point de départ, qu'un nombre très limité de textes, ce qui conduit à fausser les perspectives et à subjectiver les résultats; le procédé de la superposition n'offre ni la généralité des " hantises linguistiques," ni le caractère prégnant et indiscutable des " textes révélateurs." D'autre part, à peine un " réseau " de métaphores entrevu, Mauron s'empresse de l'interpréter à la lumière des complexes freudiens, versant ainsi dans une psychanalyse littéraire qui manque à la fois d'originalité et de base. Quant aux déchiffrements sartriens, il est visible qu'ils n'ont pas encore trouvé, sur le plan de la critique littéraire, leur point d'équilibre.

Reste le problème de la valeur. Deux attitudes sont ici possibles, et ont été formulées. D'une part, mettant entre parenthèses la question de la vérité, on peut souligner le caractère neuf et éclairant des analyses que sous-tendent les méthodes weberiennes. On pourra trouver ainsi qu'aucun

---

[1] Il s'agit du fantasme du retour du père mort, venant retrouver la mère de l'écrivain. *Si le grain ne meurt*, 28, Cf. *Genèse*, 188, n. I. Notons qu'il y a une légère contradiction entre le récit des *Domaines* et le début du chapitre sur Baudelaire (*Genèse*, 185).

[2] *Domaines*, 17.

[3] *Ibid.*, 15.

[4] Weber annonce, en effet, une étude analytique thématique sur Bergson.

[5] *Des Métaphores obsédantes au mythe personnel*, 1963.

critique n'a encore réussi à mettre en évidence avec autant de clarté la hantise horlogère chez Poe, pourtant indiscutable et omniprésente. On pourra insister sur l'intérêt d'une étude qui propose du *Cimetière marin* une interprétation particulièrement simple, d'accord à la fois avec les données biographiques et l'ensemble de l'œuvre valéryenne. On pourra mettre en valeur l'originalité et le caractère surprenant d'une analyse comme celle de Gogol, dont il serait malaisé de trouver l'équivalent dans la critique littéraire, et qui aboutit à " expliquer " le fantastique du *Nez* de façon plausible. Il semble bien que, quelle que soit la position ultérieure des érudits, il serait difficile de contester aux résultats et aux méthodes de Weber leur nouveauté et leur intérêt, disons, de curiosité.

Pourtant ce n'est pas ainsi que Weber lui-même conçoit l'intérêt de ses études : visiblement il pense que ces dernières ne sont pas seulement curieuses, mais qu'elles offrent au moins une approximation de la vérité. Pour contester sérieusement ce point de vue, il ne suffit pas de nier en bloc, sous prétexte que le " weberisme " ne parvient à rejoindre ni l'érudition lansonienne, ni l'orthodoxie freudienne. Il ne suffit pas d'isoler quelques textes demeurant extérieurs à l'interprétation proposée. Il faudrait viser plus précisément au centre même de la doctrine et de la méthode : s'opposer, par exemple, à l'intervention de l'inconscient, de l'enfance, du symbolisme ; s'inscrire en faux contre l'idée de faire appel à des *analogies* en rapprochant des textes d'un même auteur, en apparence éloignés les uns des autres. Essayons de scruter ces différents points.

Il est impossible de négliger le rôle que joue l'enfance de l'écrivain dans son œuvre. Au reste, nul n'y songe ; les critiques fouillent à l'envi dans les mémoires et autobiographies ; l'enfance de Gide, celle de Rimbaud, celle de Balzac ont été étudiées dans cette perspective, et l'on est d'accord que de telles recherches jettent sur le destin ultérieur de l'artiste, de très importantes clartés. Toutefois, les analyses weberiennes font généralement état d'événements qui peuvent paraître de minime importance ; et quelquefois le souvenir de ces événements, même s'il est pleinement conscient, semble hors de proportion avec le rôle qu'il joue, selon Weber, dans l'imagination créatrice des écrivains. Comment expliquer l'importance, pour un Mallarmé, d'un oiseau blessé, tombé ; pour un Poe, d'une horloge ; pour un Hugo, d'une image et d'une légende rhénane ?

A cette objection deux réponses sont possibles. D'une part, quoique Weber ne le dise pas expressément, il paraît bien établi que l'enfant ne voit ni n'apprécie le monde et les événements comme l'adulte. Que chacun fasse son examen de conscience : n'apercevra-t-il pas, dans sa lointaine enfance, quelque incident—la mort d'un animal familier, par exemple—qui, tout en laissant les adultes indifférents, a eu le don de provoquer dans son âme des bouleversements profonds ? On sait que l'enfant est volontiers animiste, vitaliste, artificialiste. L'adulte l'est moins, et autrement. Les acquisitions les plus sûres de la psychologie de l'enfant montrent ainsi que l'attention à certains détails pour nous insignifiants, loin d'être l'exception, doit être la règle.

D'autre part, il serait facile de prouver que parfois des souvenirs évanouis dirigent, à notre insu, les secrètes stratégies de notre imagination.

Dans un article remarquable,[1] paru un an après la thèse de Weber, Etienne Souriau décrit un souvenir " qui remonte plus haut que l'âge de deux ans... tout a pu en être contrôlé." [2] Voici ce souvenir. " Imaginez un vitrail de cathédrale, dans une foret, un vitrail ruisselant des plus magnifiques couleurs. En deçà, retombant sur lui, de splendides draperies écarlates. Au-delà, appuyés sur lui, des feuillages d'arbres, ensoleillés, jaunes et dorés. Et puis, en profonde perspective, l'intérieur de la forêt, une vaste futaie traversée par les rayons du soir. Et au fond, la lisière même de la forêt: de hauts troncs verticaux; à contre-jour. Et le long de cette lisière, en dehors de la forêt, de droite à gauche, un par un ou par petits groupes, des hommes mystérieux qui, de temps en temps, tout à coup, se retournent et se mettent à défiler en sens inverse." [3]

Ce souvenir est en réalité très proche d'une œuvre d'art: " La description fantasmagorique du vitrail, dans la forêt, confirme Souriau, et des passants mystérieux," " n'est pas à proprement parler une image mentale." [4] C'est plutôt ce que Weber appellerait un " thème ": puissant aimant mental enfoui dans les profondeurs du passé. Aussi bien, ce " thème " a-t-il d'abord été " induit "[5] de toute une série d'expériences psychiques présentant, avec la description faite après coup, des ressemblances globales, ou de détail: " une patrouille allemande qui s'en venait l'arme à la main, le long d'une lisière de bois illuminé par le soir "; " des ponchos suspendus à des branches d'arbres, près de la lisière, qui évoquaient des draperies "; " une gravure de Gustave Doré pour l'Arioste, avec draperies et vitrail ": et Souriau conclut: " C'est (la) constance (de cet effet mental), sa netteté, sa persistance, son caractère énigmatique, et la parenté structurale de tous les spectacles ainsi précisés, sans oublier aussi certains effets esthétiques dans la composition ou les coloris, qui m'ont amené à la conviction que tout cela avait une clef commune, située vers la lointaine extrémité de la vie." [6] Il a fallu donc rechercher cette clef dans l'enfance. La voici: " Elle est très simple et familière. Mes parents habitaient, dans la ville du Nord où je suis né, une petite maison devant laquelle était une véranda vitrée, dont les verres blancs étaient bordés, comme c'est classique, d'une bande large comme la main de verres rouges, bleus, jaunes, des plus vulgaires. Tel est le ' vitrail.' Une bande de drap rouge, découpée en festons, était suspendue en haut pour arrêter un courant d'air (détail précis qui suffit à authentifier la donnée). Dehors il y avait une étroite cour-jardin, avec vigne-vierge et arbustes, le tout allant vers la rue. Sur la rue une grille, de toute la largeur du jardin. On imagine aisément un gosse de dix-huit mois s'accrochant au bas du vitrage pour hisser sa petite tête et regarder

---

[1] E. Souriau, " Le Souvenir de l'enfance," *Journal de Psychologie*, 1962 (janvier-juin), 15-57.

[2] *Ibid.*, 55.

[3] *Ibid.*, 56.

[4] *Ibid.*, 56.

[5] *Ibid.*, 57.

[6] *Ibid.*, 57.

vers la rue, l'effet que faisait l'apparition inopinée tantôt â droite, tantôt à gauche de la perspective, des passants qui débouchaient et suivaient la grille, venant dans un sens ou dans l'autre. Les silhouettes, le soir, étaient à contre-jour devant la lueur solaire, car il n'y avait pas de maison de l'autre côté de la rue, et le soleil se couchait en face." [1]

Par quel mystère un spectacle banal, commun, a-t-il pu frapper indélébilement la mémoire d'un homme? Nous l'ignorons. Toujours est-il que nous sommes en présence d'une observation topique, remarquablement précise, et qui confirme de façon rigoureuse l'un des principes fondamentaux de l'analyse thématique de Weber.

Passons maintenant à la question des *analogies*. Dans quelle mesure est-il possible d'affirmer que des ressemblances, si elles sont nombreuses et précises, renvoient à une source commune? La position extrême consisterait ici à postuler que les ressemblances " ne comptent pas "; seules compteraient les identités, comme celles qu'on retrouve entre tel vers de Pétrarque et telle adaptation en français de ce vers au XVIe siècle. " On nous a objecté, écrit Weber, que la lune, dans tel poème des *Orientales*, ne peut ' moduler ' le soleil, puisque la lune et le soleil sont deux êtres très différents; qu'entre la cagoule d'un pénitent et la perruque d'un marquis il n'y a aucun rapport, etc." [2] Mais, continue, Weber, " en nous opposant de tels arguments on oublie que l'inconscient créateur d'un poète, d'un écrivain, voire d'un dormeur, ne fonctionnent pas comme la raison démonstrative d'un savant. Nous savons bien que la lune n'est pas le soleil, que la cagoule n'est pas la perruque. Mais rien n'empêche de prendre le soleil pour la lune, dans certaines circonstances; ni de ranger cagoule et perruque dans la catégorie des couvre-chefs—surtout lorsque, comme c'est le cas, la cagoule recouvre la tête d'un *pénitent*, et la perruque, celle d'un *pêcheur*. Comment raisonne l'inconscient? Nous n'en savons pas grandchose, pour l'instant; assez pourtant pour pouvoir affirmer que le principe de son fonctionnement n'est pas l'identité, mais la ressemblance—comment, sinon, expliquer que le village circulaire (dans *Le Diable dans le Beffroi*) *module* un cadran d'horloge? " [3]

Il n'apparaît donc pas, dans l'état actuel des choses, que les bases théoriques de l'analyse thématique aient été ébranlées par la critique. Tout au contraire, en parcourant les réfutations qui se trouvent dans l'introduction aux *Domaines thématiques*,[4] ainsi que les appendices de cet ouvrage [5], on est obligé d'avouer que les nombreuses objections suscitées par les thèses weberiennes ont trouvé en leur auteur un défenseur coriace non moins que subtil. Sans doute le jugement dernier appartient-il à l'histoire littéraire, à l'histoire de la critique. Mais d'ores et déjà nous croyons pouvoir affirmer que la doctrine analytique de Weber est un ensemble

---

[1] *Ibid.*, 56.

[2] Verlaine, *Sur l'herbe*. Cf. *Genèse*, 319.

[3] *Domaines*, 25.

[4] *Ibid.*, 19-32.

[5] *Ibid.*, 329-338.

cohérent et solide de faits, d'idées et d'applications, que l'analyse thématique a renouvelé la plupart des problèmes qui s'offrent à l'historien de la littérature, présenté un complexe d'interprétations d'un haut intérêt et d'une grande originalité, bref que nous nous trouvons en présence d'une " idée-force " qui non seulement séduit par sa nouveauté et sa vigueur, mais qui fait encore qu'involontairement le lecteur se pose, à propos d'elle, la question inévitable en ces domaines, la question de principe: " Et si c'était vrai ? ".[1]

---

[1] Quelques mots au sujet de l'*Esthétique* de Weber. Elle s'inscrit dans la tradition de Wordsworth, de Baudelaire, de Rilke, ne différant guère des *Esthétiques* de ces auteurs que par son esprit systématique et, pour ainsi dire, technique. L'émotion esthétique serait le souvenir affectif inconscient de l'enfance, chaque art aurait pour base un certain ensemble de réminiscences relatives à l'acquisition d'une fonction cognitive ou existentielle. Ainsi la musique renverrait à l'horizon des perceptions sonores *avant* les significations verbales; la poésie ressusciterait l'apprentissage du langage, etc. On voit comment la théorie des thèmes personnels s'encadre dans une telle Esthétique, fondée, comme l'analyse thématique, sur la persistance et la modulation d'un souvenir.

# LA NOUVELLE CRITIQUE
## OU LA MÉSENTENTE CORDIALE *

Vous souvenez-vous du conseil donné par Bartholo à Figaro ? " Et cherche à présent qui t'adopte... " La Nouvelle Critique française, elle, n'a que l'embarras du choix. Non pas qu'elle représente le vrai, le beau, et toutes les valeurs. Mais les jeunes, de nos jours, n'admirent guère que ceux qui parlent avec autorité, extravagance et éclat. Et qui donc, parmi les critiques et les philosophes d'aujourd'hui, affirme et fulmine avec plus d'originalité et plus de force que les nouveaux critiques et ceux qui leur ressemblent ? L'avouerai-je ? Celui qui vous parle a commis l'imprudence, il n'y a guère, dans une grande et célèbre Université, de faire une conférence, très classique, très " vieux jeu," sur certains aspects du XVIIIe siècle français. Tout en parlant, j'observais mon auditoire. Si mes collègues aux chefs blanchis par l'âge faisaient semblant de m'écouter avec un intérêt passionné, il n'en allait pas de même des jeunes. Les uns bayaient aux corneilles, les autres regardaient le plafond, ou jouaient pensivement avec leur barbe: ils s'ennuyaient à périr, et cherchaient à peine à le cacher. C'est qu'il n'était question, dans la conférence de votre serviteur, ni de structuralisme, ni de Roland Barthes, ni de Lucien Goldmann, par exemple.

Et pourtant, ce dix-huitiémiste dépassé, cette vieille baderne de la critique lansonienne a plus d'une fois, au cours de ces dernières années, tourné ses regards vers la Nouvelle Critique.[1]

Pourquoi ? Tout simplement parce que le dix-huitiémiste en question s'intéresse à cette Nouvelle Critique, que la lecture des critiques structuralistes et thématiques le passionne, et qu'il est prêt à en défendre les positions—*jusqu'au feu, exclusivement*. En somme, il y va de la liberté de pensée. Puisque la Sorbonne, par la bouche de certains de ses maîtres, crie haro sur la Nouvelle Critique, Voltaire l'eût sans doute défendue, comme il avait défendu Calas. En m'intéressant à la néo-critique, je suis en apparence infidèle à ma spécialité; en fait, je reprends le flambeau de la libre pensée, je dis non, fièrement, à toute tyrannie intellectuelle; je me montre fidèle

---

\* Causerie faite à Columbia University le 11 juillet 1967.

[1] Cf., en particulier, nos remarques sur les *Domaines thématiques* de Jean-Paul Weber, dans la *Romanic Review* de 1965; l'article *Un Critique de la Nouvelle Vague, Jean-Paul Weber* publié d'abord dans *Studi e ricerchi di letteratura francese*, Torino, V, 196, et reproduit ici (179). Voir aussi la Préface à Robert E. Jones, *Panorama de la Nouvelle Critique en France*, Paris, SEDES, 1968.

à la leçon la plus noble de ceux dont je me plais à me déclarer un admirateur et un disciple; je cesse momentanément d'étudier la lettre pour m'inspirer de l'esprit.

Non, rien, aucune menace, aucun danger—sauf le bûcher peut-être—ne m'empêchera de lire les ouvrages et d'examiner les systèmes relevant de la Nouvelle Critique, et d'en parler devant des " jeunes " admiratifs.

Systèmes? La Nouvelle Critique en France est donc une critique à systèmes?

Pour moi qui ne suis pas de naissance française, pour moi spectateur désintéressé autant que passionné, et qui observe de l'extérieur—comme à travers les grilles—les bonds prestigieux et les danses cérémonieuses de la culture la plus raffinée du monde, il ne fait pas de doute — c'est là mon opinion et, comme disait Joseph Prudhomme, " je la partage "—que la notion de système exerce sur les Français de souche une attraction des plus vives. Remontons, voulez-vous, au siècle du Roi-Soleil: cet âge classique est coupable d'au moins deux systèmes ingénieux, sinon toujours solides, ceux de Descartes et de Malebranche. Le dix-huitième siècle voit naître, pour me borner aux plus connus, les systèmes de Maupertuis, de Buffon, de Rousseau, des physiocrates et des idéologues. Je passe rapidement sur le dix-neuvième, qui a commis le positivisme de Comte, les phalanstères de Fourier, et tant d'autres crimes contre l'expérience terre-à-terre. Au vingtième siècle, c'est l'avalanche. Partout où porte le regard, on ne voit que systèmes, réfutations, querelles, dogmes, excommunications et conciles. Le surréalisme lui-même est un système, ou du moins une folie systématique. Le cas de l'existentialisme mérite examen. C'est d'abord un système, et un système clos: " No exit," " Huis-clos." Mais bientôt, à l'intérieur de l'enceinte hermétiquement close, naît la discorde: Sartre supporte mal la présence, dans son domaine, de cet " étranger " qui s'appelle Albert Camus. Camus est-il parti de son propre gré, ou fut-il expulsé de cet enfer qui est " les Autres "? Toujours est-il que Camus n'a pas voulu jouer " les Autres ": *Exit* Camus. Mais la révolte même, et le culte de l'absurde, auxquels s'associe le nom de Camus, revêtent une forme systématique. Tant il est vrai que le Français, qui pourtant ne prise rien tant que la fantaisie et la grâce, quand il s'agit de sa vie quotidienne, et qui, en politique, a " le goût désordonné de l'ordre," dès qu'il s'agit de la vie de l'esprit, *pense systématiquement.*

Ainsi, les intellectuels français aiment à échafauder les systèmes. Mais, attention: chacun a son système à lui, et, par principe, déteste celui de son voisin. Ces êtres doux savent se montrer violents quand il s'agit de défendre le système qu'ils ont eux-mêmes bâti. Volontiers ils donneront tout ce qu'ils ont, se dépouilleront de leur dernière chemise: mais ils seront intraitables sur une question de principe. Les faits ne cadrent-ils pas avec un système? Ce sont les faits qui ont tort. Ils aimeraient mieux voir s'écrouler l'univers plutôt que de céder un pouce de leur doctrine. Il y a en tout Giraudoux un Saint-Just qui sommeille, les rêveries les plus innocentes aboutissent à la Terreur, et tel brave professeur qui ne ferait pas de mal à une mouche se révèle soudain doctrinaire assoiffé de sang. Que voulez-vous? Il en a toujours été ainsi, et il en sera toujours ainsi, tant que la France sera la France.

Les raisons en seraient trop longues à développer ici. Mais nous pouvons citer, un peu pêle-mêle: la tradition cartésienne, longue et glorieuse, de la logique et de l'idée claire; l'individualisme bien connu des habitants des Gaules, et dont il est déjà question dans César; enfin la passion bien française qui consiste à tout intellectualiser, depuis l'omelette au fromage jusqu'aux armes atomiques.

Mais système ne veut pas dire stabilité, immobilisme. Je l'ai dit ailleurs: " Le renouvellement est la loi fondamentale de la littérature. Que serait le roman français si nous en étions restés à Maupassant ou à Anatole France? Que n'aurions-nous perdu si les poètes, au lieu de se métamorphoser au gré des découvertes, s'étaient bornés à répéter docilement les leçons délectables des romantiques? "

Où en serions-nous aujourd'hui si nous acceptions toujours la cosmologie de Descartes, avec ses tourbillons, l'horreur du vide et la matière subtile? Et la génération spontanée de tant de savants du dix-huitième siècle? On ne se moque plus, heureusement, de Louis Pasteur. De même, on ne tourne plus en dérision la musique de Wagner, comme on l'avait fait du temps de Baudelaire. Quelle tête auraient fait les amateurs les plus ouverts de 1850, par exemple, devant la poésie d'un Saint-John Perse, devant l'univers anonyme et tendu de Nathalie Sarraute, l'art des peintres tachistes, ou même, plus simplement, la relativité d'Einstein?

A temps nouveaux, nouvelles idoles: le renouvellement n'est pas seulement la loi de l'esprit, c'est la loi d'airain de l'évolution humaine. Appliquons cette loi à la critique littéraire. Si je suis, pour ma part, et tout au long de mes travaux, un disciple lointain, mais fidèle, de la méthode lansonienne, celle qui met l'accent sur l'histoire et la biographie, je puis m'enthousiasmer également pour d'autres méthodes, pour d'autres systèmes que je vois naître autour de moi. Vous connaissez tel système stylistique, qui s'en tient à la minutieuse observation de ce que dit ou écrit un auteur, et où l'explication du texte joue un rôle prépondérant. Vous êtes au courant du système caractérologique où, selon les principes de Le Senne, en particulier, on analyse l'émotivité, la primarité ou la secondarité d'un grand écrivain du passé. Il y a aussi des systèmes, fort répandus, qui nous éclairent sur les poètes et les romanciers d'une époque en analysant scrupuleusement les faits politiques et sociaux qui la caractérisent. Tous ces systèmes font la transition entre la critique classique et la Nouvelle Critique, nous permettent de nous sentir moins dépaysés en abordant les doctrines de celle-ci.

Envisageons maintenant la question d'un point de vue différent. S'il existe des dons qui nous individualisent, qui ne sont pas l'apanage de tous — ainsi ces talents particuliers qui sont nécessaires pour réussir dans la carrière de médecin, d'avocat, de banquier ou d'officier de marine—il me semble que deux dons sont également partagés parmi les hommes. Le don d'enseigner est très biologique et très profond. Déjà les oiseaux enseignent à leurs petits l'art de voler, les chats adultes apprennent aux chatons celui d'attraper une proie... De même, dans l'espèce humaine, la mère instruit la fille dans l'art de plaire aux hommes, le père apprend à ses fils à réussir dans les affaires et dans le monde; et tout le monde enseigne à tout le monde la politesse et les bonnes manières, ce qui se fait et ce qui ne se fait pas. Oui, l'enseignement est bien la chose du monde la mieux partagée, pour paraphraser René Descartes. Et, sur un autre plan, comme l'a dit si bien Bernard Shaw, ceux qui savent, agissent; ceux qui ne savent pas, enseignent—ou, si vous préférez, deviennent professeurs.

L'autre don le mieux partagé est, semble-t-il, la critique. Critiquer est aussi nécessaire, aussi essentiel qu'avoir son pain quotidien. La critique ! Chose la mieux partagée—et aussi le plus calomniée.... Au dix-huitième siècle, Philippe Néricault, dit Destouches, nous assène déjà cette flèche empoisonnée: " La critique est aisée, et l'art est difficile." Et, cent ans plus tard, Gustave Flaubert, dans une lettre à Louise Colet, décoche cet autre trait, non moins mortel: " On fait de la critique quand on ne peut pas faire l'art." A les entendre, nous serions les eunuques, les impuissants, les voyeurs de la littérature: et tout le monde peut être eunuque. En fait, tous critiquent tout, et à tous les niveaux: la mère critique sa fille trop prude, la fille critique sa mère, aux atours trop voyants; le père critique son fils, qu'il trouve trop colombe, et le fils critique son père, trop vautour. Et, naturellement, on critique ses critiques ! De là vient, sans doute, que notre champ clos, d'ordinaire si calme, celui de la critique dite universitaire, est aujourd'hui le théâtre de critiques et de contre-critiques à la fois spirituelles et violentes.

M. Raymond Picard, professeur en Sorbonne, énumère les nouveaux systèmes dans son petit livre *Nouvelle critique ou nouvelle imposture*, systèmes qui lui déplaisent fort: " Psychanalyse ou psycho-critique, analyse marxiste, analyse structurale, description existentielle ou phénoménologique." Il ajoute que la nouvelle critique " se pose en s'opposant à ce qu'elle appelle, pour les besoins de la cause, la *critique universitaire*, ou *critique positiviste*, ou encore *lansonisme*." Les doctrines de la nouvelle critique sont, selon M. Picard, fragiles—qu'il s'agisse de celles de Jean Starobinski, de Lucien Goldmann, de Roland Barthes, de Jean-Pierre Richard, de Charles Mauron et de Jean-Paul Weber. Voilà donc notre petite bande de coupables. Mais, comme la plupart des critiques universitaires, M. Picard se montre un peu plus indulgent vis-à-vis des trois derniers: Richard, Mauron, Weber. Leurs péchés sont moins graves: eux du moins sont plus près des faits; comme il dit, chez eux, " l'intérêt pour l'anecdote est grand."

Tout amateur des arts sait que souvent, trop souvent, la valeur d'une œuvre ne commence à devenir évidente que bien après la mort de l'artiste. Balzac, que Sainte-Beuve traitait de romancier de troisième ordre, est pour nous l'un des géants du premier dix-neuvième siècle; Baudelaire, à qui Lanson consacre un seul paragraphe dans la première édition de son *Histoire de la littérature française*, a fait depuis l'objet d'innombrables études; Cézanne, bizarre barbouilleur de toiles pour ses contemporains, est considéré aujourd'hui comme le précurseur génial de toute une pléiade de styles et d'écoles qui font la gloire de notre temps. La liste est longue de ces créateurs vilipendés, que la mort a transfigurés et vengés.

C'est moins vrai, semble-t-il, dans le domaine de la critique littéraire; ou du moins ce n'est pas encore vrai, peut-être. La célébrité des critiques est rarement posthume; il n'y a pas encore eu de " critiques maudits "—

malgré les louables efforts que fait la Sorbonne en cette direction; et c'est de leur vivant que la plupart des critiques jouissent du peu de gloire que le destin leur accorde.

Ainsi Gaston Bachelard, l'ancêtre vénéré, dont la *Psychanalyse du feu* a déclenché le mouvement de la Nouvelle Critique. Déjà de son vivant n'était-il pas considéré comme un critique remarquable, un pionnier, un chef d'Ecole?

De même, prenons le cas de Georges Poulet. Vous le connaissez bien, vous l'avez entendu ici-même peut-être. Peut-on contester qu'il s'agisse d'un historien des plus considérables? Pourtant, ses recherches le situent résolument dans le domaine de la Nouvelle Critique. Qui, avant lui, et mieux que lui, a parlé de l'espace et du temps, du cercle et de la perle, chez Proust et chez Pascal, chez Vigny et chez Edgar Poe? On chercherait en vain, chez un Lanson, des descriptions et des analyses analogues: le renouveau de la critique contemporaine est, en grande partie, l'œuvre de Poulet.

Plus près de la Nouvelle Critique proprement dite, nous trouvons Jean Starobinski. Comme Sainte-Beuve, ce critique possède la double et rare culture de médecin et d'historien de la littérature. Et, comme Sainte-Beuve, Jean Starobinski est philosophe, bien que son barycentre se place plutôt du côté de l'existentialisme que de Port-Royal. A la confluence de l'existentialisme et de la psychanalyse, M. Starobinski nous a offert un Rousseau inoubliable, neuf, et surtout *vrai*. Or, tout hommage rendu à *La Transparence et l'obstacle* transcende nécessairement l'ancienne critique et constitue un hommage à la nouvelle. M. Starobinski résout, comme en se jouant, des problèmes dont la paléo-critique ne soupçonnait même pas l'existence!

M. Doubrovsky, qui a opté pour New York après être sorti de l'Ecole Normale Supérieure, voit déjà plus loin, et prône ce qu'il appelle la Nouvelle Nouvelle Critique. Pourtant, c'est un ouvrage d'ensemble, sur la Néo-critique, où l'érudition le dispute à la hauteur des vues philosophiques, qui l'a fait connaître; et sa thèse sur Corneille se situe résolument sur le plan du structuralisme.

Faut-il rappeler ce que la Nouvelle Critique doit à Barthes? Déjà il fait figure d'ancêtre, déjà il apparaît, pour employer un terme sociologique, institutionnalisé, et chef de file. On se rappelle l'ardente polémique qui l'avait opposé à Raymond Picard, et qui a soudain polarisé toute l'intelligentsia française en une droite picardiste et une gauche barthiste. Ce critique, le plus intéressant de notre génération, selon Miss Susan Sontag, n'a pas fini de nous étonner et de nous éblouir.

La Nouvelle Critique a éprouvé récemment une perte notable en la personne de Charles Mauron, mort il y a quelques mois sans avoir achevé son œuvre. De tous les psychanalystes de stricte obédience freudienne il était certes le plus original, le plus passionnant à lire et à discuter. Même si sa doctrine paraît aujourd'hui quelque peu étriquée, dogmatique, dépassée par l'évolution de la psychologie et de la psychanalyse, il serait difficile de nier que ses études sur Racine—qui avaient inspiré celles de Barthes—sur Nerval, sur Mallarmé surtout, n'aient posé des jalons nécessaires sur la route qui mène à la compréhension en profondeur des auteurs et des œuvres.

Vous connaissez tous, je suppose, les remarquables ouvrages de M. Lucien Goldmann. Vous avez admiré la patience de l'historien, la dialectique ingénieuse du philosophe, le tact sûr du sociologue. Les textes de M. Goldmann resteront longtemps des modèles, tant par la nouveauté de leur approche de l'œuvre que par la précision du système partout présent. Peut-être regrettera-t-on seulement que, dans son ardeur de sociologue, M. Goldmann oublie quelquefois la spécificité de l'œuvre et de ses structures propres: les idées de ce néo-critique, pour user d'une expression de Bergson, sont plutôt du tout-fait, qui pourrait s'adapter à une foule de textes semblables; tandis que nous souhaiterions pour notre part, des analyses plus précises, mieux ajustées à chaque personne et à chaque personnage.

Et nous en venons enfin à Jean-Pierre Richard, dont l'œuvre nombreuse, variée, ciselée, nous a valu déjà de mémorables " paysages intérieurs " thématiques. Le Mallarmé de M. Richard domine de très haut toutes les thèses qui ont été consacrées récemment à ce poète difficile. Et, tant dans la recherche des thèmes et des motifs, que dans l'exploration psychologique il est évident que le talent de Jean-Pierre Richard ouvre partout des chemins nouveaux, offrant au lecteur des points de vue non moins exquis que rares.

Tous ces noms, toutes ces œuvres, toutes ces doctrines nous autorisent à dire, je pense, qu'il n'y a pas *un* structuralisme, mais plutôt *des* structuralismes. Les attitudes sont nouvelles et variées; ce qu'elles ont en commun, c'est peut-être l'idée que rien n'est intelligible à moins d'être structuré d'une certaine façon; et cette idée s'enracine dans la thèse, commune à Platon et à Aristote, selon laquelle toute différenciation, partant toute intelligibilité, réside dans la forme plutôt que dans la matière. Ce qui est neuf, c'est l'ensemble des techniques utilisées. Elles sont rarement inventées par les critiques eux-mêmes; bien plutôt participent-elles de l'immense explosion doctrinale qui a conduit, au XIXe et au XXe siècle, à la constitution des Sciences humaines. Et ainsi la Nouvelle Critique, en dernière analyse, semble puiser sa validité et sa valeur dans ce simple fait que la Critique, avant Bachelard et avant Freud, était la seule discipline littéraire qui fût désespérément en retard sur l'ensemble des Sciences de l'homme.

Barthes, Bachelard, Sartre, Richard, Goldmann, Mauron: ces noms, encore une fois, vous sont bien connus, et tous ces écrivains ont certes bien mérité du structuralisme et de la néo-critique. Pourtant, ce n'est pas d'eux que j'ai l'intention de vous entretenir aujourd'hui. C'est d'un autre structuraliste, d'un autre " thématique, " philosophe d'origine et new-yorkais d'adoption, auteur de quelques romans pleins de fantaisie et d'une ou deux thèses extrêmement sérieuses—bien qu'on ait dit que ses thèses sont des romans, et ses romans des traités de philosophie: je voudrais vous présenter aujourd'hui notre collègue et presque concitoyen, Jean-Paul Weber.

Pourquoi Jean-Paul Weber? Peut-être parce qu'il s'agit d'un extrémiste, voire d'un terroriste. Son livre sur la *Genèse de l'œuvre poétique*, à peine paru, a fait sensation, scandale. La vieille Sorbonne, qui pourtant l'avait couronné, eut soudain l'impression de trembler sur les bases. L'Olympe des crânes chauves et des barbes grisonnantes sentit courir sur ses cimes un vent d'incroyance, et eut peur. Le philosophe sceptique leur disait poliment qu'il ne croyait pas au lansonisme, qu'il croyait à l'inconscient, aux grandes forces aveugles qui, sourdement, façonnent notre œuvre et notre destin. L'aéropage solennel des historiens et biographes n'en croyait pas ses oreilles, lui qui avait sucé le lait de la logique cartésienne, et qui avait accoutumé de se repaître d'idées claires et distinctes. Les théories de Jean-Paul Weber, ne craignons pas de le dire, ont répandu la terreur dans les enceintes vétustes des Facultés des Lettres. Il y eut des cris, un tumulte, un commencement d'émeute.

Mais aussi parce que Jean-Paul Weber est un esprit systématique. Il a un système bien à lui, et qui ne ressemble à aucun autre: en deux mots, il consiste à affirmer que l'œuvre tout entière d'un poète, d'un romancier, d'un philosophe, s'enracine dans le souvenir d'un événement singulier, unique, et qui avait marqué, profondément, l'enfance du créateur. Le terroriste se révèle ainsi homme à système; le théoricien sème la terreur. Ce mélange étonnant, et détonnant, me paraît extrêmement français. Ce sont les Français du dix-huitième siècle qui, armés de leurs systèmes, ont fait la Révolution et démoli l'Ancien Régime. Jean-Paul Weber n'éveille peut-être ma curiosité et mon intérêt que parce qu'il me rappelle par certains côtés—et toutes proportions gardées—ces écrivains que moi, dix-huitiémiste, j'ai étudiés et pratiqués toute ma vie durant. Et, certes, il y a du terrorisme et de l'esprit systématique chez tous les néo-critiques français. Mais il me semble que Jean-Paul Weber représente, au sein de la Nouvelle Critique, à la fois la terreur absolue et le système absolu. Aucune œuvre n'a suscité plus de cris de peur et de haine; aucune théorie n'est plus étroitement, rigidement et absolument système, avec tout ce que ce mot comporte à la fois d'aveuglement, de droiture un peu maniaque et de puritanisme intellectuel. Si Bachelard est le Voltaire de la Nouvelle Critique, si Georges Poulet en est le Rousseau, sublime et pervers, Jean-Paul Weber en serait le Robespierre, le Marat et le Saint-Just: l'esprit jacobin, intolérant et doctrinaire, qui fait tomber des têtes et construit, dans les décombres, un monde nouveau et appelé à triompher.

Pardonnez ces images et ces comparaisons, qui sentent le spécialiste du Siècle des Lumières.... Me replongeant dans le vingtième, je vois d'abord que M. Weber, qui a fait toute sa carrière en France, et qui a raflé tous les titres universitaires français, a puisé la première notion de son système chez un auteur américain, le seul, avec Faulkner, qui éveille plus d'échos peut-être dans le cœur d'un lettré français que dans l'esprit d'un lecteur américain: Edgar Allan Poe. Sans aucun doute, s'il n'y avait pas eu Poe, il n'y aurait pas eu non plus de Weber... J'ajoute que l'essence de l'Esthétique weberienne, comme l'indique sa *Psychologie de l'art*, offre une parenté indiscutable avec les intuitions du poète anglais Wordsworth. Rien d'étonnant, dans ces conditions, que ce Français systématique ait fini par venir enseigner et vivre parmi nous.

L'interprétation que Jean-Paul Weber donne de l'œuvre poesque est suffisamment connue, des deux côtés de l'Atlantique, pour qu'il soit besoin de s'y attarder longtemps. Je me bornerai à vous rappeler comment la lecture de *The Devil in the Belfry* a d'abord suggéré au néo-critique l'idée que le village circulaire, bordé de soixante petites maisons, et au centre duquel se dresse le beffroi majestueux, pourvu de sept horloges, n'est sans doute qu'un *symbole inconscient du cadran circulaire d'une horloge.* Relisant par la suite les contes complets de Poe, M. Weber n'a eu aucune peine à y discerner cent allusions, diverses et subtiles, à l'Horloge, à l'Heure, au Cadran. Ainsi, comme les aiguilles tournent autour d'un centre, l'œuvre de Poe se révèle tourner autour d'un *thème* unique: qui est l'Horloge. Et ce thème, M. Weber croit que Poe l'avait rencontré dans son enfance; c'est du moins ce que nous apprend *Néo-critique et Paléo-critique.* Désormais, rien ne pouvait plus arrêter M. Weber. Puisque Poe gravite autour d'un thème unique, il fallait que d'autres écrivains le fissent aussi. Que dis-je: d'autres? *Tous* les écrivains; tous les poètes, tous les conteurs, tous les romanciers; et finalement tous les philosophes, et peut-être tous les hommes. Quand je vous disais que M. Weber est un terroriste! Vous tous, qui avez lu *le Diable dans le beffroi,* cette histoire grotesque, amusante, a dû vous paraître sans grande portée; vous avez dû hausser les épaules; vous avez dû penser: décidément, ce pauvre Edgar avait bien de l'imagination.... Jean-Paul Weber, lui, y avait vu la première pierre d'un édifice imposant, le premier atome d'une doctrine totalitaire, et qui, après avoir fait exploser les explications traditionnelles, finirait par nous priver de notre liberté en nous apprenant que nous sommes tous d'inconscientes victimes d'un thème original et unique, tapi dans la pénombre d'une enfance oubliée. *Le Diable dans le beffroi* est comme le diable dans la boîte: à peine a-t-on soulevé le couvercle qu'un diablotin noir vous saute à la figure.... Et chaque fois que Jean-Paul Weber soulève ainsi le couvercle qui cache l'œuvre et l'inspiration d'un auteur, un diablotin nous saute au nez. Mais, chaque fois—ou presque: Vigny, lui aussi, d'après M. Weber, a, sinon le diable au corps, du moins l'Horloge à l'âme—chaque fois, ce diablotin est différent. A chacun son thème....

Considérons, pour prendre un exemple, le " diable " de Mallarmé. Mallarmé, cela est tout à fait sûr, est un poète *hanté*:

*Je suis hanté. L'Azur, l'Azur, l'Azur, l'Azur....* Mais cette hantise, cette obsession, M. Weber montre qu'elle concerne un être ailé: l'Oiseau; un Oiseau planant, volant dans l'azur, tombant, mourant.... Des centaines d'exemples, patiemment réunis par l'auteur, établissent la réalité, l'impérialisme de cette hantise. Pensons à l'admirable poème en prose intitulé *Le Démon de l'analogie.* Nous y trouvons des ailes, des chutes, des glissades, des morts ailées; jusqu'à ce que, à la fin du texte, le poète hanté s'arrête pile, frappé de stupeur—devant quoi? Devant la vitrine d'un luthier, où gisent des oiseaux morts, empaillés.... Songeons aussi au *Tombeau d'Edgar Poe,* dont le vers le plus chargé de sens et de destin invoque une chute, toute semblable à la chute d'un oiseau blessé à mort:

*Calme bloc ici-bas chu d'un désastre obscur...*

Mais rappelons-nous aussi, à côté de tant de poèmes dont la signification profonde s'élucide en fonction du thème, du mythe de l'Oiseau tombant, mourant, rappelons-nous la lutte soutenue par Mallarmé, selon ses termes, " sur l'aile osseuse " d'un Dieu redoutable, souvenons-nous de l'admirable et étrange courbe dessinée par l'évolution de la poésie mallarméenne, d'abord " humaine, trop humaine," puis atteinte comme d'une aphasie progressive, comme d'une incapacité progressive de parler, et qui débouche enfin, après les derniers sonnets, divinement inintelligibles, sur " Un coup de dé jamais n'abolira le hasard." Ne dirait-on pas, affirme Jean-Paul Weber, que toute l'œuvre de Mallarmé vise, graduellement, à supprimer le langage humain, et à lui substituer un langage tout autre, à la fois mélodieux et sans signification apparente, comme l'est précisément, à nos oreilles imparfaites, le langage d'un oiseau chanteur? Mallarmé, obsédé toute sa vie durant par l'Oiseau, n'a-t-il pas tenté, inconsciemment, de s'identifier lui-même, d'identifier l'ensemble de son œuvre et la totalité de son destin, avec l'Oiseau chanteur dont, sans le savoir, il déplorait la mort—comme nous le suggère déjà Le Démon de l'analogie, dont il a été question tout à l'heure? Une fois par semaine, le mardi soir, rue de Rome, Mallarmé subissait l'étrange métamorphose: devant un cercle muet d'admirateurs, il parlait, mystérieusement, musicalement, de sujets obscurs et un peu futiles: il se faisait Oiseau, il devenait l'Oiseau mystique dont, toute sa vie, il avait porté le deuil.

Chaque écrivain a son thème, propose M. Weber. Mais chacun poursuit, cerne, approche, symbolise, " module "—selon un terme weberien—différemment ce thème nucléaire. Le poète qu'est Mallarmé module son thème en poète, à grands renforts d'images poétiques et de rythmes mystérieux. Un romancier comme Stendhal vivra, lui aussi, son thème, décrivant autour de celui-ci mille arabesques. Mais il le fera autrement, en romancier, voire en philosophe. L'ouvrage de M. Weber s'intitule, bizarrement—mais tout est bizarre dans le système de ce terroriste—*Stendhal ou les Cristallisations de la Morsure*.[1] Ce livre épais—plus de 600 pages!—n'est pas encore paru. Mais il est sous presse, et vous pourrez le lire—ou ne pas le lire—d'ici à quelques mois. J'en ai lu une grande partie en manuscrit, et je dois dire que, de toutes les monographies de Jean-Paul Weber, c'est la plus minutieuse, de loin, et peut-être la plus convaincante.

Quel est le " thème " de Stendhal? M. Weber, qui a étudié attentivement l'exquise *Vie de Henry Brulard*, inventaire précis des souvenirs d'enfance de Stendhal, en découvre trois, mais qui se tiennent étroitement, " forment système," comme dit l'auteur, et finalement remontent à une source commune unique, qui est le souvenir de la Morsure. Morsure? Mais oui; à l'âge de trois ans, le petit Beyle, déjà agressif, invité à embrasser sa charmante et jeune " cousine " (en réalité tante), se rebiffe et, " piqué," dit-il, par le " rouge " insolent couvrant la peau de la jeune femme, lui mord cruellement la joue.... Souvenir cuisant; non seulement pour la Cousine, mais aussi, et bien davantage, pour le petit Beyle lui-même, aussitôt baptisé " assassin," " criminel " et " monstre." Jamais Beyle ne pardonnera à son père et à sa tante Séraphie de l'avoir ainsi, systématiquement, vilipendé et maltraité à cause d'une malencontreuse et puérile morsure.

---

[1] Cet ouvrage s'appellera en définitive *Stendhal, les grandes structures de l'œuvre et du destin*.

Or, cette " morsure " sur la joue, et la trace—bleue, verte, colorée—que l'une a dû laisser sur l'autre, cette " morsure " et cette tache réapparaîtront, soit directement, soit indirectement, dans l'œuvre romanesque de Stendhal. Le cas le plus clair est peut-être celui de Lamiel. Vous rappelez-vous cette jeune fille ambitieuse, sorte de Julien Sorel en jupe, dont un roman inachevé retrace les aventures provinciales et parisiennes? Vous souvenez-vous du stratagème ingénieux qu'elle emploie pour se débarrasser des assiduités importunes de commis-voyageurs? Elle s'enlaidit, volontairement, en étendant sur sa *joue* une décoction de vert-de-houx, qui dessine sur cette joue une large *tache* déplaisante et verte.... Or, cette tache verte sur la joue n'est pas seulement une obsession de Lamiel, qui se l'inflige parfois quotidiennement. C'est aussi une obsession de Stendhal. Combien de taches sur les joues ne découvrons-nous pas dans l'œuvre stendhalienne! On en voit sur les joues de Mina de Vanghel, dans le récit du même nom; sur celles de Mina Wanghen, dans le roman inachevé intitulé *Le Rose et le Vert*. Et l'on notera, avec M. Weber, que Vanghel et Wanghen, tous deux, ne peuvent avoir qu'une seule signification: *Wange*, " joue " en allemand, signification d'autant plus plausible que les deux jeunes Mina sont Allemandes, que l'action se passe, au début, dans les deux cas, en Allemagne, et que Stendhal savait passablement l'allemand.... Rappelons-nous également la tache bleue que laisse, sur la joue de Fabrice cette fois, la poignée de l'arme de Giletti, au cours du ridicule et tragique duel qui devait sceller la destinée de Fabrice. Notons encore, entre autres textes, deux épigraphes du *Rouge et Noir*, où il est question de *rouge sur les joues* d'une jeune fille: en voilà assez, selon M. Weber, pour dépister une hantise—tache sur la joue—et en même temps pour déchiffrer le titre, toujours un peu énigmatique, du roman, où le *Rouge* symboliserait finalement la joue d'une jeune femme, et le *Noir*, la trace colorée de la Morsure sur cette joue. (Et de même, entre parenthèses, dans *Le Rose et le Vert*, et dans un grand nombre de titres demeurés à l'état de projet.) Or, toutes ces taches sur toutes ces joues—comment se fait-il qu'on ne se soit encore jamais aperçu d'une hantise aussi évidente?—tout cela serait incompréhensible, selon Jean-Paul Weber, si nous ne remontions à la haute enfance de Beyle, si nous ne songions, d'emblée, à une certaine " morsure " laissant sur la joue d'une jeune et jolie femme, une trace douloureuse et enlaidissante. Vous souriez? J'avoue que la conclusion ne laisse pas de surprendre. Mais ne croyez-vous pas que la critique littéraire a tout à gagner, et rien à perdre, à s'évader parfois du cercle étroit auquel la condamnent, depuis Sainte-Beuve, les érudits? Ne vous êtes-vous jamais demandé comment il se faisait que la littérature dite d'imagination, domaine du fantasque, du fantastique, de l'émouvant, de l'intéressant, du passionnant, bref de l'imprévu, n'ait donné naissance, jusqu'à présent, parmi les critiques chargés de l'élucider et de l'analyser, qu'à des œuvres dégageant presque toujours un puissant ennui, et toujours rigoureusement dépourvues de la moindre fantaisie? Les œuvres les plus ailées, les plus passionnantes, emprisonnées dans l'étroit carcan d'ouvrages critiques les plus plats et les plus ennuyeux! Quels que soient par ailleurs les mérites ou les défauts des livres de Jean-Paul Weber, on ne leur contestera pas l'inattendu de leurs conclusions, l'humour ou l'ironie de leurs prémisses. Pour la première fois peut-être, l'on est en présence d'ouvrages de critique qui se lisent avec autant d'intérêt, autant de surprise, antant d'amusement, pour tout dire, que dans le cas des récits, romans ou poèmes examinés par le critique. Pour ce qui me concerne, j'avoue volontiers que la lecture des *Cristallisations de la Morsure* m'a intéressé presque autant que la lecture d'un récit de Stendhal.

On se doute bien que l'œuvre puissamment originale, provocante, révolutionnaire à certains égards du terroriste des Lettres qu'est Jean-Paul Weber a suscité une foule de réactions négatives, parfois furibondes.... Je vous ai déjà parlé du petit livre de Raymond Picard; il faut mentionner également—à côté d'analyses sympathiques et élogieuses—l'article de Jean Pommier, paru dans le dernier numéro d'une Revue d'histoire littéraire. Ces réactions étaient attendues; elles étaient nécessaires. Elles permettront à l'analyse thématique—car tel est le nom que Jean-Paul Weber a donné à sa méthode—de mieux prendre conscience de sa valeur et de ses limites. Je ne m'attarderai pas sur ces objections, que vous connaissez du reste peut-être: elles ont été partiellement réfutées par M. Weber lui-même dans une brochure parue dans la même collection ("Libertés") que le petit livre de M. Picard. Et il est curieux d'observer que ces deux pamphlets, où s'affrontent furieusement deux esprits antagonistes, poursuivent aujourd'hui une carrière parallèle: n'a-t-on pas publié, en Italie, une traduction de l'attaque de M. Picard et de la réponse de M. Weber, sous la même couverture? Il semble ainsi que se transforment en frères siamois des frères ennemis qui s'entre-déchirent: quel sort affreux pour deux pensées qui se jettent l'anathème, réciproquement!

Qu'il me soit permis de remarquer, néanmoins, que, à mon sens, la plupart des critiques adressées par les disciples de Lanson à l'analyse thématique de M. Jean-Paul Weber, n'ont pas beaucoup de portée. Ou bien ces objections montrent que leurs auteurs n'ont qu'une connaissance des plus vagues des notions et des faits acquis, depuis une cinquantaine d'années, par les sciences de l'homme. En particulier, il suffit d'admettre, avec les psychologues d'aujourd'hui, la réalité de l'inconscient, pour que certains reproches perdent toute signification. Ou bien encore, les arguments proposés sont de pures chicanes, qui manifestent, comme on l'a dit (Roland Barthes), l'incapacité de certains lecteurs de s'élever au niveau général et symbolique de la pensée adulte.

Ainsi, lorsque M. Picard reproche à Jean-Paul Weber de placer l'œuvre d'un auteur sous la domination d'une fatalité (celle du thème), et de supprimer par là la liberté de l'écrivain—objection qui n'est pas sans fondement, en un sens—, il ne s'aperçoit pas que la prépondérance du thème n'est pas mécanique et absolue, qu'elle laisse place à toutes les ruses et à toutes les inventions de l'inconscient aux prises avec la volonté consciente; de même, il ne discerne pas que toute liberté est nécessairement *engagée*, qu'elle n'existe qu'en surimpression sur un fond qui la limite et la rend possible—et ce fond, c'est, d'abord et avant tout, l'inconscient du créateur.

Lorsque M. Pommier, de son côté, objecte que, dans une image de Vigny interprétée par Jean-Paul Weber, l'élément meurtrier n'est pas l'aiguille parcourant un cadran d'horloge, mais la branche d'un compas transperçant la poitrine du sujet, il ne voit pas que ce n'est pas tel ou tel élément de l'horloge qui est, chez Vigny, meurtrier, mais bien l'horloge tout entière—ainsi le cadran sur lequel est placée la lettre fatale de *Laurette ou le Cachet rouge*.

De telles objections, encore une fois, témoignent plutôt d'un approfondissement insuffisant des thèses de M. Weber, ou d'une farouche ignorance des données de la psychologie contemporaine. Aussi bien, pour ma part, je refuse de les prendre tout à fait au sérieux—sauf l'argument suivant, reproduit dans l'article de Jean Pommier: " L'Horloge, chez Edgar Poe, et chez Alfred de Vigny. ... Pourtant, ni l'un ni l'autre n'étaient Suisses ! "

Ce qui ne veut pas dire, bien évidemment, que les thèses de M. Weber soient au-dessus de tout reproche et de tout soupçon.

Tout d'abord, je reprocherai à M. Weber le caractère parfois incomplet de ses analyses. Dans l'étude sur Edgar Allan Poe, pour ne donner que cet exemple, bien des contes s'élucident à la lumière du thème de l'Horloge, du thème du Temps. Mais d'autres paraissent relever d'une thématique assez différente: ainsi les contes marins, les récits où il est question de chutes, de rivières, d'eau ordinaire ou d'eau lourde... Il me semble que la question mériterait d'être reprise et approfondie. Mais du reste M. Weber en est lui-même conscient, et il nous promet, dans son *Contre Picard*, de compléter ses analyses dans un proche avenir.

D'autre part, je crois que M. Weber, dans les ouvrages publiés, n'a pas bien précisé les rapports existant entre sa doctrine et celle de ses confrères en Nouvelle Critique. Que pense-t-il, par exemple, des efforts du marxiste Goldmann ? Comment envisage-t-il ses relations avec la critique strictement freudienne, comme celle de Charles Mauron ? Il eût été intéressant de connaître la position de notre critique face à ces problèmes.

Mais surtout, je reprocherais à M. Weber l'absence d'une théorie des modulations. Nous voyons bien ce qu'il entend par thème; et, dans bien des cas, les thèmes qu'il découvre dans l'enfance et dans l'œuvre d'un auteur paraissent plausibles, au moins à titre d'" hypothèse de travail." Mais pourquoi ces thèmes sont-ils modulés précisément comme ils le sont, chez l'écrivain hanté ? Comment expliquer que le thème—à supposer qu'il en existe un—soit symbolisé, dans l'œuvre, selon telle technique, de préférence à tant d'autres également possibles ? C'est là une question qui me paraît capitale, et dont je voudrais bien que M. Weber traitât dans un de ces prochains ouvrages.

Pourtant, ces objections ne doivent pas nous faire oublier l'essentiel. L'essentiel, c'est que la critique littéraire est en train de se transformer profondément sous nos yeux, qu'elle ne sera plus jamais ce qu'elle a été avant l'apparition de la Nouvelle Critique. L'essentiel c'est que, parmi tous les systèmes néo-critiques, la doctrine terroriste de Jean-Paul Weber est une de celles qui nous font le plus réfléchir, remettre en question, repenser les bases même de notre savoir. L'essentiel enfin est que bien des études de M. Weber, dès maintenant, paraissent emporter la conviction, et fournir les fondements d'une discipline nouvelle, capable d'éclairer toutes les œuvres et tous les destins dans une lumière tout à fait neuve et probablement juste. Faisons confiance à Jean-Paul Weber : comme le bon vin, il s'améliore en vieillissant et en voyageant; nul doute, si on le laisse faire, qu'il ne parvienne à nous dire, sur une foule d'auteurs, des secrets insoupçonnés, et peut-être la formule d'un aspect au moins de la création littéraire.

*Achevé d'imprimer
sur les presses
de l'Imprimerie du « Journal de Genève »
en mars 1970
pour le compte des
ÉDITIONS DROZ S.A.*

# HISTOIRE DES IDÉES ET CRITIQUE LITTÉRAIRE

54. STONE (J.-A.), Sophocles and Racine: A comparative Study in Dramatic Technique 1964. 162 p.
55. MAY (Gita), De Jean-Jacques Rousseau à Madame Roland: Essai sur la sensibilité préromantique et révolutionnaire, 1964, 275 p. 4 ill.
56. BAILEY (H.P.), Hamlet in France, from Voltaire to Laforgue (with an Epilogue), 1964, XVI-180 p., 12 ill.
57. SOULIER (J.-P.), Lautréamont — Génie ou maladie mentale, 1964, 160 p.
58. ROGERS (B.-G.), Proust's Narrative Techniques, 1965, 216 p.
59. SEYLAZ (J.-L.), Les *Liaisons dangereuses* et la création romanesque chez Laclos, 1965, 3e tirage, 160p.
60. CORNELIUS (P.), Languages in Seventeenth- and Early Eighteenth-Century Imaginary voyages, 1965, 178 p.
61. COLBY (A.-M.), The portrait in Twelfth-Century French Literature. An example of the stylistic originality of Chrétien de Troyes, 1965, 206 p.
62. ALLART (H.), Nouvelles lettres à Sainte-Beuve (1832-1864), avec une introduction et des notes par L.-A. Uffenbeck, 1965, XVIII-178 p.
63. MULLER (M.), Les voix narratives dans la *Recherche du Temps perdu*, 1965, 188 p.
64. AUTRET (J.), Ruskin and the French before Marcel Proust. (With the collected Fragmentary Translations), 1966, 134p.
65. DEGUISE (P.), Benjamin Constant méconnu: le Livre De la Religion, 1966, x-310 p. 4 pl.
66. WEINSHENKER (A.-B.), Falconet: his Writings and his Friend Diderot, 1966, x-140 p., 15 pl.
67. GINDINE (Y.), Aragon prosateur surréaliste, 1966, x-120 p.
68. SCHWARTZ (J.), Diderot and Montaigne. The *Essais* and the Shaping of Diderot's Humanism, 1966, 160 p.
69. ALTER (J.), La vision du monde d'Alain Robbe-Grillet. Structures et significations, 1966, VIII-124 p.
70. NICOD (M.), Du réalisme à la réalité. Evolution artistique et itinéraire spirituel de Ramuz, 1966, 212 p.
71. SHOLOD (B.), Charlemagne in Spain: The Cultural Legacy of Roncesvalles, 1966, 232 p.
72. BROWDER (C.), André Breton, arbiter of Surrealism, 1967, 214 p.
73. SAREIL (J.), Essai sur *Candide*, 1967, 106 p.
74. MAY (G.), Diderot et Baudelaire, 2e éd., 1967, 210 p.
76. TRICAUD (M.-L.), Le Baroque dans le théâtre de Paul Claudel, 1967, 284 p.
78. GOCHBERG (H.-S.), Stage of Dreams. The Dramatic Art of Alfred de Musset (1828-1834), 1967, 222 p.
82. ROGERS (B. G.), The novels and stories of Barbey d'Aurevilly, 1967, 268 p.
77. HARDEE (A. M.), Jean de Lannel and the pre-classical French Novel, 1967, 152 p.
79. GOODRICH (N.-L.), Charles of Orléans, 1967, 222 p.
80. HYTIER (J.), Questions de littérature, 1967, 234 p.
81. DULAIT (S.), Inventaire raisonné des autographes de Molière, 1967, 128 p. et ill.
83. BRADY (P.), « L'œuvre » d'Emile Zola, 1967, 506 p.
84. HOLDHEIM (W.-W.), Theory and Practice of the Novel. A study on André Gide, 1967, 274 p.
85. PUTTER (I.), La dernière illusion de Leconte de Lisle, 1968, 176 p.
86. MARMIER, X., *Journal (1848-1890)*. Etablissement du texte, présentation et notes de E. Kaye, 2 tomes, 1968, 400+412 p.
87. HAIDU, P., Aestic Distance in Chrétien de Troyes: Irony and Comedy in Cliges and Perceval, 1968, 275 p.
88. DASSONVILLE, M., Ronsard. Etude historique et littéraire. I: Les enfances Ronsard (1536-1545), 1968, 296 p., ill.
89. PRINCE, G.-J., Métaphysique et technique dans l'œuvre romanesque de Sartre, 1968, 152 p.
90. PAXTON, N., The Development of Mallarmé's Prose Style, with the original textes of twenty articles, 1968, 176 p.
91. Benjamin Constant. Actes du congrès Benjamin Constant (Lausanne, octobre 1967), édités par P. Cordey et J.-L. Seylaz, 1968, 232 p.
92. GIRAUD, Y. F.-A., La fable de Daphné. Essai sur un type de métamorphose végétale dans la littérature et dans les arts jusqu'à la fin du XVIIe siècle, 1968, 576 p., ill., 21 pl.
93. MEYLAN, J.-P., La Revue de Genève, miroir des lettres européennes, 1920-1930, 1969, 528 p.
94. PERKINS, J.-A., The Concept of the Self in the French Enlightenment, 1969, 162 p.
95. MORTIER, R., Clartés et ombres du Siècle des Lumières. Etudes sur le XVIIIe siècle littéraire, 1969, 166 p., 6 pl.
96. NESSELROTH, P.W., Lautréamont's Imagery. A Stylistic Approach, 1969, 134 p.
97. BESSER, G. R., Balzac's Concept of Genius. The Theme of Superiority in the *Comédie humaine*, 1969, 288 p.
98. SPENCER, M. C., The Art Criticism of Théophile Gautier, 1969, x-126 p.
99. BONARD, O., Peinture et création littéraire chez Balzac, 1969, 191 p.
100. CHATEAUBRIAND. Actes du Congrès de Wisconsin... éd. par R. Switzer, 1970, 300 p., 14 pl.
101. TREMBLEY, G., Marcel Schwob, faussaire de la nature, 1969, 135 p.
102. SAREIL, J., Les Tencin. Histoire d'une famille au dix-huitième siècle d'après de nombreux documents inédits, 1969, 440 p.
103. ALTER, J., L'esprit antibourgeois sous l'Ancien Régime. Littérature et tensions sociales aux XVIIe et XVIIIe siècles, 1970, 210 p.
104. CONLON, P.M., Prélude au Siècle des Lumières en France. Répertoire chronologique de 1680 à 1715: I, 1680-1691., 1970, 680 p.

## ÉDITIONS DROZ